The Crisis of
Multiculturalism
in Europe

The Crisis of Multiculturalism in Europe

A History

Rita Chin

Princeton University Press
Princeton and Oxford

Copyright © 2017 by Princeton University Press

Published by Princeton University Press,
41 William Street, Princeton, New Jersey 08540
In the United Kingdom: Princeton University Press,
6 Oxford Street, Woodstock, Oxfordshire OX20 1TR

press.princeton.edu

Cover art: Jon Arnold Images Ltd. / Alamy

All Rights Reserved

First paperback printing, 2019

Paper ISBN 978-0-691-19277-2

Cloth ISBN 978-0-691-16426-7

Library of Congress Control Number: 2017936617

British Library Cataloging-in-Publication Data is available

This book has been composed in Dante MT Std & Sabon Next LT Pro

Printed on acid-free paper. ∞

Printed in the United States of America

For Lay and Mari Chin
Jay Cook and Oliver Chin Cook

Contents

Acknowledgments

This is a book about the migration of non-Europeans to Europe after World War II and the massive upheavals (social, economic, political, and cultural) that accompanied the process. Although I have no direct connection to the particular groups described here and have lived in Europe only as a researcher, these issues are of immediate interest to me as a first-generation immigrant to the United States and a person whose entire life has been shaped by the social and political debates surrounding multiethnic societies. In many respects, my parents have lived this process more than anyone I know. Their decision to leave Malaysia was prompted by race riots against ethnic Chinese in the late 1960s, as well as their worries that their newly born daughter would not have access to opportunities (especially higher education) due to the fraught politics that followed the end of British rule. They have navigated various multicultural societies throughout their lives, operating in many languages and moving through different cultural worlds as students, employees, colleagues, neighbors, friends, and in-laws. As I have tried to make sense of the debates about European multiculturalism, I have often thought about the courage and resolve it took my parents to make these life-transforming choices. It required an enormous leap of faith for them to leave everything they knew, bearing an infant, two suitcases, seventy dollars, and the promise of a job. My hope is that if this book succeeds on any level, it will help to historicize and denaturalize assumptions about immigrants in postwar Europe that have made it harder to see them as three-dimensional human beings, as well as to better understand their struggles in a world where much of the political discourse is quick to demonize them as groups. Making multicultural societies successful *anywhere* is enormously hard work. It is an ongoing project that requires empathy, patience, and resolve—a lesson that has only become clearer in the aftermath of the US presidential election of 2016.

Even though the words of this book were committed to paper in a relatively short span of time, I have spent many years absorbing and sharpening the ideas contained in it. For this reason, I have many debts to acknowledge: institutional, intellectual, and personal. In 2007–8, I received support from the Wilson International Center for Writers and Scholars for another project, but some of the key questions for this book were raised during my time as a fellow there. Much of the reading and intellectual groundwork took place while I held an ACLS Frederick Burkhardt Fellowship for Recently Tenured Scholars at the Institute for Advanced Study, School of Social Sciences in Princeton in 2010–11. In 2014–15, I wrote the first draft of this manuscript with the combined support of a sabbatical from the University of Michigan and a History Department Hudson Professorship. The project was significantly enhanced by research grants from the University of Michigan's LSA Associate Professor Support Fund, Institute for Research on Women and Gender, and Weiser Center for Europe and Eurasia. UM's College of Literature, Science, and the Arts and History Department generously provided funds to defray some of the book's production costs.

By far my greatest debt is to Jay Cook, who has been my best friend, primary interlocutor, and partner for more than twenty years. For this book, he helped me see connections and through-lines in my work on race and gender that ultimately gave this project its specific shape. He listened to my ideas, discussed my arguments, scrutinized every transition, offered critical interventions at key moments, and selflessly set aside his own work during the final stages of this project to get in the trenches with me over a number of months. He is an incredibly talented historian, blessed with the ability to see the forest for the trees on issues well beyond his immediate areas of expertise. He is also the smartest and best editor I know. I have been truly lucky to have such a sharp, yet generous intellect by my side as I was working through this material.

Geoff Eley has been an important critic and sounding board for my work over many years. I sincerely thank him for his insightful reading of the entire manuscript and providing important feedback, especially on the British aspects of the project. I also want to express my gratitude to Mrinalini Sinha, who read the manuscript from beginning to end at the conclusion of an exhausting Michigan semester. She offered encouragement as well as critiques of my arguments about gender that made the book stronger. I thank Joshua Cole for giving me some key French citations and lending me books. I am also grateful to Uljana Feest for assistance with a tricky translation question. As History Department chair, Kathleen Canning offered support in numerous ways at especially critical moments. For friendship, conversation, and various forms of intellectual support at UM, I thank Pamela Ballinger, Howie Brick, John Carson, Juan Cole, Clem Hawes, Kali Israel, and Paolo Squatriti.

Some of the first ideas for this book began to take shape while I was a fellow at the Wilson Center in the months after my son was born. During the weekly seminar and over a number of lunches, Frances Hagopian asked tough questions, many of which I have sought to answer here; Anthony Messina generously shared sources; and Robin Muncy offered intellectual, professional, and practical advice to a new and extremely harried mother. I had originally planned to write a book about the European New Left and its responses to postwar immigration, but I eventually realized that such an ambitious archival project was not feasible with a new baby or even a young child. The fellowship from ACLS helped me shift directions (saving the bigger project for a later moment), and it was as a member of the IAS School of Social Science that I began to develop a number of this book's core arguments. I thank Joan Scott, Didier Fassin, Judith Surkis, Cécile Laborde, Tanya Erzen, and the other members of the 2010–11 Social Science Seminar for stimulating weekly discussions. I am also grateful to numerous individuals around the country whose invitations to give talks allowed me to try out many of the ideas that ultimately found their way into this book. These include Michelle Egan at American University; Philipp Gassert at the German Historical Institute in Washington, DC; Judith Surkis at the Center for European Studies, Harvard University; Gundolf Graml at Agnes Scott College; Brittany Lehman, Konrad Jarausch, and Karen Hagemann at the University of North Carolina at Chapel Hill; Cynthia Paces at the College of New Jersey; Cornelia Wilhelm at Emory University; and Yasemin Yıldız at the University of Illinois at Urbana-Champaign. Samuel Moyn deserves thanks for his friendship and support of this project from a very early moment. I am grateful to Martin Jay for championing my work over many years. I appreciate the early intellectual exchanges with Claudia Koonz on headscarves and veils. I thank Heide Fehrenbach for her crucial contributions to our joint effort to puzzle out the problem of race in postwar Germany and Atina Grossmann and Geoff Eley for their commitment to the collective project. Beyond the United States, I want to express my appreciation for the intellectual engagement and critical feedback offered by Bill Schwartz and Eleni Varikas.

This book benefitted enormously from the enthusiasm and strong advocacy of Brigitta van Rheinberg, my editor at Princeton University Press. I thank her for recognizing the potential in this project, providing encouragement while I was writing, and masterfully shepherding the book through the review and production processes. Two anonymous readers for the press gave me important feedback that had a major impact on my revisions of the book. I have benefitted as well from an excellent editorial and production staff at Princeton, including Quinn Fusting, Amanda Peery, Jenny Wolkowicki, and Joseph Dahm. I am grateful to Rebecca Bonner, who spent a chunk of her senior year at Michigan organizing and annotating my collection of newspaper articles and media coverage on European multiculturalism. I also thank Martha Schulman for her stellar copyediting work, and Sarah Mass and Connie Cook for helping me correct the page proofs.

Although writing is mostly a solitary endeavor, it is sustained and strengthened through the fellowship of friends and family. I thank Ernie Poortinga and Larissa Larsen for providing relief from the work grind with dinner-playdates that afforded both adult relaxation and kid entertainment. Maria Montoya and Rick Hills have offered generous hospitality and companionship in New York for nearly a decade. While I was writing the first draft of this book in Brooklyn, I was grateful to have the company of such good friends. I am especially pleased to be able to thank Peggy Burns and Phil Deloria for the delicious meals, moral support, sensible advice, and abiding friendship that have enriched my Michigan life in too many ways to count. I owe a huge debt of gratitude to Connie and Jim Cook, who have bolstered me and my work with countless kindnesses, especially time in northern Michigan and childcare help. Finally, I thank my immediate family, to whom I dedicate this book. My parents, Lay and Mari Chin, made choices and sacrifices that have had a profound impact on my life. They have encouraged and supported my academic endeavors and life choices, even though these did not always seem "natural" or practical to them. My husband, Jay Cook, has inspired and sustained me; he has picked me up and cheered me on. I admire his intelligence and ethical commitments, and I have benefitted tremendously from his generosity. His grace, resilience, and love have been enormous sources of strength for our ongoing partnership. Our son, Oliver Chin Cook, has lived with this book for much of his life. He embodies the multicultural in all kinds ways, both obvious and surprising. It has been a joy to watch his clear pride in the many cultures, cuisines, and traditions that contribute to his sense of self. It has been hard to explain to him the new political moment we are entering, where the basic conviction that diversity enriches and the values of mutual respect and common good seem to be giving way to a hardening of boundaries between peoples. But it is in the manifest gift of people like Oliver that I see the promise of a better future.

—Ann Arbor, January 2017

The Crisis of Multiculturalism in Europe

The Multicultural and Multiculturalism

The question of how European nations deal with racial and ethnic diversity has become inescapable in recent years. For some, the issue emerged in the fraught political climate of 9/11. For others, it surfaced with the establishment of the European Union (EU) and its efforts to define a collective identity. For still others, questions of difference and national belonging assumed special urgency with the succession of homegrown terrorist acts: the London bombings, the killings at *Charlie Hebdo*, the attacks at the Bataclan, the assaults in Brussels, and the rampages in Nice and at the Berlin Christmas market. Even before the most recent acts of violence, the leader of the EU's largest state, Angela Merkel, had pointedly declared the "failure" of multiculturalism in 2010. Meanwhile, the increasing strength of populist movements explicitly antagonistic to diversity—Germany's Patriotic Europeans against Islamicization of the West (PEGIDA), Austria's Freedom Party, Hungary's Jobbik, and Britain's United Kingdom Independence Party (UKIP), to name just a few—underscored growing anger toward migrant communities. In

2015, the issue resurfaced with particular force as a massive influx of refugees fleeing Syria, Iraq, and other parts of the Middle East and Africa renewed public debate about "foreigners" once again.

This question of how Europeans understand themselves in relation to different ethnic and racial groups is not actually new. Indeed, one might argue that there has *never* been a moment in which Europeans did not define themselves against some group perceived as "other." The very idea of "Europe" (and a distinctive European culture) emerged in the process of launching the Crusades against the infidel, "discovering" the New World, defending eastern territories against the Ottomans, and establishing trading posts and colonies in unfamiliar lands. In each case, Europeans became more self-conscious about who they were, and what distinguished them from the populations they encountered. But developments after the Second World War significantly altered this interaction. Instead of Europeans moving outward into the world as they had done for hundreds of years, people from around the world began to settle in Europe, filling the demand for labor created by wartime destruction. This reversal of migratory patterns shifted the process of European self-definition in a dramatic way. In the past, groups perceived as incompatible with European identity were usually located beyond European borders. But now they are firmly established within Europe itself.

There are, of course, important precedents for collective anxieties about internal "others." Jews, especially, occupied a fraught position for many centuries. They were relegated to ghettos. They were barred from certain professions. They were subjected to pogroms. In more extreme cases, they were expelled altogether. In 1935, the Third Reich promulgated the Nuremberg Laws, which progressively stripped German Jews of their social, economic, and legal rights. And from there, a hyper-racialized German state pursued a "final solution" to rid Europe of its historic "enemy within." The most recent concerns about internal "others," by contrast, have been exacerbated by the free movement of people within the EU, escalating homegrown threats, and large waves of refugees. These conditions have made the problems associated with "foreigners" seem particularly pervasive and intractable.

Strikingly, during the mid-1990s when I first began a previous book on the topic of ethnic diversity in Germany, it was still possible to believe that the question of "multiculturalism" was peripheral to the central narratives of European history. As late as 2005, one of the most prominent historians of modern Europe could write a grand synthesis of the postwar period in which these issues were a minor subplot.[1] In retrospect, one might read this selective portrait as a deliberate ideological choice, an effacing of racial and ethnic "others" in relation to the very considerable demographic diversity clearly rooted in every major Western European country. The charged politics of the past decade, however, has made it increasingly difficult to wish these issues away. As it happens, 2005 was also the year of the 7/7 London bombings, carried out by British-born sons of Pakistani immigrants. After this tragedy, it was no longer possible to pretend that immigrants and ethnic diversity were irrelevant, or even external, to European history.

Yet even as Europeans have come to define multiculturalism as a central fault line in their society, history, and politics, the meaning of the word has remained difficult to pin down. In many cases, critics and heads of state talk past each other, using very different definitions of multiculturalism and the various "issues" and "problems" it is perceived to encompass. But the ambiguities are historical as well as definitional. For much of the 1960s and 1970s, nationality (and legal status) served as the crucial marker of difference for newcomers, whereas in the 1980s culture began to assume this role. Today, by contrast, religion—and especially Islam—has become the key divider. To a surprising extent, however, these changes in the term have hardly registered; indeed, they have been largely unconscious. Despite decades of fraught debate, we do not really have common definitions or starting points for understanding the politics of multiculturalism in Europe.

What follows here is a series of specific frameworks for making sense of European multiculturalism. Above all, this book offers a critical history of the present, one that takes a comparative approach and insists on a longer temporal arc of half a century. It proceeds from the realization that since the 1950s at least, most Western European democracies have grappled with the question of what to do with ethnic, racial, and religious minorities within their borders. This shared history cuts across multiple immigrant groups—those who arrived as recruited guest workers, postcolonial settlers, and asylum seekers of various sorts. It includes people from the Caribbean, India, Pakistan, Bangladesh, Algeria, Morocco, Tunisia, Senegal, Mali, Turkey, and the former Yugoslavia. It encompasses those who count themselves as Christian, Orthodox, Muslim, Hindu, and Sikh. And it involves every major country in Western Europe: from Great Britain, France, and Germany to the Benelux states and the Scandinavian nations.

As a way into this complex terrain, I examine the efforts of European leaders and policy officials to apprehend and manage these radical demographic transformations taking place on the ground. But I also trace the manifold ways Europeans debated diversity—and especially how the terms of these discourses changed over time. Rather than providing an exhaustive account of multiculturalism country by country, I bring together the three largest national cases—Great

Britain, France, and Germany—that shaped the broader contours of the European debate. At times, I include Switzerland and the Netherlands as useful foils for my primary stories. By virtue of my own research expertise, I am able to flesh out the British and German arguments through archival sources, whereas I rely more heavily on secondary literature to develop the French analysis. Despite these constraints, I believe the comparative approach is absolutely crucial to our understanding of European multiculturalism. Such a perspective allows us to grasp the clear differences in migration patterns, colonial legacies (or lack thereof), and conceptions of citizenship, but also the 1980s consolidation of political discourse across Europe that has been less visible within the framework of individual national history. One key question for the book is this: how do we make sense of each country's distinct historical contexts, ideologies, and policies for dealing with diversity, on the one hand, and the fact that these efforts largely converged into a European-wide discourse on multiculturalism, on the other? If these states initially approached the issue of immigrants from different starting points, that is, how did they end up in the same place?

Treating immigration as a longer postwar story enables us to see that the variegated patterns of response to newcomers have not just pushed in a linear direction. Instead, the trajectories of public debate and policy making indicate that European reactions to non-European migrants vacillated between different forms of openness and exclusion at different junctures. In the 1950s and 1960s, Western European nations typically welcomed those who arrived from their colonies, former colonies, and other foreign countries to help rebuild after the massive destruction of World War II. In this way, questions of immigration and ethnic diversity were always interwoven with the postwar economic boom that drove a quarter century of prosperity and affluence. While governmental authorities in certain countries worried about the long-term effects of ethnic and racial difference on their societies, most suppressed such concerns by focusing instead on the immediate economic benefits of foreign manpower or by insisting that guest workers would eventually return home. For much of the 1960s and 1970s, Britain, France, and Germany pursued distinctly different approaches to dealing with their multicultural societies. It was only around 1980, in fact, that all three openly acknowledged the massive social consequences of immigration and ethnic diversity. At virtually the same moment, though, each country *also* began to pursue a new politics of national belonging that was at least partially framed in relation to non-European settlers. With growing intensity, British, French, and German political leaders identified immigrants as bearers of alien cultures that now rendered them "inassimilable" to the nation.

The 1989 furors over Salman Rushdie's *The Satanic Verses* and the expulsion of French school girls for wearing headscarves marked a major watershed in this cycle because they helped knit together what had been distinct processes of national boundary drawing. Together, the Rushdie and headscarf affairs kindled serious doubts about coexistence with the multiethnic populations that had established themselves in Europe over the previous four decades. These events drew attention—for the first time—to Islam as the common cultural and religious tradition among many different immigrant groups across Europe, groups that had previously been understood as distinct. These included Pakistanis and Bangladeshis in Britain; Algerians, Tunisians, Moroccans in France; Turks in Germany and the Netherlands. They also sparked skepticism about the "capacity" of Muslim immigrants to adapt to Western liberal values, a process supposedly undermined by religious fanaticism and the oppression of Muslim women. A second key question for this book, then, is this: how precisely did the growing preoccupation with religion as the central marker of ethnic and racial difference dovetail with concerns about gender relations and sexuality?

Doubts about the compatibility of Islamic culture and the principles of liberal democracy continued to fester during the 1990s, spurred by the establishment of the EU (and resurgent questions about a specifically European identity), the collapse of the Cold War's bipolar system, and the triumph of neoliberal values that celebrated individual "freedoms" as core tenets of Western culture. Precisely because Islam was understood as antithetical to European freedoms, critics from across the political spectrum focused on Muslims as the crucial litmus test for the viability of multiculturalism. Even those on the left often explained the seemingly oppressive treatment faced by some Muslim women as the product of religion, identifying Islam itself as the major barrier to integration. They wondered whether it was possible for European societies to manage such differences, if tolerating Muslim cultural practices required them to turn a blind eye to what they perceived as gender discrimination. The attacks of 9/11 and subsequent acts of localized terrorism, in turn, crystallized these doubts into a conclusion that is now understood as simple common sense: the oft-stated pronouncement that European multiculturalism has "failed." But what exactly have the costs of this conclusion been? Why did multiple heads of state affirm it publicly in 2010? And how do we parse the myriad problems that the acceptance of "failure" seemed to target? The goal of this book is not to prescribe a specific form of multiculturalism that might serve as a cure-all for an enormously complicated politics. Rather, my hope is that the history I chronicle here may help us to become more self-conscious about what multiculturalism is, has been, and might be in the future.

———

To that end, it seems useful to begin by clarifying when the term "multiculturalism" emerged, and how its meanings have changed over time. As numerous scholars have noted, "multiculturalism" is a notoriously slippery word.[2] Its definitions and meanings have proliferated exponentially since it came into common usage in the 1970s, first in the United States and then in much of Europe. Multiculturalism has been most commonly invoked in societies where different cultural communities live together: the United States, Canada, Australia, New Zealand, Yugoslavia, and, more recently, Britain, Germany, and France. But the term itself has become, according to one prominent critic, a "floating signifier" that connotes anything from touchy-feely celebrations of cultural differences to the political demand for minority rights, from gay and lesbian studies in the academy to public funding for community projects.[3]

It is important to note at the outset that the word was an American invention, one subsequently adopted in Britain and some of its former settler colonies such as Canada and Australia. The term first appeared as an adjective in the title of a 1941 American novel, *Lance: A Story about Multicultural Men*, written by scientist and author Edward F. Haskell. The book received a number of major reviews in the US press, including the *New York Herald Tribune*, *New York Times*, and *Saturday Review*. Many of these reviews featured efforts to use and flesh out the new word. One described the book as "concerned with people who are multicultural, who give their allegiance to no single nation or race or church, but to humanity at large."[4] Another summed up the novel as "a fervent sermon against nationalism, national prejudice and behavior in favor of a 'multicultural' way of life."[5] Among these commentaries, the *New York Times* review stood out for attempting to clarify the word through the story itself. "Though English born," the critic explained, the protagonist "spent his childhood . . . on the Continent, believing himself to be . . . the son of a kindly old German." The experience led the boy to become "multi-cultural," a mind-set exemplified by "facilities in various languages and an appreciation of national cultures that is more than skin-deep."[6] In its initial articulations, then, the idea of the "multicultural" served as a somewhat vague conceptual foil for chauvinistic nationalism. It connoted a concern for humanity in its most expansive sense, as opposed to a subset of humanity bounded by race, nation, or religion. Significantly, the need to introduce this term came at a very specific historical conjuncture: the moment when the United States was being pushed to the brink of war by the territorial advances of Nazi Germany.

The first invocation of "multiculturalism" as a noun, according to the *Oxford English Dictionary*, did not come until 1957, when it was used in the journal *Hispania*. The word appeared in a report on the Modern Language Association's foreign language program in the United States. Edward A. Medina, New Mexico's director of elementary education and supervisor of Spanish, explained that his state is "a land . . . where good will, understanding and cooperation are not only desirable but essential. For here its Indians, its Americans of Spanish descent, and its 'Anglos' meet in daily contact. They must not only co-exist but contribute to each other's lives. The key to successful living here, as it is in Switzerland, is multilingualism, which can carry with it rich multicultural-ism."[7] In this context, too, the word had a distinctly positive connotation, treating a diversity of languages and cultures as an opportunity for enrichment and engagement. It suggested a particular strategy for dealing with diversity: namely, that the "successful" coexistence of multiple cultures is best promoted by persons of linguistic facility—and by implication, those open to a variety of experiences and ways of thinking. In its early formulations, then, multiculturalism required a cosmopolitan frame of mind.

But this attitude toward diversity did not appear out of nowhere. It actually resembled ideas articulated by the New York intellectual Randolph Bourne on the eve of the First World War. Employing the concept of cosmopolitanism (drawn from the Ancient Greeks) as a rebuttal to the xenophobia and jingoism then dominant in American public discourse, Bourne championed the United States' exceptional diversity.[8] He viewed the multiplicity of immigrant cultures as one of the country's greatest strengths and argued against the conventional zero-sum logic that saw any openness to difference as a dilution of Americanism. Indeed, it was precisely through reciprocal interaction across lines of class, religion, and ethnicity that he imagined American identity expanding.

Neither "multicultural" nor "multiculturalism" appeared in the national press again until 1962, when the *New York Times* reported on an experiment in Detroit's public schools. Teachers wanted to replace the "Dick and Jane" reading primers set in a "nice suburban home" with new books about "Negro" and "Caucasian" children who live in a large metropolitan area.[9] The article quoted extensively from the announcement made by the Detroit teachers' committee: "The pre-primers which are in general use in American schools have many strong points for middle- and upper-class white children. . . . However, if children learn to read best when they can identify with the environment, the characters and the situations presented in their readers, then current pre-primers do not offer the best starting point for children in the great cities. These children need beginning reading materials that present family-life patterns resembling those found in multicultural areas."[10] In this context, the term "multicultural" served to describe places—especially major metropolitan locales—inhabited by people of diverse cultural and economic backgrounds. The teachers drew attention to the fact that large segments of the American population resided in cosmopolitan urban communities, rather than the "all-white, antiseptic world" of the suburbs.[11] In their efforts to legitimize the life experiences of children in the "great cities," they echoed Bourne, who had valorized New York as a unique environment where the collision of different cultures and religions routinely forced individuals to broaden their self-understanding.

In 1964, the term surfaced again, this time in relation to Nathan Glazer and Daniel Moynihan's landmark book, *Beyond the Melting Pot*. Glazer's section on American Jews, according to one commentator, convincingly demonstrated that "the image of 'the melting pot'" had been "dethroned in favor of the multicultural and multiethnic community of 'cultural pluralism.'"[12] Here, the "multicultural" community was explicitly linked to "cultural pluralism," a familiar concept often associated with the American philosopher Horace Kallen. A contemporary of Bourne, Kallen likewise extolled the diversity of US cultures and regarded differences across immigrant groups as a positive attribute. But where Bourne emphasized the transformative interactions forged between natives and immigrants—a process he believed would productively enrich both parties—Kallen stressed the autonomy of each group and envisioned the United States as a "federation" of enduring ethnic communities that would contribute to the national fabric without losing their particularity.[13] Following Kallen, the reviewer of *Beyond the Melting Pot* welcomed Glazer's report on the low rate of intermarriage between Jews and

other groups as a sign that the Jewish community was resist-
ing the assimilationist demands of "Americanization." Multiculturalism, in other words, was now deployed as an antidote
to the homogenizing overtones of the melting pot analogy.[14]
It contained a kind of preservationist impulse, a desire to retain and pass down cultural differences as a bulwark against
assimilation.

It should be clear at this point that there were already
multiple inflections of the word "multiculturalism" in play.
What they shared was a celebration—or at the very least,
a basic acceptance—of diverse cultures within a single nation, a fundamental tolerance of heterogeneity rather than
a defense of homogeneity. In this respect, the initial uses of
multiculturalism operated within a broadly leftist intellectual tradition of arguing for the value of diversity in modern society. This tradition had been especially galvanized by
the emergence of American nativism and xenophobia in the
1910s and the rise of fascism in Europe in the 1930s. Where
these invocations of multiculturalism diverged was in their
understanding how exactly different cultures should relate.
While the cosmopolitan strand emphasized cultural mixing
and the expansion of identities, the cultural pluralist strand
stressed the integrity of groups and the need to maintain
their distinctiveness. These earliest references to "multiculturalism" suggest, above all, that the word's meanings were
not fixed, consistent, or even always coherent. Indeed, they
were often loose and messy.

By the 1970s, the term began to be seen in a more explicitly political light, as activist groups adopted it to contest
accepted narratives of American history and national belonging. In 1974, for instance, the National Education Association (NEA), an independent teachers' union, announced a
"checklist for selecting and evaluating U.S. history textbooks."
Among the criteria were recommendations that such text-

books "portray the multicultural character of our nation" and "present the sexual, racial, religious and ethnic groups in our society in such a way as to build positive images, with mutual understanding and respect."[15] As the *Baltimore Afro-American* explained, this checklist was part of a "multifaceted plan to influence publishers to produce textbooks and other instructional materials which reflect the pluralistic nature of American society."[16] At the most basic level, the NEA deployed the term "multicultural" to make a point similar to the one that had been made by the Detroit teachers a decade earlier: both highlighted the diverse makeup of the United States and sought to introduce textbooks that would represent that diversity. Yet the NEA guidelines went further, stressing a broad spectrum of groups and the importance of cultivating "mutual understanding and respect" among them. In the context of the changing civil rights movement, moreover, this demand to acknowledge the multiplicity of American society assumed bigger stakes.

During the civil rights struggle's early years, the goal had been to combat the segregationist color lines of Jim Crow by pursuing a more "integrationist" program in which all citizens would be valued and protected equally under the law. In the late 1960s, however, a younger generation of activists extended the movement's initial demands for democratic freedom and political rights to more autonomous forms of self-determination, race pride, and strategic essentialism (such as Black Power). In the process, the older calls for social equality paved the way for a major transformation in the educational mission and curricula of American public schools: from a model that sought to socialize children to white middle-class values to one that encouraged students to appreciate and preserve their own unique ethnic cultures and histories. This latter curricular impulse came to be defined as "multicultural."

As an effort to revise the national history curriculum, the NEA textbook guidelines quickly provoked a major backlash among conservative parents that began in West Virginia and spread across the country to Florida and Vermont. An eighty-seven-page study conducted by the NEA on the controversy characterized the West Virginia protests as posing "another threat to rights that have been newly won: the right of racial and ethnic minority groups to be included in the textbooks and the right of all students to learn that in the world and in this society, white is not always right, that white, middle-class values are not the only, nor even always the best values, and that the history of the United States is not one long, unblemished record of Christian benevolence and virtue."[17] This defense of multiculturalism made explicit a set of engagements that had previously only been implied. The concept now not only included the expectation that minority groups be "represented"—in textbooks, school curricula, and American history itself—but the belief that challenges to the structural dominance of "white, middle-class values" carried ideological and cultural authority. In this way, multiculturalism became an important weapon against antiblack and other forms of racism, but this new function tended to push the concept toward its more cultural pluralist, federalist inflection.

It is in the related context of bilingual education in the United States that we find the first reference to multiculturalism in a European publication. Writing for the Manchester *Guardian* in 1974, a British journalist detailed the effects of recent US legislation supporting bilingualism in American public schools: "Anyone brought up on the idea of the United States as the great melting pot, bound together by the English language, would find the number of shop signs in Spanish in parts of Texas, Miami and New York city faintly alarming. For anyone interested in education, the extent to which the country has moved towards multiculturalism in the schools, since the passage of the Bilingual Education Act, 1967, seems to challenge any melting in the future."[18] Pressure from Mexican Americans in the southwest, explained the reporter, had spurred Congress to pass the bill and provide a hundred million dollars for bilingual programs in public schools. This campaign was part of the effort by ethnic minorities to "reassert their identity" and (as in the textbook controversy) demand respect, legitimacy, and support for minority cultures. He concluded,

> It would be easy to write off the whole bilingual endeavor as merely a passing product of the turbulent sixties.... I am not so sure. Without denying the world status of the English language, the process recognises that the United States will always contain more than the single Anglo culture, and that even a nation as powerful and self-sufficient as the United States must go further to meet the smaller language communities. And I suspect, too, that there is a message for Britain here: that local authorities outside Wales might think more seriously of offering a genuinely bilingual option at a few schools—in languages like Urdu, as well as French.[19]

In drawing lessons for British society from this account of American education, the journalist was making a series of pivotal choices. Arguing not only that bilingualism might be a useful educational policy in Britain, he went on to suggest that the American term attached to it—multiculturalism— might be productively applied to the UK context. It is worth noting that as early as 1966 British Home Secretary Roy Jenkins had already articulated crucial features of this concept in a speech to the National Committee for Commonwealth Immigrants, although he did not explicitly invoke the term.[20] Outlining the Labour government's stance on "race relations,"

Jenkins recommended the integration of recent arrivals from New Commonwealth countries in the Caribbean, Africa, and South Asia (as opposed to those from Old Commonwealth countries such as Canada, Australia, and New Zealand who presumably had no problem fitting in). He proclaimed "integration" a national goal, defining it as the preferable option to assimilation. Where assimilation involved a "flattening out process," integration stressed "equal opportunity accompanied by cultural diversity, in an atmosphere of mutual tolerance."[21] In this statement, we can detect clear traces of a Kallenesque model of multiculturalism. Explicitly describing Britain as a diverse country, home to the Welsh (Jenkins himself was Welsh), Scots, Irish, Jews, and more recent arrivals, Jenkins endorsed providing "equal opportunity" and cultivating "mutual tolerance" as key strategies for dealing with the coexistence of multiple cultural groups.

Meanwhile, the American uses of multiculturalism were becoming increasingly politicized as they gained heightened visibility on the national stage. By the late 1960s and early 1970s, developments in US higher education radicalized the meanings and effects associated with the demand for multiculturalism, now firmly linked to curricular reform and contests over history and memory. Ethnic minority activists on university campuses, in particular, began to push for fundamental changes in the academy. In November 1968, the Black Student Union and a coalition of student associations known as the Third World Liberation Front organized a strike at San Francisco State University.[22] Students demanded equal access to public higher education, more diversity among the professoriate, and a new curriculum that would embrace the history and culture of all people, including minority groups. After a five-month walkout, they won a major concession from the university: the creation of a College of Ethnic Studies, the first in the United States. Similar events occurred the following year at Berkeley, where the standoff with the university administration turned violent, leading Governor Ronald Reagan to call in the California National Guard to quash the strike. Faculty support of the strikers helped pave the way for the establishment of a separate ethnic studies department at Berkeley. As a by-product of these and subsequent struggles during the 1970s and 1980s, US institutions of higher learning gradually incorporated the values of a highly politicized multiculturalism into their curricula, hiring practices, and structure. In this way, education—and specifically, its role in sustaining the distinctive cultures of ethnic and racial groups—became the ground on which the increasingly contentious debates about multiculturalism were fought in the United States.

What's important for our purposes is that "multiculturalism" migrated across the Atlantic as a specifically "American" term, one with its politics already explicit. It first appeared as a topic in Britain during the early 1970s and was adapted as a model for British race relations policy in the 1980s. Only after the Rushdie affair in 1989 did multiculturalism also become an object of serious discussion in Germany and France. In adopting this term, Europeans imported not a fixed and finished understanding of diversity and its management at the level of policy, but rather a loose concept that contained both the cosmopolitan mixing imagined by Bourne and the preservationist arguments developed by Kallen. At the same time, the word came with the intensely politicized baggage of US movements for social justice, movements that sought to rewrite textbooks, revise school curricula, and fundamentally reimagine the nation's history. European critics routinely complained that multiculturalism was American, incoherent, and fraught with political overtones. Whatever its perceived deficiencies, however, the concept's arrival marked a critical new development in Europe, giving it an ideological touchstone with which to explicitly engage questions of national diversity. Indeed, it was only in the process of debating multiculturalism that Europeans began to formulate the first affirmative arguments for social diversity as a core value and policy issue.

———

One of the central complaints sometimes lodged against multiculturalism is that it fosters superficial paeans to cultural diversity as opposed to inclusive visions for how to manage it. At this point, therefore, it might be useful to think more carefully about questions of language, labels, and categories. Especially helpful on this score is British sociologist Stuart Hall's important distinction between the adjective "multicultural" and the noun "multiculturalism," a distinction too often conflated in common parlance. Multicultural, according to Hall, describes an on-the-ground situation: "the social characteristics and problems of governance posed by any society in which different cultural communities live together and attempt to build a common life while retaining something of their 'original' identity."[23] Of necessity, multicultural societies exist in the plural, rather than in the singular. They most often arise through the movement of peoples who are responding to a wide variety of factors, including imperial conquest, labor shortage, unemployment, war, and famine. Multicultural societies are thus produced by a range of historical motors, whether economic, political, social, or several in combination. In each case, the particular interplay of diverse "cultural communities" creates its own unique effects and specific manifestations.

"Multiculturalism," by contrast, denotes "the strategies and policies adopted to manage and govern the problems of diversity and multiplicity which multi-cultural societies throw up."[24] The noun, in other words, designates a programmatic statement or specific approach for dealing with multicultural societies. As such, it can be articulated in the guise of political philosophy, social ideal, or state policy. The term "multiculturalism" can be misleading, however, because it conjures a singular concept or thing. Most people do not refer to *multiculturalisms* in their conventional speech. In practice, though, there are innumerable models for managing cultural diversity—and many of them claim the label "multiculturalism."

What many critics describe as "conservative" multiculturalism, for instance, insists on assimilating minority cultures into that of the majority. "Liberal" multiculturalism, by contrast, emphasizes integrating immigrants through universal citizenship, but tolerates some forms of cultural difference as long as they remain in the private sphere. "Pluralist" multiculturalism supports and protects minority cultural groups and accords them differential rights. "Critical" multiculturalism stresses the power and privileges of the mainstream and seeks to develop modes of resistance against majority hegemony. "Commercial" or "corporate" multiculturalism celebrates diversity as a means of selling products and offers consumption as a way to resolve differences between groups.[25] If that were not enough, there is a "weak" version of multiculturalism and a "strong" one—the difference here determined by the relationship between the demand for assimilation and toleration of cultural particularities.[26] The list goes on and on. Indeed, multiculturalism has been inflected in so many ways—and enlisted to denote so many strategies and policies—that leading sociologists now argue for seven or eight distinct variants in common usage! What they all signify, however, is a political approach or social policy for regulating and managing cultural diversity.[27]

Given the sheer variety of multiculturalisms, it is not especially surprising that the concept has provoked an equally various set of criticisms, each with its own specific target. Whereas conservatives attack multiculturalism as a threat to the cultural integrity of the nation, liberals decry multicultural policies for championing cultural differences of the group rather than protecting the neutrality of the state or primacy of the individual. Antiracists reject multiculturalism because it emphasizes culture and identity while neglecting structural problems such as lived disparities of income and access to social services. Meanwhile, some minority critics condemn multiculturalism for encouraging a Kallenesque preservation of differences that ultimately isolates ethnic communities. Multiculturalism is nothing if not a contested concept!

Precisely because multiculturalism can mean so many different things, though, the term has often also been used as a kind of shorthand for the broader debate about the problem of diversity, especially in the European context. Thus, when some people invoke multiculturalism, they are using the term in a third and more discursive sense: namely, to reference how societies talk about difference. But as we have seen, this generalized invocation tends to encompass both the ground-level fact of a multiethnic society and the specific strategies for managing it.

Such indeterminacy, in turn, has made it easy for critics to vilify the concept without being especially clear about what in particular they are condemning. This imprecision has meant that people who debate multiculturalism often talk past each other, employing the same term to designate radically different ideas, doctrines, or policies. And in today's heated political debates about immigrants and immigration, conservatives' use—indeed, their exploitation—of the ambiguity has had particularly pernicious effects. It is possible to slide quite seamlessly between a blanket rejection of cultural diversity in European society (the multicultural) and a more specific critique of the strategies and policies for managing that diversity (multiculturalism). If we are to get to the bottom of the multicultural question, then, it behooves us to be as meticulous as possible in explicating the terms in play in any given debate.

At the same time, the very slipperiness of the word has led even the most thoughtful commentators to wonder about the concept's long-term liabilities. If multiculturalism contains so many meanings—some of them contradictory—does it continue to serve any constructive purpose? Might we be better off jettisoning this muddled word in favor of more precise language? This prospect, however, raises a different sort of question—namely, what would be lost if the term was actually discarded? For better or worse, the very ubiquity of the word marks an enormously valuable critical space in public discourse: it is the place where we acknowledge the lived reality of diverse societies and where we can move the discussion of diversity forward at the level of democratic politics.

Whether or not we want to wish away the messiness of multiculturalism, in other words, the basic fact of ethnic and cultural diversity in European cities, neighborhoods, and streets remains. Simply writing off multiculturalism as a "failed" experiment—or a project that has outlived its usefulness—does little to change conditions on the ground—except perhaps to create the impression of willful exclusion. One might argue, in fact, that the highly contested nature of the concept now serves a number of critical functions in democratic societies. Precisely because the term's meanings are *not* straightforward and settled, it has facilitated contentious debate about how to manage social diversity in the contexts of law and politics, education, and popular culture. In the wake of so many recent groundswells of xenophobia, isolationism, and violence, it may be that we need quite a bit more discussion about diversity—not less. Indeed, it was precisely this capacity of multiculturalism to force attention on demographic realities and disrupt commonsense categories and assumptions that ultimately made it an indispensable category for critics like Stuart Hall.[28] What Hall recognized earlier than most of us is the fundamental value of multiculturalism's messiness. Without this concept, we are left with disavowal, a stance whose logical conclusions lead to mass deportation or apartheid.

CHAPTER ONE

The Birth of Multicultural Europe

If multiculturalism ultimately became the primary trope through which Europeans debated ethnic diversity, it seems important to understand how this diversity developed in Europe in the first place. When, in other words, was multicultural Europe born? What economic and political motors drove large numbers of non-Europeans to settle in post–World War II Europe? And in what ways did different national histories, traditions, and ideas of belonging shape the diverse societies that developed—as well as the distinctive state responses to cultural diversity?

The standard answer to these questions is that Western European countries became diverse in the aftermath of the Second World War. Between the late 1940s and the early 1970s, colonial and former colonial subjects arrived in their European motherlands, while other European governments simultaneously recruited guest workers. In most cases, newcomers were welcomed—or at least tolerated—because they provided much needed manpower to help rebuild from wartime destruction and filled the massive labor shortage created by the subsequent economic boom. By and large, however, European states expected these labor migrants eventually to return home. That most remained took Western leaders by surprise. This unforeseen development, the narrative goes, forced European countries into the thankless position of having to absorb large numbers of people with foreign cultures, traditions, and religions.

Western European societies have a heavy investment in this version of the story. Before 1945, the account implies, countries in Europe enjoyed social cohesion and harmony, with few—if any—divisions. European nations were largely homogeneous and so had little or no experience dealing with cultural differences. Unlike the United States or Canada, European countries maintained neither a tradition of immigration, nor concepts of the nation that would facilitate incorporating significant foreign populations. The onset of postwar immigration, by contrast, introduced for the first time large numbers of non-Europeans into the demographic mix, which in turn forced a difficult learning curve for managing ethnic minorities and their cultural particularities. Within this narrative, the end of World War II represents a radical rupture in European society, one that helps to explain both native Europeans' resistance to the influx of immigrants, as well as the lack of preparedness among European leaders and governments to handle this social tinderbox. If 1945 marked a fundamental shift from homogeneity to diversity—and the first waves of nonwhite and non-Christian populations—then who could reasonably blame Europeans for the difficulties—and various forms of resistance—that often ensued?

The truth, however, is that this dominant image of European homogeneity was largely a myth. In fact, many scholars now argue that Europe has always been a study in contrasts, a continent marked by intense internal differences.[1]

European states accommodated—or at least, confronted—many kinds of diversity at multiple points in their histories: regional differences, religious differences, and ethnic and racial differences. In Germany, for instance, anxiety about foreign populations emerged as soon as the nation-state was established in 1871, with the incorporation of Danish Schleswig-Holstein and French Alsace-Lorraine into its territories. A diversity of religious confessions, too, was a concern for the new state. Chancellor Otto von Bismarck went to great lengths to monitor the Catholic population and ensure the dominance of Protestantism. Meanwhile, the "Jewish question" was already a major topic of debate in the German states well before unification, leading Karl Marx to pen his famous essay of the same title in 1843. Late nineteenth-century Germans, moreover, routinely worried about the flood of Polish laborers who crossed the border to work in the coal mines of the Ruhr Valley and the agricultural estates of East Prussia.[2]

This long-running experience with ethnic and religious diversity holds true in France as well. In 1870, leaders of the Third Republic were sufficiently alarmed at the lack of social cohesion among the nominally French population that they undertook a major effort to define and inculcate a national culture. The goal was to transform peasants and regional minorities such as Basques and Bretons into "Frenchmen."[3] In addition, France faced two substantial waves of immigration before the postwar period, one that brought Belgians and Italians at the end of the nineteenth century and another that created Polish, Czech, and Russian communities in the 1920s.[4] The number of immigrants was so great, in fact, that by 1930 France boasted the highest rate of foreign population growth in the entire world.[5]

The patterns in the United Kingdom were similar. If the mid-nineteenth-century Great Famine in Ireland prompted hundreds of thousands of refugees to flee to the United States, it also drove them to new parts of the British Isles: Liverpool, Birmingham, London. This mass immigration not only brought a huge underclass of laboring poor (whose "savagery" was said to rub off on English workers), but also reintroduced Catholicism as a potentially divisive factor into English society.[6] The question of religious difference was raised in somewhat different form with the arrival of a sizable contingent of Jews around the same time.[7] Significantly, the country's first immigration law, the 1905 Aliens Act, was aimed primarily at preventing the arrival of Jewish refugees fleeing the pogroms in Russia's Pale of Settlement.[8]

In contrast to most other European nations, the Netherlands actually welcomed immigrants prior to World War II. Between 1590 and 1800, newcomers relocated there in such numbers that the foreign-born population was never less than 5 percent, a sizeable figure compared to France, where foreigners composed 1.05 percent of the total population in 1851.[9] The country's relative freedom and wealth attracted those fleeing religious persecution such as French Huguenots and Jews, as well as those seeking economic opportunity. In this way, the Netherlands embraced multiple types of migrants and made the tradition of accepting new arrivals an important part of its national identity.

Most European countries, in other words, dealt with questions of immigration and cultural difference well before the Second World War. Demographic diversity was not new. Nor were tensions around ethnic and religious difference a novel development in Western Europe. Yet this master narrative of postwar rupture contains at least some seeds of useful contrast. What is perhaps most significant here is that those living through the postwar transitions perceived the demographic transformations unfolding around them as qualitatively different—a new kind of diversity. As European governments struggled to confront and negotiate these differences, moreover, many of them framed their efforts as a debate about something called "multiculturalism," a novel term in the social and political lexicons of Western Europe. Before we can grasp the significance of this linguistic shift, however, we must delve into the processes by which demographic diversity was changing on the ground, as well as how European states initially responded to these newcomers.

Empire and Labor

By most accounts, postwar immigration to Britain began on 21 June 1948, with the arrival of the SS *Empire Windrush*, to the Tilbury Docks near London. This former German troop vessel carried 492 passengers from the Caribbean, most of whom had set sail from Kingston, Jamaica, after seeing an advertisement in a local newspaper for cheap transport to England. For the costly but manageable sum of £28.10, the men and two women aboard sought economic opportunity and—above all—work in the imperial heartland.

The arrival of the *Empire Windrush* did not go unnoticed in Britain. Less than two weeks before its expected approach, the British tabloid *Daily Express* reported that Minister of Labour George Isaacs stood before the House of Commons and "confessed his worry to MPs yesterday" about the imminent landing of "500 West Indians, all seeking jobs in Britain."[10] On the day the ship made port, the tabloid announced, "Empire Men Flee No Jobs Land: 500 Hope to Start New Life Today."[11] While the steamer chugged up the Thames toward its final destination, a film crew from the British Pathé News service waited on the shore to document

the boat's docking. Once the ship was moored, the reporter
solicited a number of interviews, asking several young men
why they had come to England and what kinds of jobs they
hoped to obtain. He then turned to their fellow traveler, the
Trinidadian calypso singer Aldwyn Roberts known profes-
sionally as Lord Kitchener, who offered an a cappella version of his new song, "London Is the Place for Me."[12]

The resulting newsreel explained that the West Indian
arrivals were citizens of the British Empire. Many of them
were former servicemen who had fought with the Royal
Air Force during World War II. "They served this country
well," explained the narrator, "and they know England." Lord
Kitchener also emphasized the special ties between those
on the ship and Britain. "Well believe me, I am speaking
broadmindedly," he sang, "I am glad to know my mother
country. I've been travelling the countries years ago, but this
is the place I wanted to know. Darling, London is the place
for me."

What this short film repeatedly underscored, in short,
were colonial connections. These long-standing ties meant
that the *Windrush* passengers saw themselves not as foreigners imposing on a strange country, but rather as members of
the empire setting out for the motherland. Their legal standing confirmed the perception: they were British subjects and
thus fully entitled to seek work and settle in England. Many
of those who had fought in the armed services had actually
spent time training in the British Isles. Presumably, they felt
an even deeper bond, having risked their lives to safeguard
Britain and its larger empire. But virtually all of the migrants
viewed their journey less as a voyage into the unknown, and
more as a kind of homecoming. After all, they had spent
their grammar school years in the West Indies learning British history, geography, and literature. Their arrival in London was thus a completion of the imperial circuit.

The colonial connections were not lost on British government officials. It was the Secretary of State for the Colonies who first learned about the *Windrush*'s imminent arrival through a telegram from the Acting Governor in Jamaica.[13] The matter then became the subject of furious correspondence among these two offices, the Colonial Office in London, the Privy Council, the Ministry of Labour, and ultimately Prime Minister Clement Attlee himself. Throughout these exchanges, civil servants worried that the arriving West Indians lacked both skills and money. But the main concern for the Privy Council and Secretary of State for the Colonies was whether those aboard the *Windrush* had decided to come to England on their own or were responding to a locally organized movement in the colonies. After deciding on the former explanation, an official from the Ministry of Labour admitted, "There is no logical ground for treating a British subject who comes of his own accord from Jamaica to Great Britain differently from another who comes to London on his own account from Scotland."[14] Well aware of the open-door policy established between Britain and its imperial possessions, the prime minister echoed this position: "It is traditional that British subjects, whether of Dominion or Colonial origin (and of whatever race or colour), should be freely admissible to the United Kingdom. That tradition is not, in my view, to be lightly discarded."[15]

In most of the press coverage, however, these longer historical connections (and entitlements) were largely obscured. Rather than describing the *Windrush* passengers as imperial subjects who were undertaking an internal migration from one part of the empire to another, the media generally cast them as foreigners looking for employment in Britain. While the *Daily Express* announced "Empire Men Flee No Jobs Land" (a headline that at least acknowledged these migrants' link to Britain through the empire), the article's larger emphasis

was the flight from "no jobs land" and the description of
these newcomers as "five hundred unwanted people ... [who]
are hoping for a new life."[16] In a short notice from its "News
in Brief" section, the *Times* of London informed readers that
"492 Jamaicans had come to seek work." As these depictions
suggest, the "unwanted" arrivals appeared to be random
strangers in search of a better life in the United Kingdom.
Their long-standing ties to Britain were largely pushed into
the background.[17] For the most part, as historian Wendy Webster has argued, British perceptions of Commonwealth migrants "scarcely acknowledged the imperial history that connected them to Britain."[18]

Although the *Windrush* would later be described as the
starting point for postwar immigration to Britain, early media coverage gave little hint of the occasion's larger implications. Most reports treated the ship's arrival as a one-off,
a curious episode rather than a trigger for a massive influx
of immigrants. What seemed to capture public attention,
above all, were the questions of where to house the passengers and how to find them jobs. The *Times* reported that 236
of the Jamaicans "were housed last night in Clapham South
deep shelter. The remainder had friends to whom they
could go with prospects of work." Among the passengers, it
noted, were "singers, students, pianists, boxers, and a complete dance band. Thirty or forty of them have already vol-
unteered to work as miners."[19] Brief notices like this made
the uninvited appearance of these immigrants seem like an
anomalous event.

Government officials, though, were at least vaguely cog-
nizant of the fact that the *Windrush* passengers might pres-
age a larger flood of non-European colonials.[20] In its article
on the Labour Minister's anxiety, the *Daily Express* quoted
his hope that "no encouragement will be given to others to
follow them."[21] An internal memo from the Privy Council

office to the Colonial Office expressed fear that "successful efforts to secure adequate conditions for these men on arrival might actually encourage a further influx."[22] Indeed, the Colonial Office was right to worry. It certainly knew that the Caribbean islands were among the poorest of Britain's colonial possessions. Jamaica's economic situation was particularly wretched, with an unemployment rate between 25 and 30 percent.[23] Clement Atlee likewise understood the potential complications presented by the West Indies' dire economic circumstances, the United Kingdom's nationality policy that allowed free colonial migration, and the added factor of postwar Britain's need for manpower. It would be particularly difficult to "discard" the tradition of open borders within the empire, he admitted, "at a time when we are importing *foreign* labour in large numbers."[24]

Britain, of course, had emerged from the Second World War victorious. But within a few months of the conflict's end, it became clear that the country was suffering from a severe labor shortage that threatened to exacerbate the problems of an economy already saddled with massive national debt and a skewed balance of payments. An October 1945 report of the Trades Union Congress (TUC) stated that numerous industries were encountering "the problem of manpower scarcity at every turn, and the whole of the vital services of this country [were] very near breaking point."[25] British rebuilding efforts quickly absorbed hundreds of thousands of prisoners of war, and the TUC estimated that another half million laborers would be required in order to prevent a serious disruption of basic services. By January 1946, the government identified manpower as the most pressing national problem, especially because the lack of labor was acute in the crucial industries of coal mining, textiles, agriculture, steel, and construction. All in all, it anticipated a shortage of between 600,000 and 1.3 million workers.[26]

As first steps to address the issue, the Ministry of Labour launched a "domestic productivity drive" to urge all able-bodied citizens back to work, even granting Scottish children a fifteen-day exemption from school to pitch in with the annual harvest. It also organized a publicity campaign to encourage women to rejoin the labor force, while some members of the Cabinet pressed for a reduction in the armed services to relieve the pressure on the civilian labor force.[27] More radical solutions involved importing POWs from the United States and Canada, as well as developing resettlement schemes for European refugees and displaced persons that would eventually bring Poles, Balts, and Italians to Britain.[28] Indeed, government leaders actively recruited Europeans to fill the labor rolls, not just as temporary sojourners, but as immigrants who would help replenish the British stock.

With these programs under way less than a year after the war, knowledge of Britain's labor shortage circulated widely. The urgent need for workers in the United Kingdom, combined with extremely high rates of unemployment in the British West Indies, made the journey to England an obvious choice for colonial subjects in search of jobs. In fact, many in the Caribbean followed this path, and the evidence of a larger wave of immigration quickly mounted. The *Windrush* actually arrived after the SS *Ormonde*, which brought 108 passengers from the West Indies in late 1947. And after the *Windrush* came the SS *Orbita*, which sailed from Trinidad via Jamaica and Bermuda to Liverpool in October 1948; the *Reina del Pacifico*, carrying migrants from Nassau to Liverpool, soon followed. Between 1948 and 1953, around two thousand West Indians migrated to Britain yearly.[29]

The initial response to these developments among government ministers and civil servants was tinged with panic. Following the *Windrush*'s arrival, the Ministry of Labour scrambled to find those without friends or family initial accommodation, eventually setting them up in an old bomb shelter at the Clapham South Tube station with a warden to watch over them; from there they were sent to a labor exchange in Brixton to obtain work. A similar scenario was repeated with the landing of the *Orbita*. By the time the *Reina del Pacifico* docked, officials decided that this kind of assistance to West Indian newcomers could no longer be provided. As historian Kathleen Paul has explained, the growing fear was that "by meeting the ships, and distributing free travel warrants (in an effort to disperse the 'coloured population' throughout the country), they were in fact encouraging other colonials to migrate."[30] Particularly upsetting for government officials was this flow's spontaneous and uncontrolled nature. As British leaders from Attlee on down readily acknowledged, West Indians had every right to come to the United Kingdom for work. Yet it was one thing for limited numbers to settle over the course of many decades and quite another for thousands upon thousands to arrive expecting jobs in a short period.

Even more disturbing than the fact that neither the Ministry of Labour nor the Colonial Office could formally regulate the movements of these independent British subjects was the reversal of migratory patterns that their coming to England signaled. Historically, Britain had been a country of *emigration*. Between 1815 and 1914, over twenty-two million native white Britons ventured outward from the British Isles to settle in the colonies—from Canada and South Africa to Australia and New Zealand. During this same period, thousands more traveled to the far reaches of the empire as colonial administrators, missionaries, engineers, bankers, shopkeepers, or simply people seeking new opportunities.[31] Although less visible, there was also a simultaneous flow of colonials from the empire back to Britain, including both whites from the dominions and "coloureds" from the colonies. Black colonials often came as seamen, students, or visitors. During the two World Wars, moreover, the British government had recruited colonial men and women from the Caribbean and India to serve in the armed forces and work in war industries in the British Isles. But once the fighting was over, these recruits were quickly demobilized and returned home.[32] And overall, the numbers of black colonial migrants remained small, their flow hardly amounted to a trickle.

With the arrival of the *Windrush*, the dominant perceptions of the migration patterns shifted: Britain went from being a country of emigration to being a country of immigration that absorbed thousands of newcomers. In addition, the primary agents of migration changed: from white, native Britons to nonwhite, non-European colonials and former colonials. This reversal disrupted the traditional order of things: since the slave trade, the movement of people had been based on a racial separation between European metropole and empire. Black and Asian people were seen as belonging to the empire, but not Britain. While British leaders understood the empire (and later the Commonwealth) to be multiracial, they most certainly did not view their own domestic or social worlds this way. Black and Asian migration to Britain after 1945 was widely seen as endangering the clear boundaries between imperial center and periphery, between white and colored.[33]

Initially, the management of empire was understood to be the most relevant framework for dealing with the growing wave of postwar colonial arrivals. As the new pattern of West Indian immigration became increasingly apparent, the Attlee Cabinet took up this issue in relation to broader discussions of nationality and immigration policy. Two competing concerns emerged: on the one hand, the fear of damaging Britain's status "as the mother country, or at least the hub, of the Commonwealth" by reneging on these subjects' right of entry; and on the other, the desire to prevent unwanted colonial migration.[34] Behind the scenes, the Attlee government quietly pursued administrative strategies for controlling West Indian immigration, with Colonial Secretary Arthur Creech Jones indicating that the problem might be manageable simply because of the scarcity of suitable transport. But somewhat paradoxically, it also passed the 1948 British Nationality Act, which reaffirmed the right of all members of the British Empire to enter the United Kingdom. This legislation, Paul has argued, confirmed "Britain's position as the migratory center of the Commonwealth" and upheld "the nation's position as an important international power."[35] For the next decade, under a succession of Tory governments that followed Attlee's Labour rule, the older commitments to the empire and Commonwealth shaped Whitehall's response to the new phenomenon of labor-driven mass immigration to Britain.

If the beginning of postwar immigration to Britain can be distilled into a single iconic event, the origin story is less clear-cut in France. First and foremost, the influx of newcomers to France after 1945 was much more diffuse and diverse, fed by a variety of sources: recruited foreign workers, primarily from other European countries such as Italy, Spain, and Portugal; Algerian Muslims, who were first French nationals, then citizens, and finally foreign immigrants; and somewhat later, former colonials from the newly independent West African countries of Mali, Mauritania, and Senegal. In addition, France had already experienced two significant immigration waves, the first in the late nineteenth century, the second in the 1920s.[36] For all these reasons, the presence of a noticeable contingent of foreigners did not seem as strange or unusual in France as it did in Britain.

Despite these basic differences, a common thread runs through the development of postwar immigration to Europe:

the urgent need for labor. Primed by perennial hand wringing about the low birthrate, French government officials, demographers, and economists immediately identified manpower as the crucial obstacle for rebuilding the country after the war.[37] France had faced a similar demographic crisis after the First World War and had readily absorbed more than a million immigrants over a five-year period. In 1945, French leaders determined that the state should play a more active role in recruiting workers and matching them to jobs, rather than leaving the task to employers and the vagaries of the free market. Six months after the end of the war, anticipating a shortage of as many as five million workers, the state established the National Immigration Office (ONI) within the Ministry of Labor.

Yet filling this demand presented complications. French officials widely agreed that recruiting workers from other European countries was much more desirable than employing Africans or Asians.[38] The ONI was thus directed to open recruiting offices in Italy and later Belgium and Spain, but not allowed to pursue other countries as potential sources of labor. In addition, the French state's desire for a closely regulated policy—the goal was to monitor residence and work permits and to supervise the distribution of foreigners throughout the country—conflicted with the practical aspects of quickly recruiting large numbers of workers.[39] Employers first had to agree upon a labor contract with the Labor Ministry that specified conditions of work and housing. Once the contract was approved, the ONI sent the terms to its overseas offices to initiate the selection of appropriate candidates based on health, profession, and age.[40] The government's efforts to regulate labor recruitment, in short, slowed down the process of getting much needed manpower into place.

For prospective employers dealing with the immediate effects of too few workers, however, the most pressing issue was enlisting as many migrants as possible. They worried more about bureaucratic red tape slowing down the flow of labor and less about where foreign employees came from. As a result, French employers began to recruit workers directly, targeting populations that were not subject to ONI oversight—specifically, French nationals residing in Algeria or the overseas *départements* and territories (DOM-TOM) in the Caribbean and Indian Ocean. Algeria's proximity to the French mainland meant that Algerians were the easiest to hire. An unintended consequence of the attempt to implement a state-controlled immigration policy, then, was the exponential growth of Muslim Algerians working in mainland France. Between 1946 and 1955, the Algerian population increased tenfold, from 20,000 to 210,000. Algerian workers far outpaced the numbers of immigrants recruited by the ONI.[41]

On the face of it, the presence of Algerian laborers in France should have been relatively straightforward. After all, Algeria was not just the most important colony in the world's second largest empire, but also occupied a unique status within the imperium: it was understood not simply as a colonized land, but as an integral part of France. This status was established in 1848, when the leaders of the newly installed Second Republic declared French territory in North Africa to be an extension of the republic itself.[42] On this basis, the French state treated Algeria as administratively and legally indivisible from the metropolitan "hexagon." The territory was divided into three *départements*: Algiers, Oran, and Constantine. Under the Third Republic, moreover, each gained the right to elect two deputies to the National Assembly in Paris. For the French settler population, living in Algeria was no different than living in Alsace or Provence. For Algerian Muslims, living in France—at least in theory—was no different than living in Algeria.

Yet the place of Algerians working in the metropole was strongly conditioned by the problematic colonial relationship between France and Algeria, which, after a hundred years, continued to perpetuate structural disparities even as it promised equality. In 1830, the French invaded the city of Algiers, a military operation that ultimately paved the way for a significant influx of French and Europeans into the territory, with more than thirty-five thousand in residence by 1849.[43] The arrival of colonial settlers created a profoundly unequal hierarchy between the newcomers and indigenous Algerians, one that affected legal status, political rights, economic opportunity, and basic social welfare. Those of French and European origin were determined to preserve their monopoly on power by denying Muslims any political representation.[44] As these settlers became more entrenched in Algeria over the course of a century, moreover, they fought relentlessly to hold on to their privileges, lobbying metropolitan leaders and legislators at every turn to forestall any reform.

A complicating factor in this vexed relationship was the French state's colonial project. Ostensibly, the French justified their annexation of Algeria not as a purely self-serving land grab, but as part of their "mission civilisatrice."[45] This civilizing mission, which rested on the universal principles of democracy and color-blind citizenship enshrined in the Revolution of 1789, extended to native Algerians (and all other peoples) the possibility of becoming French citizens in exchange for assimilation. Practically speaking, the legal status of indigenous Muslims became an important testing ground for this project. As a first step in 1865, the state officially extended French nationality to all Muslim natives in Algeria. This status gave them the right to serve on equal terms in the French armed forces and civil service, as well as the right to migrate to the French mainland. The decree also granted them protection under French law, while permitting them to adhere to Islamic law in matters related to their personal status (such as marriage and inheritance). If Muslims wished to become full French citizens with political rights, though, they were required to accept the absolute jurisdiction of the French legal code and reject the authority of religious courts.[46] According to historian Todd Shepard, these new policies, which affirmed French nationality for all and outlined a process of naturalization, "gave institutional form to the promise of assimilation in Algeria."[47] Officials anticipated the eventual breakdown of local traditions that fostered superstition and ignorance, thereby freeing Algerian Muslim men to act as rational citizens capable of participating in governing the nation.[48] Muslims, however, bitterly resented this demand; indeed, most viewed the precondition for full French belonging as equivalent to being asked to commit apostasy.

Tensions around the issue were exacerbated in 1870, when the French state passed the Crémieux Decree, granting Algerian Jews—originally subject to the same policy as Muslims—full citizenship rights.[49] The justification for this shift was that Jews, a population that totaled around five thousand in Algeria, could be assimilated into French culture more easily than the Muslim majority.[50] The new policy outraged Algerian Muslims and suggested an emerging hierarchy of social—and now legal/political—distinction along religious lines that placed French and European Christians above Jews, and Jews above Muslims.[51]

This hierarchy of socioreligious groups betrayed long-held French suspicions about Islam. Already in 1843, writing about his first trip to Algeria, the famed author of *Democracy in America*, Alexis de Tocqueville, declared, "I must say that I emerged convinced that there are in the entire world few religions with such morbid consequences as that of Mohammed. To me it is the primary cause of the now visible decadence of the Islamic world."[52] Islam, in this view, presented the crucial obstacle to the civilizing mission. "To be uplifted," Muslims "had to be separated from their religion, but the project was not that easy because Islam was taken to be at once the cause *and* the effect of their inferiority."[53]

What is crucial here is that a fundamental contradiction structured how French authorities perceived and treated indigenous Algerians, both in the colony and on the mainland. On the one hand, the French state held out the possibility of equality by guaranteeing citizenship, irrespective of race or creed. On the other, it insisted that the necessary first step to attaining citizenship was to become "civilized," a process that required renouncing backward religions and assimilating to a putatively superior and more modern French culture. Even though Algeria was fully incorporated into France and enjoyed the same standing as any other region in the metropole, Muslim Algerians remained second-class colonial subjects. Muslim Algerians, in other words, were contained within the nation, yet never truly belonged to it.

Despite these asymmetries, French nationality gave Algerian Muslims the right to move to and from metropolitan France. Before 1945, relatively few did, and fewer still settled permanently in the hexagon. Nonetheless, some Algerian Muslims did find their way across the Mediterranean, and at crucial moments, France leaned heavily on indigenous Algerians for manpower. Desperate for able-bodied men during the First World War, for example, the French army conscripted more than 500,000 native troops from the colonies, over 280,000 of whom were from North Africa. Nearly 26,000 Muslim Algerians were killed on the battlefields of France and Belgium, and another 72,000 were wounded.[54] In addition, the French state recruited more than 200,000 colonial workers to help alleviate the civilian labor shortage during the war.[55] Anticipating this wartime need, metropolitan politicians even passed a law in 1914 that guaranteed free circulation between Algeria and mainland France.[56]

The flow of Algerians to France actually increased after World War I. The typical pattern was for Muslim men to come to France on their own, work for several years, and then return to their families. For each returning laborer, there was generally one ready to replace him, often a member of his own family or a neighbor from his village. This informal system of rotation characterized French labor dynamics during the interwar period, when as many as 500,000 Algerians worked temporarily in Marseille and Paris.[57] The coming of World War II curtailed this labor-driven migration. Even so, Algerian Muslims enlisted as volunteers and wartime conscripts in the French army's North African units, fighting on the mainland in May 1940 as part of the effort to stave off the country's fall. When the army was reconstituted after the liberation of Paris in 1944, the final campaigns on Germany's western front included around 250,000 colonial troops.[58] Thus, although the overall number of Algerian Muslims in metropolitan France remained relatively small compared to what came later, it is important to recognize that Algerian military and labor migrants were a familiar presence—especially in the larger cities—well before 1945.

The state's treatment of these French nationals, however, was decidedly fickle. Despite relying on Algerian labor in French munitions plants during the First World War, for instance, the state actively pursued strategies to repatriate most of them once the conflict ended. Historian Mary Lewis has noted the irony of this policy: as the police rounded up North Africans living in France in order to send them home, labor officials sought to recruit thousands of more desirable European workers for supplemental manpower.[59] At least part of this approach had to do with dynamics in Algeria itself. European settlers in Algeria actively campaigned

to bring Muslim natives home, arguing that their "expo-
sure to the metropole was potentially dangerous to both
the economic and political well-being of the colony."[60] In
particular, they worried that Algerian natives working on
the mainland would drive up wages in Algeria and possibly
even adopt metropolitan working-class militancy.

For those Muslim Algerians who resided in France during the interwar period, moreover, day-to-day existence was
often precarious. This situation seems counterintuitive: based
on their legal classification as French nationals, Muslim natives should have enjoyed a more secure position than European workers who were officially categorized as "foreigners."
Yet in the early 1920s, indigenous Algerians in the metropole were subjected to arbitrary arrests and detentions.
They were also forced to carry identification papers akin to
internal passports to prove their status as Algerian French
nationals. With the onset of economic depression in the
1930s, they quickly lost the social welfare benefits granted
them by virtue of their legal standing, as local governments
sought easy ways to reduce expenditures.[61] Even though
Muslim Algerians were bound to the French state as nationals, in practice this legal claim gave them very little benefit. Indeed, it may have actually disadvantaged them in
terms of civil rights. Native Algerian workers were sometimes treated in a far more draconian manner than their European counterparts.

Following World War II, however, the French desire to
maintain colonial rule produced the opposite effect. The
1946 constitution that created the Fourth Republic also replaced the old empire with a new French Union. The shift
in nomenclature and structure (which anticipated Britain's
1949 declaration of the Commonwealth) was part of the
French government's effort to reconcile ongoing forms of
subjugation within the empire with international outrage

at the Holocaust. As part of this effort, meaningful reform finally came to Algeria.[62] Two changes were especially important for Algerian migration to France. First, the new constitution introduced a novel legal category, "Muslim French from Algeria," a standing that granted indigenous Algerian Muslim men full political rights and allowed them to maintain their local civil status.[63] A major concession on the part of the French state (which had previously required Algerian men to renounce the authority of Islamic law as a precondition of French citizenship), this shift represented an effort to placate Algerian nationalists' criticism of French inequality.[64] Second, the French government reinstated unregulated passage between Algeria and the mainland in 1947, reopening the borders to Algerian Muslim laborers. Given the highly unequal social and economic relations in Algeria maintained by the French settler population, it is not surprising that native Algerians jumped at the chance to work in metropolitan France. Free movement allowed them to come to the mainland before securing a job. With the arduous procedures involved in recruiting European manpower through the ONI, French employers were only too happy to make the most of this labor source. For metropolitan officials, though, the principal goal of these reforms was to appease increasingly militant Algerian nationalists in the bid to keep Algeria French. In this way, a shift in colonial policy, coupled with the renewed demand for manpower, created the conditions for a major expansion of postwar Algerian Muslim immigration.

In France as well as Britain, then, preserving empire served as a primary motor for government efforts to deal with the postwar need for supplemental labor. While both countries initially sought employment rolls with more "desirable" European workers, immigrants from the colonies ultimately flocked to the metropole in response to evident demand. In

Britain, this migratory pattern led political leaders to reaffirm
the older tradition of free movement within the empire so
as to maintain the United Kingdom's stature as leader of the
Commonwealth. In France, by contrast, it required granting
a new legal status to Muslim Algerians and restoring unrestricted movement as last-ditch compromises to stave off Algerian independence. The twin concerns of empire and labor, in short, drove the emergence of multicultural societies.

Decolonization, Economic Expansion

At first glance, the Dutch immigration patterns seem similar: a need for postwar reconstruction that was filled by new
waves of workers from the colonies. The Netherlands, however, confronted the effects of a disintegrating empire and
postwar economic expansion as two distinct processes. Part
of the reason for this separation was the rapidity with which
the country lost its colonies after the Second World War. Britain and France both faced significant colonial independence
movements that began well before the war and came to fru-
ition in its immediate aftermath: India separated from Britain
in 1947, while Indochina—under the leadership of Ho Chi
Minh—withdrew from the French Union in 1946, spark-
ing the First Indochina War. But their much larger empires
meant that even with these major losses, Britain and France
fought for decades to maintain their other imperial holdings.
For the Netherlands, by contrast, the course of World War II
itself precipitated the fall of its most important colony, the
Dutch East Indies. In 1942, in a bid to control Dutch rubber
and oil resources, the Japanese invaded Indonesia. They occupied it until their surrender in 1945, in the process laying
the groundwork for the collapse of the Dutch colonial state.
Although the Netherlands tried to reestablish its colony in

1945, the Indonesian nationalist leader Sukarno declared an independent Republic of Indonesia and waged a successful military campaign that drove out Dutch forces by 1949.[65]

The process of decolonization spurred an influx of immigrants from Indonesia to the Netherlands. The first wave arrived in 1947 and consisted of the Indisch Dutch, "Eurasians" of mixed Dutch and Indonesian parentage, many of whom had been interned in Japanese concentration camps during the war. They were considered "repatriates" to the homeland, even though most of them had never set foot in the Netherlands before.[66] Additional waves of white Dutch colonial officials, businessmen, planters, and military men returned to the Netherlands between 1949 and the early 1960s. A final wave of Indonesian immigrants consisted of the Moluccans, most of them Protestant Christians indigenous to the island of Ambon who had served in the Royal Dutch Indies Army. Having fought on behalf of the Dutch against both the Japanese and the Indonesian nationalists, Moluccans were in a precarious position. The young Indonesian Republic perceived Moluccan separatist aspirations as a major threat to its sovereignty and refused to let this minority group return to their home in the Molucas Islands (an archipelago within Indonesia). The Moluccans thus had no choice but to follow the Dutch back to the Netherlands and hope for the speedy creation of an independent homeland.

In certain respects, the immigration prompted by the devolution of the Dutch East Indies was relatively seamless. There was no question that "'pure' white settlers" in the former Dutch colony, whether they had been engaged in official or unofficial sectors, would return to the Netherlands.[67] Many of these 120,000 repatriates faced difficulties obtaining housing and adjusting to the abrupt upheaval "that brought an entire way of life to an end."[68] But their private travails did not rise to the level of governmental concern.

The prospect of Indisch Dutch immigration, however, did attract the attention of Dutch officials. Initially, the government expected the mixed-race population to opt for Indonesian citizenship and strongly discouraged "Indos" (as they were commonly known) from coming to the Netherlands. But a large segment of this group identified with their paternal Dutch lineage and began to claim Dutch citizenship, especially in the 1950s as their position within an independent Indonesia grew increasingly insecure. Once it became clear that this immigration was unavoidable, Dutch authorities quickly adopted a proactive approach to head off potential social conflicts presented by the influx of approximately 180,000 mixed-race citizens. The government developed intensive "resocialization and assimilation" programs to help Eurasian newcomers adjust to living in the Netherlands, including lessons for how to behave—starting on the long voyage over![69] Upon arrival, moreover, Indisch immigrants faced enormous pressure to assimilate by adopting habits and attitudes deemed more appropriate to "good Hollanders."[70] Social workers, for example, sought to wean the Indisch Dutch from poor housekeeping practices, chronic indebtedness, and excessive generosity to visitors. In practice, this assimilation process was "neither rapid nor complete." But in retrospective narratives of postwar immigration to the Netherlands, the Indisch became the quintessential success story because they integrated so thoroughly in both economic and social arenas.[71]

More problematic was the situation of the Moluccans. When they came to the Netherlands in 1951, both the Dutch government and the Moluccans expected their stay to last only a few months until they could be returned safely to the Molucas Islands. This expectation shaped Dutch authorities' decisions about the ex-colonial soldiers and their dependents. The government did not allow the Moluccans to join the Royal Dutch Army and continue their military service, but instead discharged the soldiers as soon as they arrived.[72] Adding insult to injury, the 12,500 Moluccans were housed in the former German concentration camps of Westerbork and Vught. This meant they were kept in remote areas apart from the Dutch population, were prevented from working, and had limited possibilities for integration. While their children attended school and learned Dutch, Moluccan adults received few opportunities for language instruction.[73] At the same time, Dutch leaders refused to jeopardize their tenuous relationship with Indonesia by pressing for Moluccan independence. With no home to return to, the Moluccans remained isolated in the Netherlands through the 1950s, although they did organize sporadic demonstrations and petitions to remind the Dutch public of their ongoing demand for an independent homeland.[74]

In the 1960s, a new motor for non-European migration emerged: rapid economic expansion that required new sources of labor. This was a familiar postwar story. But where Britain and France faced manpower deficits almost immediately, the Netherlands, which saw just modest economic growth in the 1950s, did not. Only in the subsequent decade did the Dutch productivity follow the explosive trajectory of the larger Western European countries. At this point, the Netherlands experienced serious shortages of unskilled workers in industries such as shipbuilding, metalworking, mining, textiles, and agriculture.[75] Initially, businesses took the lead by recruiting Italians and other Southern Europeans on an ad hoc basis, but the Dutch government and trade unions wanted to maintain some control over the flow of foreign manpower.[76] In 1960, officials initiated a policy of guest worker recruitment, signing bilateral recruitment agreements with Italy, Spain, Portugal, Greece, and eventually Turkey and Morocco. These treaties facilitated the arrival of foreign labor migrants, who received temporary residence permits that had to be renewed every year.[77] The expectation was that these workers would not settle in the Netherlands, yet between 1960 and 1969, the number of foreign laborers increased dramatically, jumping from 5,700 to 68,900.[78]

By the time the Dutch guest worker policy took hold, though, immigration from Indonesia was largely viewed as a thing of the past. The decade separating the two migratory influxes meant that Dutch people tended to perceive guest workers as an entirely separate phenomenon from Indonesian immigrants, most of whom had already been absorbed into Dutch society. This perception was reinforced by the level of government intervention on behalf of different groups of "foreigners." Dutch authorities had expended significant public resources for newcomers from Indonesia, developing programs to help the Indisch Dutch assimilate and ultimately building special residential complexes in designated urban districts for the Moluccans.[79] These policies meant that Eurasian repatriates became more or less indistinguishable from Dutch people, while Moluccans remained segregated from Dutch society and had largely disappeared from public consciousness by the 1960s.[80] With foreign labor recruits, by contrast, authorities took a hands-off approach, relying on private companies and semivoluntary social work associations (such as a system of regional Foundations for Foreign Workers) to provide basic assistance for adjustment to Dutch society.[81] Because guest workers were seen as a temporary phenomenon, there was no reason for the government to invest in their integration. For the most part, then, foreign laborers had to navigate their new environment on their own, even as their numbers steadily escalated.

In this way, the two key motors for introducing diversity into postwar European society—imperial legacies and manpower shortage—appeared as distinct processes in the Netherlands. With the Indisch Dutch largely absorbed and the Moluccans rendered marginal, guest workers became the face of the "foreigner" in the 1960s. These labor recruits were absolutely essential for the postwar economy, but they had no intrinsic connection to the Netherlands: they were random strangers in search of employment, and they were expected to leave as soon as the need for their work dried up.

Labor and Guest Workers

The Netherlands was not the first country in Western Europe to recruit foreign workers. Both Britain and France pursued versions of this strategy in their efforts to secure a steady supply of able-bodied *European* laborers. British government leaders developed programs to bring POWs, displaced persons, and other wartime refugees to the United Kingdom, calling them "European voluntary workers." But these schemes did not follow the strict definition of a guest worker program because the goal was for these foreign workers to settle permanently in Britain, preferably taking British spouses.[82] Similarly, French officials actively sought European foreign workers to fill their country's labor gap, with the idea that they, too, might eventually become immigrants. In both cases, foreigners from other European countries were understood as preferable to West Indians, Africans, or Asians from across the empires.

Closer to the Dutch practice was the guest worker program in Switzerland. The Swiss, in fact, inaugurated the formalized practice of guest worker recruitment soon after the war was over—and on a somewhat different model than the more familiar case of West Germany. With the end of hostilities, Swiss businesses and industries immediately began the hunt for laborers, turning to neighboring countries. The Swiss convention of recruiting workers from nearby countries had been established well before World War I. But the government did not want to continue its prewar open borders policy of unregulated entry and settlement, which it viewed as leading to "overforeignization" (*Überfremdung*). Anxiety about being overrun by foreigners was particularly acute for Switzerland, a small country with a high level of regional and linguistic diversity.[83] Swiss officials thus established a recruitment program that made the systematic rotation of workers its first principle. The new guest worker program authorized two types of temporary work permits. Seasonal migrants held nine-month permits, which required them to return to their home country for ninety days before applying for a new seasonal permit. They were not allowed to bring dependents or switch to nonseasonal status. Nonseasonal migrants held one-year permits, which could be renewed indefinitely, but these workers could apply for permanent resident status only after an uninterrupted stay of a decade.[84]

The Swiss program strove to balance two competing concerns: the economic demand for additional laborers and the dangers of too many foreigners. With production expanding after the war, the number of foreign workers in Switzerland surpassed a quarter million by 1957; 60 percent were Italians.[85] Yet the stringent enforcement of the rotation policy prioritized social issues over economic imperatives. In the first decade of recruitment, seasonal hands constituted two-thirds of all guest workers in Switzerland.[86] And even for those laborers who obtained annual permits, family reunification was virtually impossible until the mid-1950s.[87] Swiss authorities and employer associations, in fact, showed "a remarkable degree of recruitment constraint—including the willingness to bear the costs of frequent labor turnover" in the effort to prevent permanent immigrant settlement.[88] Well over a decade into guest worker recruitment, most foreign laborers with annual permits still left the country after two or three years, while state officials continued to enforce the departure of seasonal workers at the end of every agricultural and construction season. Employers incurred significant expenses by rotating workers, and the annual labor turnover in some firms remained as high as 40 percent.[89]

The desire to impede the permanent settlement of foreign workers, of course, ran through all guest worker recruitment regimes. States that pursued this policy relied on foreigners to keep their economies running smoothly, but treated them as a cheap and mobile "industrial reserve army."[90] From a purely economic perspective, the guest worker model appeared beneficial to all parties. Recruiting states obtained desperately needed manpower, but without the social problems associated with integrating foreign populations. Sending countries alleviated high levels of unemployment in their own economies. And guest workers earned better wages in a stronger currency and were able to build a nest egg for financial security upon their return home.

Indeed, it was precisely this line of reasoning that drove policy makers in the newly established state of West Germany to turn to guest worker recruitment. But they didn't do so right away. In contrast to Switzerland, West Germany did not face an immediate labor crisis during the first phases of postwar reconstruction. While the loss of able-bodied German men in the war had been massive, the country was in the unique position of needing to absorb thousands of refugees who found themselves in the western occupied zones of Germany: these included ethnic Germans expelled from the eastern territories of the former Third Reich, those fleeing the invading Soviet army, persons displaced during the war, as well as Holocaust survivors. Thus, it was only in the mid-1950s that West German government officials began to think seriously about finding new sources of manpower.

The 1955 bilateral recruitment agreement between the Federal Republic of Germany and Italy shared many of the core goals of the Swiss guest worker program. Above all, by offering work permits for a single year, it sought to establish the expectation that the employment of foreign labor would be a temporary phenomenon. But unlike the Swiss government, which relied on two types of temporary labor and issued far more seasonal permits than annual ones, the German authorities mostly granted annual permits that could be renewed. West German policy makers, as Antje Ellermann has noted, "put great faith in the self-regulatory power of the market and assumed that foreign workers would voluntarily return to their home countries should labor demand slow down."[91] In the first years of guest worker recruitment, the program unfolded as imagined. West Germany opened local branches of the Federal Labor Office in Italy to screen potential workers and match them to companies seeking manpower. Most were men between the ages of twenty and forty, who were willing to come to Germany alone. Employing firms were responsible for their transport and accommodations, generally housing laborers in company barracks in industrial areas away from city centers. Overall, the numbers of Italians remained relatively low. In 1959, fewer than fifty thousand were employed in Germany, and many of those worked in agriculture.[92]

By the middle of the 1950s, the processes that would ultimately facilitate the influx of large numbers of non-Europeans to Western Europe had been set in motion. But at this point, in the first decade after the Second World War, neither the long-term trajectory of national economies nor the norms of migration were fully apparent. Western European countries were just starting to recover from wartime devastation, both psychological and physical. If rebuilding from the war helped jump-start their economies and inaugurated a period of economic boom, few imagined that prosperity would reign for nearly twenty-five years. Nonetheless, every country to the west of the descending Iron Curtain experienced significant economic expansion and struggled to maintain adequate supplies of labor. For those states with no connections to colonial territories, the solution of choice was to import foreigners through guest worker programs. Switzerland and West Germany followed this path, as did the Netherlands once its economy took off. All three countries concluded treaties with Italy that served as the template for future labor agreements with non-European nations. For states that managed to hang on to their empires into the 1960s, colonial and ex-colonial workers from around the globe arrived spontaneously to fill employment rolls in the mother country. This was the dominant pattern in Britain and France. There were, in short, two distinct reservoirs of supplemental manpower for postwar Western Europe. But they produced the same effect: a radically new diversity on European soil. And through the end of the 1950s, the growing presence of non-Europeans was accepted without much reflection.

Complications amid the Economic Boom

Soon, however, events occurred that made the stream of non-European arrivals increasingly worrisome for Western European governments and ordinary citizens alike. In France, the turning point came in November 1954, when the National Liberation Front (Front de Libération Nationale, FLN) coordinated a series of bomb attacks throughout Algeria, inaugurating the Algerian War for Independence. Unlike most other national independence struggles, this conflict did not remain within the territorial confines of the colonial state. Because Algeria was understood as an overseas extension of the metropole—and because there were hundreds of thousands of Muslim Algerians working on the mainland, the war had major repercussions in France itself.

For one thing, the war radically changed the dynamics of Algerian migration and settlement. Previously, most migrants had been lone male workers, who left their wives and children behind while they sought temporary employment in the metropole. With the outbreak of the nationalist conflict, entire families began to come to France to escape the war. New arrivals often hailed from rural areas, where massive bombings destroyed villages and forced entire communities to relocate to military camps.[93] Somewhat paradoxically, then, the fight for independence actually prompted a rapid and sizeable increase in the number of Algerians "in the metropolitan heartland of the colonial power with whom Algerians were at war."[94] During the war years, the number of Algerian immigrants grew from 211,000 to 350,000.

This significant growth transformed settlement patterns. In the immediate postwar period, France suffered from a major housing shortage, which meant that most single Algerian workers lived in government hostels or cheap lodging houses. But these accommodations were inappropriate for families, and so the arrival of tens of thousands of Algerian women and children exacerbated the housing crisis. Algerian Muslims, despite their status as French citizens, received the lowest priority in the social housing queue. For many Algerian families, the only option was the *bidonvilles* (shantytowns) that sprang up during the 1950s in the suburban areas surrounding major cities such as Paris, Lyon, and Marseille.[95] Such shantytowns were located in industrial suburbs, generally cut off by railway tracks, electrical lines, and factories from the areas that native French people inhabited. The living conditions in these overcrowded squatter camps were appalling. Large families squeezed into makeshift huts and houses, constructed on mud floors and cobbled together from wood, corrugated iron, tarred felt, and breeze blocks.[96] Most of the structures had no electricity, running water, sewers, or toilet facilities.[97]

As the war escalated, this segregated immigrant community—and the physical space of the *bidonvilles*—served as a site of struggle between nationalists and the French police in what eventually became a two-front war for Algerian independence. Working through its extensive network on the mainland, the FLN used both persuasion and force to establish control over the social and political life of Algerian immigrants. Local cell leaders in France, for instance, made monthly collections from every individual in their sector, raising around four hundred million francs to finance the Algerian Liberation Army over the course of the eight-year conflict. In addition, the FLN sought to regulate the comings and goings of its supporters as a way to maintain security of the community, but also to create a new Islamic-Socialist society that would "prove impenetrable to the operations of the police."[98]

French authorities, meanwhile, worked to infiltrate and counter this base of Algerian nationalism in the metropole. One tactic was to remove Algerians from the *bidonvilles*. In 1956, the state established the National Society for the Construction of Lodging for Algerian Workers (Société nationale de construction de logements pour les travailleurs algériens, SONACOTRAL) to build hostels and prefabricated lodgings to house Algerian workers and their families.[99] Two years later, French authorities created the Social Action Fund (Fonds d'Action Sociale, FAS) to provide aid to Algerian workers in France.[100] Ironically, it was the escalation of the conflict with Algerian nationalists that prompted the French state to begin to make good on its unfulfilled promises of social welfare for French Muslim citizens. A second tactic was to recall Maurice Papon, notorious for his service in the Vichy government, from his post as Prefect of Constantine and install him as Paris Prefect of Police. The decision not only enlisted colonial personnel to combat the FLN threat on the mainland, but also effectively sanctioned highly repressive policing techniques and revolutionary warfare tactics developed in Algeria for use in metropolitan France.[101] These efforts to intimidate the Algerian worker community, however, generally produced the opposite of their desired effect: they reinforced Algerians' resistance to colonial rule and their support for the FLN.[102]

More important for the question of diversity in France, the Algerian War had serious consequences for the perception and treatment of Muslim Algerians in the metropole. Most French people, according to C. R. Ageron, were initially indifferent to the postwar influx of Algerian workers.[103] At the most basic level, their presence was not new: the stream of Muslim Algerians to the metropole had ebbed and flowed since the interwar period. Perhaps more importantly, though, very few ordinary French people had regular contact with these newcomers, who were largely confined to factory barracks or isolated *bidonvilles*. Public opinion began to shift in 1956 when the state introduced conscription in order to raise the number of troops in Algeria from sixty thousand to four hundred thousand.[104] Resentment over military service was compounded by the internecine war between the FLN and the more moderate National Algerian Movement, which played out on French soil that same year. The violent struggle for control over the Algerian immigrant community in France led media outlets to reinvigorate old stereotypes of "Arab criminality and savagery."[105]

When the FLN decided to open a second front of the war in the metropole in August 1958, attacking mainland police patrols, French civilians witnessed firsthand acts of sabotage and police assassinations that fueled their negative views about Algerians.

The second front, in turn, provoked increasingly draconian treatment of Algerian immigrants by state authorities. In response to the FLN's terrorist attacks on the French mainland, the metropolitan police intensified their repressive measures, targeting anyone who looked Algerian for interrogation and arrest. By October 1961, police chief Papon imposed a strict curfew on all Algerians in the capital and its suburbs. When the FLN network in France organized a peaceful mass demonstration against the curfew in the center of Paris on 17 October, the police carried out a brutal massacre in which hundreds of Algerian demonstrators were beaten, shot, and clubbed to death.[106] At least fifty were thrown—unconscious, with their arms and legs bound—into the Seine and drowned. Over 11,500 more were rounded up, arrested, and detained at the Stadium of Courbevoie and the Palais des Sports.[107]

In this way, the Algerian War radically transformed the place of Muslim Algerian workers in France. The conflict produced a new demographic profile for Algerian migrants as families arrived in ever greater numbers. But in the process, Algerians were increasingly concentrated in slums and shantytowns on the edges of the major cities. Over the course of the protracted war, moreover, Algerians went from a largely invisible presence that sustained the booming economy to an enemy within the nation, whose rooting out and defeat justified all manner of violence and force.

In Britain, too, it was violence that first catalyzed public attention and significant debate on colonial immigration. On the evening of 23 August 1958, a fight broke out in the

St Ann's district of Nottingham, a midsize city in the East Midlands. The specific cause of the conflict varied from witness to witness, but all agreed that a mixed-race relationship (a West Indian man in a bar with a white woman) was at the center of the events. The scene ended with an assault on the young man, drawing nearly a thousand onlookers onto the streets. For several hours, blacks and whites attacked each other until the police dispersed both communities. The racial violence continued intermittently for two weeks.

The Nottingham disturbances were quickly overshadowed by events that began six days later in the west London neighborhood of Notting Hill. In this case, too, the pairing of a West Indian man and white woman set off a racial altercation. What began as a small fight escalated overnight into a mob of three or four hundred white Britons, many of them "Teddy Boys," white working-class youth who gathered in the streets and attacked West Indian homes and businesses. The upheaval went on for at least three days and four nights—the tensions simmering during the day and escalating into street fights between whites and blacks at night—as the police struggled unsuccessfully to contain the swelling crowds. The nighttime throngs, according to a special correspondent for the *Times*, expanded beyond the local population, as gangs of white youths from other parts of the city arrived on the Tube to participate in the attacks.[108] Ultimately, a group of mostly Jamaicans fought back by throwing homemade Molotov cocktails into the charging attackers. This action broke the white siege of the neighborhood and allowed the police to restore order.

Both the Nottingham and Notting Hill riots were widely covered in the British press, which treated these racial clashes as the natural result of friction arising from the immigration of West Indians. The city of Nottingham had a "coloured population" of about three thousand (or one in every hundred), while the Notting Hill district's black residents numbered between two and three thousand.[109] These concentrations of West Indians were not the highest in Britain, according to the *Times*, but they produced tensions similar to those of other British cities with the "same problem—envy, resentment, and sometimes fear of eventual domination of white by black."[110] In its Notting Hill coverage, the newspaper elaborated on the dominant reasons for this resentment: first, a belief that West Indians did no work and collected money from National Assistance; second, that blacks were able to find housing, while whites could not; and third, that immigrants engaged in sexual "misbehavior," especially preying on white women.[111] The influx of black colonials, according to this logic, created a combustible situation in which white Britons increasingly perceived blacks as a threat to their way of life. From here, it was easy to argue that West Indian immigration presented a major problem for British society. The events of 1958 helped lay the groundwork for a public debate about immigration controls, a debate that—as we shall see—had already been taking place behind closed doors among the political elite.

In many respects, the 1962 Commonwealth Immigrants Act was the culmination of the public hand-wringing that grew out of the Nottingham and Notting Hill racial violence. It represented the first effort to restrict nonwhite immigration to Britain. Although government leaders were motivated primarily by social tensions such as those that played out in 1958, they deflected public attention from this concern in two key ways. First, the new law imposed restrictions based on employment potential. It divided would-be immigrants into three groups: those with jobs in hand received A vouchers; those with skills or useful work experience received B vouchers; and unskilled workers in search of employment received C vouchers. This law, it is important to note, applied to all British subjects, but it imposed annual quotas only on people with C vouchers.[112] The "great merit" of the legislation, according to Conservative Home Secretary Rab Butler, was that it appeared to be color blind, even though "its restrictive effect [wa]s intended to, and would in fact, operate on coloured people almost exclusively."[113] In addition, by tying the new limits to the availability of jobs in Britain, the act suggested that economic factors—rather than social concerns—were the primary motivation for the government's decision to limit immigration.[114] This legislation was a crucial cornerstone in the development of British "race relations" policy and the state's broader strategy for dealing with postwar diversity. Significantly, this was the first attempt after 1945 by any European country to stem the flow of non-European immigrants. The policy indicated not just a growing self-consciousness about the structural effects of colonials in the metropole, but also a sense that these newcomers represented a potential problem.

In stark contrast, those states principally engaged in recruiting guest workers remained almost entirely focused on sustaining economic productivity; indeed, most actually *relaxed* the regulations for the residence of foreign laborers during the early 1960s. Within this larger pattern, Switzerland followed the most cautious course. But even the Swiss, with their resolve to prevent widespread permanent settlement, succumbed to economic imperatives. With no sign of the boom waning, businesses began to exert pressure on government authorities to ease the strict rotation policy. Swiss employers argued that endless rotation wasted tremendous resources bringing in new workers every year. By 1960, almost half of the annual permits issued were renewals. That same year, 6,700 guest workers were granted permanent resident status, having met Switzerland's stringent ten-year requirement. For the Swiss government, the reclassification of these guest workers as permanent residents signaled a major shift.[115]

At the same time, this period witnessed great Central European competition to attract guest workers. On the one hand, from the mid-1950s, West Germany had absorbed its surplus population of refugees into the labor force and began to siphon Italian workers. On the other, the establishment of the European Economic Community (EEC) with the 1957 Treaty of Rome introduced free mobility for workers among its member states. Because Switzerland did not join the EEC, it became less attractive as a destination for migrant laborers. As a result, the Swiss government agreed to renegotiate the terms of its labor recruitment treaty with Italy in 1961; the new provisions reduced the waiting period for family reunification to a single year and permanent residence to five years.[116]

Although the trend during this period was to ease restrictions on rotation, Swiss officials continued to worry about being overrun by foreigners. In 1962, despite unprecedented economic growth and continuing demand for labor, the government imposed a cap on the employment of guest workers. The new rule barred firms from hiring foreigners over and above the set number of employees already on the rolls.[117] Foreigners could replace a worker already on the books, but not increase the stipulated limit. The Swiss approach to recruitment thus remained conflicted, torn between the desire to pursue unrestrained growth and the commitment to prevent large numbers of foreigners from settling there.

West German officials, by contrast, had few qualms about importing significant numbers of foreign laborers. The guest worker program had yielded only around 50,000 Italian laborers by the end of the 1950s. Economic production—and with it, the number of unfilled jobs—continued to soar. Then in August 1961, the German Democratic Republic erected

the Berlin Wall, and West Germany lost its steady stream of
East German laborers. Perceiving the shortage of manpower
as a major threat to the booming economy, the West German
government promptly signed additional guest worker treaties with Spain and Greece in 1960, Turkey in 1961, Portugal
in 1964, and Yugoslavia in 1968.[118] By 1964, there were over
764,000 foreign workers in the country. By 1966, that number had risen to over 1,126,000.[119]

Throughout this period, West German policy makers insisted to both themselves and ordinary Germans that guest
workers would ultimately return home. Yet they did not
follow their Swiss counterparts in enforcing measures to
prevent temporary workers from becoming immigrants. Although the recruitment treaties initially limited the dura-
tion of work permits to a year or two, West German officials
quickly bowed to pressure from industry leaders' complaints
about the added costs of worker turnover. In the early
1960s, they stopped adhering to the rotation principle and
began renewing permits more or less automatically.[120] Similarly, while German recruitment officers generally favored
male guest workers, who were single or were willing to leave
their families behind, they also increasingly tolerated family
reunification.[121] Some policy makers actually argued for the
advantages of family migration—a model they hoped would
produce lower worker turnover, maintain public order, and
preserve family values.[122] Recent research suggests that a
large proportion of married guest workers did migrate with
their wives, many of whom were ultimately hired by their
husbands' German firms.[123] By 1968, 30 percent of the adult
foreign population in West Germany had entered the country as a dependent spouse, while 57 percent of the male guest
worker population had been in residence for at least four
years.[124] Nevertheless, politicians and policy makers alike re-

fused to face the possibility that migrant workers would opt to stay.[125]

A key explanation for this blindness was West German leaders' perception that economic health played a crucial role in their efforts to distinguish the democratic Federal Republic from its Nazi predecessor. Leaders of the Federal Republic believed that building a strong, stable economy and boosting prosperity would help establish the new state's political legitimacy in the eyes of the West German population.[126] In fact, as Minister of Economics, Ludwig Erhard made the guest worker program a signature policy initiative, part of his attempt to ensure economic strength and dynamism. The bilateral recruitment treaties also helped to solidify ties with other European countries. Economics was thus the linchpin for both democratization and forging close relations with the Western powers in the emerging Cold War.

West German commitments to prolonging expansion remained, moreover, even though as early as 1961 government officials had an inkling that the so-called guests were becoming permanent residents. In 1964, members of the cabinet under Erhard (now Chancellor) debated revising the recruitment treaty with Turkey, which originally restricted the residence period to a maximum of two years and prohibited family reunification.[127] While the Interior Ministry argued for maintaining and enforcing these limits, the Labor Ministry and the Confederation of German Employers vehemently opposed them. Ultimately, the cabinet relaxed both provisions, fearful that singling out Turks with these restrictions "would set back the government's efforts to enhance West Germany's image abroad."[128] In this way, the continued success of the economy and foreign policy imperatives took precedence over mounting evidence that guest workers were becoming permanent immigrants.

It was around this time (early 1960s) that the Netherlands joined the ranks of countries with national guest worker programs. Following both the Swiss and West Germans, Dutch authorities initially signed treaties to obtain workers from Italy, Spain, and Portugal. Because the Netherlands began its program somewhat later than Switzerland (fifteen years) and Germany (five years), however, it did not attract nearly as many Southern Europeans. It thus turned to Turkey, Greece, Morocco, and Yugoslavia, with Turkey and Morocco ultimately providing the bulk of its foreign labor population.[129] Despite the differences in timing, the basic hallmarks of guest worker recruitment appeared in the Netherlands as well. The Dutch Ministry of Foreign Affairs issued temporary residence permits that had to be renewed every year, the goal being to create a reserve army of manpower that could be adjusted to the demands of the labor market.[130] In 1965, as non-European migration was ramping up, the Dutch Parliament passed the Aliens Act and General Administrative Orders, which formalized rules for admitting immigrants, established a system of work permits, and imposed a five-year period of uninterrupted residence in order for a foreigner to apply for permanent resident status.[131] Ultimately, the Netherlands pursued what political scientist Eytan Meyers has described as a "relatively liberal immigration control policy," an assessment supported by the numbers.[132] Guest workers skyrocketed from 6,600 in 1960 to 84,200 in 1970; of that total, there were 100 Turks and Moroccans in 1960 and 41,000 a decade later.[133]

Much like those of Switzerland and West Germany, Dutch policies around guest workers during this period were driven almost exclusively by the economic boom. What needs to be emphasized here is that these states were not passive bystanders to the demographic transformation of their societies. Foreign migrants from outside the continent did not simply flood these countries while the Swiss, West German, and Dutch authorities were not paying attention. These states and their political leaders actively sought—and even competed with each other for—nonwhite and, increasingly, non-Christian workers to propel economic prosperity. But this approach created the conditions for future complications: namely, the unexpected and unwanted long-term settlement of large numbers of brown, Muslim foreigners.

The Long Shadow of Empire

The desire to promote economic expansion was not just limited to countries that recruited guest workers. The French government also sought to encourage economic growth by opening the door to foreign able-bodied laborers. This priority meant that France agreed to preserve the principle of free circulation of people with Algeria in the 1962 Evian Accords, which established Algeria as a fully independent state.[134] That both former colony and colonizer endorsed allowing the continuing migration of Algerian workers to France might seem somewhat surprising. For Algerian leaders, after all, the outward flow of precious human resources was "a product and symbol of colonial dependency."[135] But the influx of Algerian workers was no less problematic for French authorities: Algerians had been the enemy within and were living testaments to the country's humiliating colonial defeat. Yet for both parties, economic considerations were decisive.

The Algerian economy emerged from the nationalist struggle in shambles. During the eight-year conflict, nearly half of the rural population in Algeria had abandoned homes, fields, and livestock as a result of forced military displacement. Independence, moreover, prompted the mass exodus of around eight hundred thousand French settlers. Their departure effectively drained the ranks of engineers, technicians, and administrators from the country, since indigenous Algerians had been barred from these professions under colonial rule. As a parting shot, the Organisation de l'armée secrète (OAS), Secret Army Organization systematically destroyed much of the country's capital equipment, as well as public buildings, schools, and oil depots. With all these problems, the new government under Ahmed Ben Bella struggled to expand job opportunities. It thus viewed the emigration of unemployed workers to France as a necessary measure to relieve pressure on its efforts to recover economically and establish a stable independent state.[136]

With the distraction and expense of the Algerian War over, the French economy began to take off. During the boom years under President Charles de Gaulle, government authorities and policy makers alike believed that foreign workers were absolutely necessary for economic prosperity, and they therefore adopted a laissez-faire approach to immigration. What began as an effort to secure enough labor quickly became "an open process whereby employers had virtually unlimited access to new supplies of immigrant labor."[137] One Labor Ministry official specifically championed the advantages of young Algerian immigrants, who had "the 'merit' of being mobile and taking positions" for which using "French labour risk[ed] inflexibility; for example, in terms of increases in salary and redundancies in the event of restructuring."[138] Thus, the French, too, embraced the free movement of Algerians to their country even after the bitter nationalist conflict. The result was that between 1962 and 1965, around 111,000 Algerians came to France, significantly more than the annual average of 11,000 during the years of the Algerian War.[139]

On the surface, the Algerians who sought work in France after the Evian Accords appeared to be following the well-established migration path across the Mediterranean. After all, they could still come to France without obtaining work or residence permits. But unlike in the colonial period when Algerians were French nationals and eventually citizens, after 1962 Algerian laborers were described as foreigners, immigrants from a wholly separate country (although according to the terms of the peace treaty, Algerians could claim French nationality until the end of a five-year transition period).[140] Their tenuous status made them especially vulnerable to unscrupulous employers. Because Algerians could enter France outside the regulatory mechanisms of the ONI that governed other foreign workers, they could be recruited at the factory gates and paid below-market wages. Firms that employed a foreigner through independent channels were supposed to register the hire with the state in order to regularize the worker's legal situation. However, many chose not to register Algerians, which technically rendered them illegal. Most Algerians, though, were unaware of this rule—which became applicable to them only with their post-Evian status— and they often had to live as highly vulnerable illegals (clandestins) because their employment had not been reported.[141]

Significantly, both the Algerian and French governments regarded Algerian labor migration after 1962 as a temporary phenomenon—in much the same way that the signatories of bilateral labor treaties saw guest worker migration. As far as the newly independent Algerian state was concerned, the large number of Algerians in France was a neocolonial arrangement, an expedient measure to be terminated as soon as possible. Under the leadership of Ben Bella's successor Houari Boumediene in the early 1970s, in fact, the government began to restrict skilled workers from leaving the country. French officials, too, insisted that the continuing presence of Algerian workers would be short-lived. As they had since 1945, state authorities favored European laborers to relieve the ongoing manpower shortage and signed labor agreements with Spain in 1961 and Portugal in 1963 as part of a concerted effort to attract more immigrant workers from Europe.[142] The commitment to diversifying the immigrant labor pool was so great that they also concluded treaties with Morocco, Tunisia, Mali, and Mauritania in 1963; Senegal in 1964; and Yugoslavia and Turkey in 1965.[143] With the numbers of Algerians rapidly escalating after 1962, moreover, leaders enacted the 1964 Nekkache-Grandval accord that imposed an annual quota of twelve thousand Algerians.[144]

Even though the colonial relationship with Algeria came to an end in 1962, then, the legacy of empire continued to influence the course of postwar labor migration in France and the ground-level ethnic diversity it helped engender. The severing of the formal legal relationship did not mean that previous ties simply disappeared. Indeed, France remained deeply reliant on well-established colonial networks to keep its economy supplied with willing laborers.

Older imperial connections also had a major impact on the contours of the multiethnic society taking shape in Britain during the 1960s. The reverberations of a disappearing empire were exemplified most vividly in the so-called Kenyan Asian crisis. This crisis came as the country was beginning to experience initial signs of economic downturn (a first for Western European countries in the postwar period). The slowdown ultimately forced the government to devalue the pound in 1967. But the roots of the crisis went all the way back to the mid-nineteenth century, during the height of imperialism, when the British had encouraged Asians from the Indian subcontinent to move to Kenya (and East Africa more generally) to establish a colonial infrastructure for their expanding empire. Asians initially went to Africa as railroad builders, traders, and laborers, but by 1945, the Kenyan Asian community was firmly rooted and working in diverse occupations, including business, the police force, and the bureaucracy. Asians were major contributors to the economic development and prosperity of Kenya and greater East Africa.

Complications began to emerge in 1963, when Kenya became independent. Among the country's first acts was the abolition within its territory of British nationality law and the establishment of Kenyan nationality. Most Asians chose not to apply for Kenyan citizenship, instead retaining their status as citizens of the United Kingdom and Colonies (UKC). This meant that the Asians who remained in Kenya after 1965 faced an uncertain existence. As non-Kenyans, they were unable to obtain or even retain work permits, and were permitted to trade only in restricted areas of the country. Those who held civil servant jobs were fired in favor of Africans.[145] With neither a future in Africa, nor the right (or, in many cases, inclination) to migrate to India or Pakistan, Kenyan Asians traveled to England. By early 1967, nearly a thousand were arriving monthly.[146]

This influx of Asians came on the heels of the 1962 Commonwealth Immigrants Act, which had been designed to slow the pace of immigration from the former colonies. Faced with an increasingly difficult situation in Kenya, British lawmakers assumed that the 1962 bill would apply to all Commonwealth immigration. This idea, however, as political scientist Randall Hansen points out, was based on two false assumptions: first, that all citizens of the UKC outside Britain would become citizens of an independent Commonwealth nation once their country of residence achieved independence; and second, that only British passports issued under a colony's authority would need to be subject to immigration regulation.[147] These presumptions did not apply to the Kenyan situation or take into account the complex labor migration patterns fostered and facilitated by the British during colonial rule. Most Kenyan Asians had no wish to become Kenyan citizens, and the Kenyan state—increasingly committed to Africanization policies—was not inclined to grant it to them. These desires, however, would have had little impact on the demographics of postwar immigration to Britain, except that after Kenyan independence in 1963, all British passports issued to citizens of the UKC in Kenya had been granted by the authority of the British government, not the colony. As a result, some 13,600 Kenyan Asians arrived freely on British soil in 1967.[148]

Throughout that year, British nightly news programs showed Asians queuing at travel agencies to buy one-way tickets out of Kenya. British public sentiment had already begun to favor restrictions in the wake of the racial violence in Nottingham and Notting Hill. With the numbers of arriving Kenyan Asians mounting, between 69 and 72 percent of the population supported tightening immigration controls even further.[149] Harold Wilson's Labour government responded by rushing what became the 1968 Commonwealth Immigrants Act through Parliament in a single week. The new bill exempted from quota only those who had a "qualifying connection" to the United Kingdom: citizens of the UKC who were themselves—or had a parent or grandparent who was—born, adopted, or naturalized in the United Kingdom.[150] The 1968 legislation effectively halted the flow of Kenyan Asians, restricting the entry of heads of households from this group to fifteen hundred annually.[151]

Three years later, a second crisis developed around Ugandan Asians, who faced a similar predicament as their Kenyan counterparts. In this case, though, the newly independent state took a much harder line toward its Asian community. Uganda's leader Idi Amin announced in August 1972 that all Asian UKC citizens would be expelled in three months' time. After just over a week of intense diplomatic negotiations, in which Amin refused to budge and India agreed to take in only a limited number of refugees, Conservative Prime Minister Edward Heath announced that Britain would accept full responsibility for the Ugandan Asians. This was a particularly tricky predicament for Heath, whose government was strongly committed to tighter immigration controls and had just passed the 1971 Immigration Act. This act formally distinguished between patrials and non-patrials—those who were native and those who were not—for right of entry to Britain. Studiously avoiding all reference to the Kenyan Asian crisis just four years before, the prime minister argued that the situation of the Ugandan Asians was a special case that warranted exceptional treatment. Heath invoked "our obligations," by implication to former colonial subjects, but emphasized "holding out a friendly hand to people in danger and distress": ultimately around twenty-eight thousand Ugandan Asians were allowed to settle permanently in the United Kingdom.[152]

Above all, the crises around East African Asians underscored the extent to which older—and in many cases, forgotten—imperial arrangements shaped the emergence of multicultural Britain. Yet even though East African Asians were the product of migratory patterns established by the British to further their interests, these causal connections were largely missing from subsequent public discussion. Politicians like Heath argued behind the scenes that Britain needed to honor its obligations, but they tended to frame their public comments in terms of immigration. This turned refugees of decolonization into just another group of aliens clamoring for entrance into a more prosperous country. The arrival of East African Asians in the United Kingdom, moreover, also marked a major shift already under way in postwar British demographics. While settlers from the Caribbean had dominated in the late 1940s and 1950s, people originally from the Indian subcontinent began to immigrate to Britain in significant numbers in 1958 and constituted the largest group of newcomers during the 1960s and 1970s.

For the two old colonial powers, the 1960s marked a significant expansion of the pattern whereby the empire returned home. French businesses actively sought out Algerian workers as a crucial source of cheap labor even after the colonial ties between the two countries had been severed. The result was that the population of Algerians in France more than doubled between 1962 and 1975.[153] British authorities, by contrast, scrambled to deal with the unanticipated consequences of previous imperial decisions. Large numbers of immigrants from India and Pakistan raced to "beat the ban" on free movement within the Commonwealth, signaled by increasingly restrictive legislation in 1962 and 1968. Meanwhile, East African Asians expelled from Kenya and Uganda had no place except the United Kingdom to go. For both France and Britain, though, the expansion of postcolonial migration produced virtually the same results as the guest worker recruitment in Central Europe: more nonwhite people, more non-Christian people, and more people coming from outside the continent.

Oil Crisis and the End of Prosperity

By the early 1970s, Britain was no longer the only nation experiencing economic slowdown. The changing conditions across Western Europe cast the now established presence of large numbers of non-European workers and their families in a new light. The strength of Western European economies had been the crucial linchpin that fueled the arrival of diverse populations and allowed the growth of multicultural societies to go largely unnoticed. Sustained economic prosperity provided the unimpeachable rationale for continuing to encourage the immigration of foreign laborers to France and the importation of guest workers to Switzerland, Germany, and the Netherlands. Unprecedented levels of affluence also made it easier for European governments and populations to focus on economic benefits and ignore the social consequences of these labor-driven policies—especially the mounting evidence that foreign labor migrants who had been envisioned as temporary residents were becoming permanent immigrants.

Throughout the twenty-five-year period of unparalleled economic expansion and large-scale labor migration, Switzerland hewed to the most conservative path. Following the 1962 efforts to limit foreign workers, the Swiss Federal Council defied the strong opposition of organized business and imposed a "global ceiling system" that capped the employment of foreign laborers for the country as a whole.[154] Yet intense competition for Italian labor also forced Swiss leaders to relax the rules on family reunification and permanent residency, concessions that pushed the country's foreign population to 18.4 percent in 1973.[155] Somewhat ironically, many foreign workers achieved legal security and sent for their families in 1973, just as the Organization of the Petroleum Exporting Countries (OPEC) announced an embargo that drove up the price of oil and brought Western Europe's extended era of economic growth to an abrupt end.

While Swiss authorities constantly worried about the social effects of guest worker recruitment, many French officials uncritically championed the benefits of immigration. Michel Massenet, the head of the Population and Migrations section of the Ministry of Labor, extolled the advantages of young Algerian workers—namely, their mobility and willingness to accept poorly paid or precarious positions that their French counterparts would not.[156] The December 1969 issue of *Revue politique et parlementaire* (Political and Parliamentary Review), a key public policy journal for French legislators and bureaucrats, asserted, "We can therefore claim that by underplaying its demographic potential and constituting itself instead as an immediate economic resource, foreign labor has clearly been an important factor in economic stability. We might even go so far as to regret the fact that, in terms of French economic growth, this resource has not been even more substantial."[157] This perspective deliberately sidelined "demographic" considerations in favor of economic expediency.

By the end of the 1960s, however, a handful of policy makers—most notably Massenet himself—began to express serious concern about social tensions caused by recent Algerian immigration.[158] These worries echoed a growing hostility of French workers toward immigrants and a sense among the general public that "immigration was contributing to a rapid deterioration in urban living standards and conditions."[159] Government authorities, in turn, proposed a new quota system for immigrants that favored ethnic and national groups who were seen as more likely to adapt to French norms. In early 1972, moreover, Ministers of the Interior and Labor outlined new restrictions on work and residence permits. The Marcellin-Fontanet circulars, as they came to be known, stated that foreign laborers would now be regularized only if they provided evidence of a twelve-month work contract and decent housing. Failure to produce satisfactory documentation was grounds for expulsion. The goal was to force all foreigner workers to use the state-controlled ONI to obtain employment in France, so that the state could better determine the hiring of foreigners according to its economic needs and social concerns. But this new policy also affected long-resident foreign workers if they suddenly became unemployed. The change provoked immediate protests among foreign workers, including hunger strikes, office sit-ins, demonstrations, and a major wildcat strike of 367 foreigners at the Renault car factory in Boulogne-Billancourt in April 1973.[160] Nevertheless, when conservative Valéry Giscard d'Estaing became president in 1974, his government went even further, suspending all immigration.[161] Between 1968 and 1974, then, France gradually tightened immigration controls. The shift was motivated not so much by economic decline or rising unemployment, but rather by the desire to achieve "ethnic balance" and the fear of social tensions that would arise if Algerians continued to dominate the foreign workforce.[162] In this respect, France began to follow Switzerland's lead in prioritizing social cohesion over economic growth as it reshaped immigration policy.

The period of liberal immigration policy was comparatively short in the Netherlands, framed by a slow economic expansion that didn't take off until 1960 and an economic recession that began at the end of 1973. Beyond the 1965 Aliens Act that set out the basic parameters for guest workers, there was relatively little high-level political engagement with the business of recruitment until 1970. In that year, the Dutch government published its first policy paper on migrant labor with recommendations for reform. It suggested that an admission quota for foreign workers be established and firmly tied to the country's economic needs. It endorsed measures to encourage return migration. And it made official the de facto practice of delegating the oversight of migrants' social needs to nongovernmental welfare and social work associations. Dutch authorities also tried to tighten admissions standards for guest workers. But neither reform effort produced much effect. In fact, the recruitment of foreign labor reached its peak in 1970–71.[163]

Dutch citizens, meanwhile, were becoming increasingly restive to the large numbers of foreigners living in their towns and cities. There had been sporadic acts of violence against Italians and Spaniards in the early 1960s, as well as attacks on Turks and Moroccans in the late 1960s and early 1970s.[164] In August 1972, a Turkish landlord summarily evicted a Dutch woman and her three children from their Rotterdam house. A confrontation between Turks and Dutch locals soon ensued that sparked rioting throughout the city of Rotterdam, with Turkish restaurants and hostels destroyed over several nights.[165] This unrest, which the media quickly dubbed Holland's first race riot, transformed isolated incidents of anti-immigrant violence into a growing sense that there were too many foreigners in the Netherlands.

Yet, according to most accounts, it was the onset of the economic recession provoked by OPEC's oil embargo that prompted Dutch lawmakers to take action. In 1974, government officials issued a second policy paper, "Memorandum in Reply to the Law on Foreign Workers," which again proposed tighter controls on the entry of foreign laborers, efforts to promote return to the country of origin, and limits on the stay of Mediterranean workers to two years.[166] In 1976, these recommendations produced a new law: a cap on the employment of foreigners that barred Dutch firms from hiring more than twenty Mediterranean laborers.[167] While the government did not officially end recruitment, it issued a significantly lower number of new work permits.

In West Germany, growing doubts about the unexpected settlement of guest workers began to surface around 1970. At that point, there were nearly two million foreign laborers in the Federal Republic. Major industrial and urban areas, furthermore, increasingly struggled to meet the housing and education needs of guest workers and their children, a strong indication that family unification had transformed transient laborers into permanent settlers.[168] But these concerns were mitigated by a spontaneous drop in the number of guest workers following a short-lived decline in economic production during 1966 and 1967. The fact that the drop occurred without forced rotation suggested to some policy makers that guest worker recruitment could still regulate itself according to labor-market needs.[169]

By 1973, however, there were unmistakable signs that the nature of migration had changed. That summer, the West German automotive industry experienced a series of major work stoppages. In June, female workers—native German and foreign alike—walked out at the Pierburg factory in Neuss to protest low wage categories that specifically disadvantaged women. In August, Turkish laborers struck at the Ford factory in Cologne, demanding extended vacation time that would allow them to visit their families in Turkey. These wildcat strikes were part of a broader pattern of labor unrest during the early 1970s, but they drew attention to a new role for guest workers. Even as foreign laborers were making demands unique to their specific situation (e.g., extended summer holidays), they were also staking claims in Germany. They expressed their grievances not by appealing to the Turkish consulate, but rather by organizing strikes among and sometimes even in conjunction with their German colleagues. In taking labor action, recruited workers demonstrated a commitment to and broader participation in West German society.[170] Essentially, guest workers were behaving a lot more like immigrants.

In November 1973, just weeks after OPEC triggered the oil crisis, the West German government suspended all foreign labor recruitment. Chancellor Willy Brandt's cabinet made its decision after a Ministry of Labor report concluded that guest worker recruitment no longer made sense "from a macroeconomic and socio-political perspective."[171] Once West German leaders began to absorb the fact of immigrant settlement and the social and infrastructural costs associated

with it, importing foreign labor could not continue. The recruitment halt, of course, came too quickly on the heels of
the oil embargo to have been a direct response to tangible
economic decline. But officials used the developing crisis to
justify their decision. The economic rationale was crucial
as a way of avoiding hard questions about the guest worker
program, not only from the sending countries, which understood recruitment in terms of an economic calculus, but also
from ordinary Germans, who had been repeatedly told that
the presence of foreigners was the price of the prosperity they
enjoyed.

By the time West German officials suspended guest worker
recruitment, all the Western European countries that had experienced large-scale migration—whether colonials or guest
workers—had implemented some version of immigration
control. Some of these states imposed restrictions in response
to explicit worry about the social tensions created by large foreign communities. Switzerland began with an unusually restrictive guest worker recruitment regime in order to preempt
social complications from foreign settlement. Meanwhile,
Britain clamped down on Commonwealth immigration in
the early 1960s, prompted by urban unrest in Nottingham and
Notting Hill, and reduced the entitlements of ex-colonials for
another decade. For France, the Netherlands, and, above all,
West Germany, economic growth largely trumped social concerns. In France, Algerians had been an easy source of labor
first as colonial subjects, then as citizens, and, after the Algerian War, as foreign (guest) workers. Only in the late 1960s did
French officials begin to worry openly about the difficulty of
Algerians in adapting to French norms. At this point, public concern about social cohesion prompted authorities to
restrict Algerian immigration. For the Netherlands and West
Germany, however, it really took the prospect of economic

downturn to break through the status quo of unhindered and increasingly, unregulated, foreign labor recruitment.

With the possible exception of Britain, whose political leaders admitted behind the scenes that colonial migration could produce permanent settlement, Western European countries operated under the assumption that halting the flow of immigrants or suspending foreign labor recruitment would prevent significant numbers of non-European workers from putting down roots in their societies. Policy makers further imagined that this strategy would stave off any social issues introduced by the influx of all these foreigners. In particular, those states that had relied on the guest worker framework to address their labor shortages—and this included France after 1962—took for granted a core expectation: namely, that imposing tighter rules for entry or ending recruitment programs altogether would signal temporary guests to return home. From the perspective of recruiting nations, after all, the very presence of guest workers was predicated on manpower shortage. Thus, when short-term laborers were no longer needed, they would simply go back to where they came from. But if Western European countries expected to be able to reset their demographic profiles to 1930 or even 1945 by closing their borders, these measures—coming after decades in which social concerns were all but ignored in favor of economic growth—were too little too late.

CHAPTER TWO

Managing
Multicultural
Societies

In many respects, 1973 marked the end of postwar prosperity. More specifically, it marked the end of an unspoken assumption—shared by most Europeans—that collective economic expansion would continue unabated. Whereas the dominant discourses of the late 1940s and early 1950s had focused on heroic wartime survival and rebuilding from the rubble, the enduring theme of the mid-1970s was a contracting society saddled with intractable problems and intrusive new constraints. The five-month OPEC embargo quadrupled the price of oil, and its effects rippled throughout Western Europe in the form of escalating prices, fuel shortages, and massive unemployment. Governments, in turn, imposed speed limits, Sunday driving bans, and heating restrictions. The optimistic boom years of the 1950s and 1960s were over.

The oil crisis sent an unequivocal message about the vulnerability of European financial systems to global forces and plunged every Western European country into recession for the rest of the decade. It also significantly affected people's mood: a sense of crisis and malaise reigned. As one popular historian of the era has suggested, Britain was a "seedy, shabby, downbeat" world in the mid-1970s.[1] The state of emergency in the United Kingdom may have appeared particularly intractable, but the outlook in Western Europe as a whole was characterized by similar frustration and pessimism.

One notable (and understudied) effect of this malaise was a strengthening of Western European leaders' resolve to curb immigration and guest worker recruitment. Nearly a quarter century of expanding labor migration came to a grinding halt: by 1974, both Britain and France had closed their borders to most foreign workers and severely curtailed immigration from the former colonies. Switzerland, West Germany, and the Netherlands, meanwhile, suspended their guest worker recruitment programs. The countries that had actively imported manpower expected that these measures would significantly reduce the number of non-European residents. Here, after all, was a clear signal that foreign labor was no longer needed. But the numbers initially remained steady and then—much to the dismay of most Europeans— actually rose, as foreigners realized that the opportunity for bringing over their families was closing. For Western European leaders, the fact that guest workers did not return home at this juncture was not simply a logistical problem of supply exceeding demand. It also constituted a breach of the basic premise on which labor recruitment had been based. As they saw it, guest workers—and not European governments— were failing to follow through with their side of the bargain.

Largely missing from the public announcements of immigration control and the suspending of recruitment was any explicit acknowledgment of the now significant migrant communities that existed across much of Western Europe.

Given the extensive hand-wringing about the effects of the recession and the new sacrifices that it required, one might have
expected some public statement about what state authorities
planned to do with the tens of thousands of foreign workers
who had been brought to Western Europe. Yet there was no
open discussion about how these two issues fit together. Nor
was there any acknowledgment that European states themselves had created the conditions for migrant laborers to stay.

In retrospect, the mid-1970s should have been a collective
moment of European reckoning. The nearly twenty-five-year
scramble to procure foreign workers had resulted in the permanent settlement of transient labor that was increasingly
nonwhite, non-Christian, and non-European. Temporary
guest work, in short, now began to resemble long-term immigration. Communities of different ethnicities, cultures,
and religions increasingly lived side by side with the British,
French, Dutch, and Germans, spawning multicultural societies throughout Western Europe. But with the notable exception of Britain, few European countries immediately grasped
the effects of these developments.

Fewer still were willing to discuss openly how the protracted residence of multiethnic labor forces might impact
or even alter their societies. Indeed, the government officials
who addressed the various policy issues generated by the inflow of foreign workers operated almost entirely behind the
scenes, striving to make their initiatives largely opaque to
ordinary citizens. Above all, European leaders did not want
these initial efforts at multicultural management to draw
the notice of curious journalists or become targets of public scrutiny. They therefore tended to adopt abstract pro-
cedural terms such as "race relations," "insertion," and—in
the Dutch case—"pillarization" that effaced the complexity
of what was actually happening on the ground. The goal
was to make the process of managing new diversity cold,

efficient, and largely invisible—in order to attract as little attention as possible.

For our purposes, however, this bureaucratic process of ground-level management intermixed with disavowal is a crucial part of the larger story. In narrative terms, it requires a certain patience on the part of the reader: this was policy language explicitly designed to drain the politics of human drama and efface the broader stakes—so it is easy to become a little numb to the shifting categories and technocratic abstractions. But without a clear understanding of these initial policy efforts, it is simply impossible to make full sense of the volatile controversies to come. Only by unpacking the management strategies first developed in the wake of recessionary downturns can we assess the more explosive politics around particular immigrant practices (such as wearing headscarves) and often blistering critiques (from opponents of Muslim immigration more generally) that more typically serve as the starting points for scholarly analysis of European multiculturalism.

Race Relations

If Britain was the first Western European country to experience large-scale non-European immigration, it was also the first to confront the social implications of that migratory movement. The process of dealing with what the British called "race relations" began in the late 1950s and unfolded for almost two decades before neighbors like West Germany finally admitted that guest workers had become permanent residents. In many respects, Britain's early acknowledgment of the broader effects of immigration was not especially surprising. When people from Jamaica, Trinidad, and Barbados landed on British shores in the late 1940s, they did so as

British subjects with the same rights of residence, work, and political participation as any English-born citizen. This status meant that there was little talk of sending West Indians back. While British authorities clearly favored Europeans as a supplemental workforce and went to great lengths to encourage such laborers to immigrate, they also understood that West Indians were entitled to settle permanently in the United Kingdom.

Because these newcomers came spontaneously and were not recruited as part of a government scheme or guest worker program, most arrivals beyond the initial *Empire Windrush* passengers had to fend for themselves in securing jobs, housing, and basic social services. They were forced to navigate British society and grapple with British prejudices with little buffering from government agencies or even employing firms. Ordinary Britons, in turn, came face to face with black neighbors, black coworkers, and black customers. In general, West Indians had no problem finding employment in the 1950s, but many encountered hostility in their search for lodging. With publicly subsidized council housing regulated by strict residency requirements and subject to long waiting lists, new arrivals from the Caribbean were forced to seek accommodations on the private market, where they faced open prejudice and discrimination. As one early immigrant explained, "They always put on the board, 'Blacks—Niggers not wanted here,' . . . 'No Niggers' or 'No Colour,' things like that. So it's very hard to get a room."[2] From the very beginning of postwar immigration, West Indians and British natives interacted over social issues in a climate of tension. But at least they interacted.

British authorities kept close tabs on this unsolicited immigration and privately expressed concern about its long-term implications. But settlement from the Caribbean proved to be a trickle at first, with the 1951 census noting only around

15,000 British residents who had been born in the West Indies.[3] Things changed in 1952, when the US Congress passed the McCarran Walter Act, severely limiting the number of Caribbean migrants entering the United States.[4] After that, West Indian arrivals in Britain escalated, with some 240,650 Caribbeans coming between 1953 and 1961.[5] Despite the relatively low initial numbers, the Labour government convened a secret committee as early as 1950 to discuss the rising black population. Five years later, with the Conservatives now in power, Prime Minister Anthony Eden asked his aides to explore legislative ways to curb immigration.[6] Right from the start, then, both parties worried about an emerging pattern of postcolonial migration.

Their emphasis was on preventing the entrée of West Indian and other "undesirable" New Commonwealth migrants because once they were on British soil, they enjoyed full rights of citizenship. Indeed, these entitlements meant that most British officials quickly grasped the broader social implications of immigration. They feared that "a large coloured community as a noticeable feature of our social life would weaken ... the concept of England or Britain to which people of British stock throughout the Commonwealth are attached."[7] At the same time, political leaders also recognized that discriminatory controls would be seen by the world as a form of state-sanctioned racism and, perhaps more importantly, as an insult and provocation by the former colonies. Because the Commonwealth was an important symbol of Britain's global authority and provided a counterweight to the threat of Soviet encroachment, politicians remained reluctant to adopt aggressive policies such as immigration quotas that might diminish Britain's place at the center of this international community of nations.[8]

In this respect, the 1958 racial violence in Nottingham and Notting Hill was a clear turning point. The riots made immigration an issue of public debate and prompted a more open discussion of the topic at all levels of society. Scholars have argued that many factors played into these uprisings: the postwar housing shortage, white working-class deprivation, Teddy Boy delinquency, public irritability about migrants, as well as the more transparent racist activism by far-right agitators such as Sir Oswald Mosley.[9] In 1958, however, most contemporary journalists stressed the race and immigration angle, echoing public officials who tended to interpret the violence "as a spontaneous and inevitable reaction to the mere presence of migrants."[10] Two MPs from Nottingham, for instance, explicitly criticized the country's open-door policy that allowed the unrestricted entry of people from the Commonwealth. While the Labour MP argued that "keen competition for housing" and "ominous unemployment trends" required the government to curtail immigration, his Conservative counterpart called for "a quota or definite restrictions on people from overseas."[11] The Notting Hill uprising prompted the Labour representative for that London district to assert: "The government must introduce legislation quickly to end the tremendous influx of coloured people from the Commonwealth.... For years white people have been tolerant. Now their tempers are up."[12]

This racial unrest did not produce an immediate change in policy, however. For the remainder of the decade, Harold Macmillan's Conservative cabinet privately debated such possibilities, but remained divided and did not introduce legislation in the House of Commons. In the meantime, new pressures were building. Migration from the Indian subcontinent began to increase in 1958, generating fear that Britain would have to absorb a second major influx of New Commonwealth immigrants.[13] The Colonial Office had already approached the Caribbean colonies in 1952 about informally withholding passports to slow the rate of West Indians entering Britain. And when migration rates from the subcontinent began to rise, the Commonwealth Relations Office made a similar suggestion to the Indian government. By 1960, however, it was clear that informal restrictions were failing. West Indian governments were increasingly reluctant to comply because migration to Britain offered a crucial safety valve for dealing with unemployment in their own lands. The Indian Supreme Court, in turn, ruled that it was illegal to withhold passports from Indian citizens, creating the specter of massive Indian migration.

The looming prospect of still more non-European settlers ultimately compelled political leaders to move ahead with restrictive legislation. In 1962, Parliament passed the Commonwealth Immigrants Act, imposing a quota on the entry of citizens of the United Kingdom and Colonies (UKC) with no special job skills or job in hand. The Conservative Party under Macmillan was united in its support, but the Labour Party was divided. The "intellectual and anti-colonialist element in the party" objected to any action that smacked of racial prejudice and vehemently opposed the legislation, while the trade unionist wing was increasingly skeptical about large-scale immigration and the potential for integration.[14]

Significantly, when Labour returned to power in 1964, the new government had the chance to allow immigration control to lapse. In both 1963 and 1964, however, over fifty thousand people from the New Commonwealth landed on British soil, with a large percentage now coming from India and Pakistan.[15] These numbers suggested that the 1962 restrictions had failed to reduce substantially the influx of non-European arrivals. At the same time, racial upheaval across the Atlantic influenced the thinking of leaders from both parties. "What we are debating this evening," declared

Conservative MP Henry Brooke during the House of Commons discussion about the expiring restrictions, "is nothing less than whether we shall be able in this country to avoid the atmosphere of racial bitterness and outbreaks of racial hatred which hang like a menacing cloud permanently over America."[16] In an effort to prevent the type of social conflict seemingly rampant in the United States, the Labour-controlled Parliament ultimately renewed the legislation, even lowering the visa quota.

Still, the party's more progressive wing remained uneasy about limiting immigration. Home Secretary Frank Soskice and other Labour leaders sought to alleviate these doubts by linking tighter border control with positive measures that would help integrate immigrants already settled in the United Kingdom. The argument went something like this: The British people were naturally tolerant, but their capacity for absorbing alien cultures only went so far. If the government did nothing to curb the flow of colonials and former colonials, race relations would inevitably explode. By limiting new immigration, the government could ensure that non-whites already in Britain would not be treated as second-class citizens. Labour officials thus presented their support for immigration controls as working hand in glove with a second piece of legislation that they intended to propose, one aimed at protecting those already on British soil: what would become the 1965 Race Relations Act. This two-pronged approach served as the bedrock of Britain's initial strategy for dealing with the social effects of immigration—that is, its emerging multicultural society.

An important reason that the Labour Party agreed to restrict immigration was the outcome of the 1964 election in the Midlands town of Smethwick. Here, the veteran Labour MP, Patrick Gordon, fell victim to the use of race as a political weapon by his Tory challenger, Peter Griffiths. Not only did the political novice Griffiths paint a dire picture of New Commonwealth immigrants "deciding Smethwick's future," but his campaign was also accused of producing posters that blazoned a highly inflammatory slogan: "If you want a nigger neighbour, vote Liberal or Labour."[17] Confronted by the media about this slogan, Griffiths responded, "I would not condemn anyone who said that. I would say that is how people see the situation in Smethwick . . . I would say it is exasperation, not fascism." The tactic worked: the Conservative Griffiths achieved a 7.2 percent swing in his favor even as the national vote gave a 3.5 percent advantage to Labour.[18] Labour leaders responded, in turn, by pushing for intensified immigration restriction (a pattern exemplified by the renewal of the 1962 Commonwealth Immigrants Act, support for a second act in 1968, and passage of the Immigration Act in 1971).

On one level, then, Labour now seemed to accept the public's "ultimate verdict" on immigration. But they also sought to introduce "positive legislation" to protect ethnic minorities from discrimination—part of their effort to mitigate the "most extreme manifestations" of public opinion.[19] The 1965 government white paper on "Immigration from the Commonwealth" framed the situation starkly: "[I]t must be recognized that the presence in this country of nearly one million immigrants from the Commonwealth with different social and cultural backgrounds raises a number of problems and creates various social tensions in those areas where they have concentrated. If we are to avoid the evil of racial strife and if harmonious relations between the races who now form our community are to develop, these problems and tensions must be resolved and removed."[20] The underlying assumption was that "social tensions" inevitably resulted from the presence of immigrants "with different social and cultural backgrounds" (and conversely, that such friction would not arise if not for the "coloured" presence). In order to create more "harmonious relations," the white paper put forward a program to integrate immigrants, which included efforts to address discrimination. Junior Home Office Minister Roy Hattersley explained the rationale for Labour's proposed antidiscrimination legislation, which ultimately became the 1965 Race Relations Act: "Integration without control is impossible, but control without integration is indefensible."[21] The bill outlawed discrimination based on race and ethnicity in public places (hotels, public houses, restaurants, places of entertainment or recreation) and prohibited incitement to racial hatred.[22] This was the first law of its kind anywhere in Europe—a first both in acknowledging the existence of racial discrimination and in making overt acts of racial bias illegal. No European country had ever legislated to protect basic equality among different ethnic groups.[23]

The concept of "race relations" relied on a number of basic assumptions. First, it accepted race and ethnicity as valid categories—not only as a means of identification, but also for understanding how those groups behaved both internally and with others.[24] Second, it posited a fundamental difference between "coloured" immigrants and white Britons, despite the fact that colonial immigrants were actually British.[25] And third, it drew upon older strategies for overseeing and ruling radically different colonial peoples across a vast empire. Under colonialism, the crucial task had been to manage public order as well as differences between majority and minority groups that were often figured as racial. The principal strategy had been to rely on the leaders of local racial or ethnic communities as mediators, that is, to use existing hierarchies to finesse the process of negotiation.[26]

The passage of the 1965 act signaled the beginning of what scholars have called the "liberal hour" in British politics,[27] a period in which "racial harmony" was understood by both major parties as an unquestioned "public good."[28] Even in the House of Commons debate about the bill, bipartisan consensus was notable. Home Secretary Soskice summed up the discussion: "[T]here has been disclosed in the course of the debate a very great degree of unanimity on the broad aspects of the problem with which we are faced. . . . [First,] the Government accept that there must be—simply because of the scale of possible immigration— effective control of numbers. . . . [Second,] our aim should be to see that there is only one class of citizen, each with equal rights, each with equal respect, each with equal opportunity and each with an equal career of happiness and fulfillment in his life in the community. We all agree that we should aim [at] that."[29] With ongoing US racial strife providing a powerful counterexample of race relations gone wrong, British leaders from both parties agreed to prioritize immigration restriction, while simultaneously combatting discrimination—a dual strategy they hoped would promote peaceful coexistence.

As a follow-up to the 1965 bill, the Local Government Act of 1966 included a single sentence—under Section 11—that extended the possibility of central government funds to local authorities with "substantial numbers of immigrants from the Commonwealth whose language or customs differ[ed] from those of the community."[30] This new provision represented the first time grants were specifically earmarked to support the needs of newcomers. But its emphasis lay on the undue pressures borne by communities where large numbers of immigrants had settled.

Ironically, the right-wing Tory politician Enoch Powell's infamous Rivers of Blood speech inadvertently strengthened the emerging liberal consensus. Addressing a conservative group in Birmingham on 20 April 1968, Powell vehemently criticized New Commonwealth immigration and a second piece of antidiscrimination legislation (what would become the 1968 Race Relations Act) that was due for a parliamentary vote. If Britain did nothing and continued to allow an "annual inflow of 50,000 dependents," he warned, an intolerable outcome was inevitable: "In this country in fifteen or twenty years' time the black man will have the whip hand over the white man." Powell ended his dire predictions with an apocalyptic flourish from Ovid: "As I look ahead, I am filled with foreboding. Like the Roman, I seem to see 'the River Tiber foaming with much blood.' That tragic and intractable phenomenon which we watch with horror on the other side of the Atlantic but which is there interwoven with the history and existence of the States itself, is coming upon us here by our own volition and our own neglect."[31]

The response to this bleak vision was immediate. Conservative Party leader Edward Heath dismissed Powell from his Shadow Cabinet and vociferously condemned the speech as "racialist in tone and liable to exacerbate racial tensions."[32] Other prominent members of the Tory leadership also rejected his statements. Nevertheless, Powell received huge popular support: his poll numbers shot up; his office was deluged with sympathetic letters; and London dock workers and Smithfield meat porters staged widely publicized demonstrations on his behalf.[33] That Powell became the most popular Conservative politician for views that many of his party colleagues deemed "offensive" seemed to bear out Heath's prediction, spurring the Tories to redouble their support of the dual approach underlying the initial Race Relations Act.[34]

Although this speech effectively ended Powell's political career (he had aspired to the Conservative leadership), his inflammatory rhetoric on race and immigration continued to reverberate across the political establishment. Members of his own party feared that his "Anglocentric unionist nationalism against immigrants" might exacerbate the already simmering tensions between English nationalism and the "periphery nations" of the United Kingdom.[35] This anxiety provided added incentive for them to go along with the liberal efforts to pass subsequent race relations laws in 1968 and 1976, even as they pressed for tighter immigration regulations and floated the idea of repatriation.[36] Once the Tories returned to power in 1970, they put forward the Immigration Act of 1971, the goal being to tighten immigration control still further by introducing the distinction between so-called patrials (persons born in the United Kingdom or who had at least one parent or grandparent with UK citizenship) and non-patrials. While Labour leaders protested the law as racist and "a concession to prejudice," the party didn't prevent its passage.[37] Mindful of Powell's populist appeal, Labour, too, cleaved to the consensus forged on the twin policies of immigration restriction and integration of those already settled.

The government's efforts to manage different ethnic communities, however, was not received passively by newcomers. To a greater extent than in any other Western European country, immigrants in Britain took an active role in shaping the way diversity was managed. Part of their leverage in this process derived from their legal status. Unlike in France, all colonials and ex-colonials were citizens of the UKC. Even those who were subject to entry quotas because they arrived after 1962 enjoyed the same rights as every other British citizen once they landed. This security no doubt made immigrants in Britain somewhat bolder in their critiques and more efficacious in their demands. Another reason for early immigrant activism was the network of self-organized associations already established in the mother country during the empire. In 1936, for example, black workers in Cardiff formed the Coloured Seamen's Union to fight racial discrimination on the docks. Two years later, laborers from the subcontinent established the Indian Workers' Association (IWA) in Coventry to collect funds for the nationalist cause, quickly spawning similar groups throughout England. Most IWAs went dormant after 1947, when India achieved independence, but the network revived in the 1950s, consolidated into a national organization in 1958, and served as the crucial spearhead for political activism among Asian immigrants for the next two decades.[38]

The first waves of immigrant associations generally embraced a working-class orientation. And their immediate experiences as new immigrants only reinforced a working-class politics. In many cases, organizers and members of these groups had been active in the anticolonial, trade union, and socialist movements in the West Indies and India.[39] They often worked the poorest paying positions, settled primarily in industrial areas, and occupied the least desirable housing. Not surprisingly, many fought for acceptance from established British trade unions, despite hostility and resistance from white workers and local union leaders, but they also coordinated industrial actions themselves. During the mid-1960s, for instance, the IWA led the first major postwar immigrant strike of Indian, Pakistani, and Caribbean workers at Courtauld's Red Scar Mill in Preston before playing another generative role in the 1974 strike by Asian women workers at Imperial Typewriters in Leicester.[40]

Some immigrant organizations addressed specific areas of discrimination. One major target was education. The issue first came to public view in 1969, when West Indian parents and community organizers orchestrated a campaign against an initiative by the London Haringey school district to place pupils in specific groups based on academic ability. The educational authority's plan was to impose quotas on immigrants, especially West Indians, who were believed to lower educational standards.[41] The North London West Indian Association rallied London's Caribbean population to protest the policy and succeeded in killing it. Out of this activism emerged organizations devoted to fighting racism in education, as well as the Black Supplementary School Movement, a grassroots effort by teachers, community activists, and parents to offer additional classes (often meeting on Saturdays) to teach black children their own culture and history. But ethnic associations tackled other forms of discrimination as well. Immigrant groups organized by Birmingham's Coordinating Committee Against Racial Discrimination (CCARD), for instance, tested the limits of the 1965 Race Relations Act by demanding to be served at establishments in the Midlands that openly refused to wait on colored people.[42] In 1971, the Pakistani Progressive Party joined the Universal Coloured Peoples' Association to demonstrate outside the House of Commons against Peter Shore because of the MP's ongoing refusal to address complaints of assault, robbery, and even murder of Pakistanis in his East London constituency.[43]

What's notable about minority activism in Britain, especially as it flourished during the 1970s, is that it cut against the political establishment's assumption that each immigrant community should be treated as a separate entity. To be sure, immigrants did organize along ethnic or racial lines to address issues that affected a specific group disproportionately. But they also forged cross-ethnic partnerships and collaborations, among both fellow minorities and white British activists. In part, this coming together was an unanticipated consequence of the racialized populism unleashed by Powell and taken up by National Front (NF) street fighters. Throughout the decade, NF thugs mounted provocative demonstrations and terrorized immigrant neighborhoods across the country. Such far-right activities drew immigrants into "a new relationship with the politics of their environment," underscoring the need for vigorous "antiracism" campaigns that engaged the loyalties of white activists.[44] Initially, these new forms of cross-ethnic cooperation aimed to oppose the NF on the streets, but they also produced movements like the Anti-Nazi League and Rock Against Racism. Nothing, however, crystallized the new multiracial coalitions more than the adoption of the term "black" as a political strategy; indeed, by describing themselves as part of a single rubric, West Indians and Asians marked their shared struggles against British racism.

The rise of Margaret Thatcher in the mid-1970s is typically remembered as marking a sea change in British national politics, and this assessment holds true as well for her management of the British transition to an explicitly multicultural society. Her larger approach was far more hard-line than any of her predecessors' attempts to work within the parameters of bipartisan consensus. Even before she became prime minister, Thatcher signaled her intent to clamp down on immigration by publicly sympathizing with people's sense of being "swamped" by alien cultures. Upon taking office in 1979, she tightened the rules of family reunification and, two years later, presided over the passage of the British Nationality Act. The law abolished the categories of citizen of the UKC and British subject, as well as the principle of jus soli, which had granted automatic citizenship to anyone born on British soil. It also created a new definition of citizenship exclusive to the United Kingdom.[45] Such measures built on earlier efforts to curb the flow of New Commonwealth immigrants, but they were far more extreme, leaving few legal avenues for ex-colonials to settle in Britain.

This tough-minded approach applied to "race relations" as well. Thatcher's neoliberal domestic agenda—which included weakening the trade unions, cutting taxes, and privatizing national industries as well as state-owned public housing—hit Britons from the Caribbean and South Asia especially hard. Privatization pushed already high unemployment figures even higher, with a disproportionate number of those laid off coming from immigrant communities. At the same time, Thatcher's gutting of the welfare state meant that social service agencies had fewer resources with which to help alleviate the worst material effects on the swelling ranks of those made redundant. Her efforts to neutralize the trade unions, moreover, forced working-class and left-oriented activists into retreat, an assault that undercut the two major contexts supporting the minority protests of the 1960s and 1970s. Above all, second-generation youth bore the brunt of Thatcher's harsh policies. Many younger Asians, whose parents had worked in the factories and mills of the English Midlands, encountered a ravaged manufacturing industry with virtually no job prospects. West Indian youth faced even slimmer chances. Disadvantaged in the educational system, few ethnic minorities had the skills to find employment in a post-Fordist economy that favored the service and financial sectors.

These consequences of Thatcher's economic program, moreover, dovetailed with new images of minorities in the press. As economic woes escalated in the 1970s, the media increasingly emphasized the dangers posed by certain elements of the black population: young militants, criminals, Rastafarians, and the unemployed. Newspapers frequently reported incidents of petty street robberies with a novel term, "mugging," which they linked almost exclusively to young West Indians.[46] According to sociologist John Solomos, this new rhetorical category gave rise to the belief

that "pathological" black cultures produced "special" problems among the young, including "unemployment, poverty,
homelessness, crime, and conflict with the police." In this
way, mugging became a "racial crime"[47] and conditioned
British police to treat all black youngsters as potential criminals.[48] Soon, authorities began to rely on the so-called "sus"
law, a relic of the 1924 Vagrancy Act that allowed police
to stop, search, and arrest based on any "suspicious" behavior.[49] The net result, as we might expect, was a tense and
increasingly hostile climate between law enforcement and
the West Indian community, which now accused the police
of racialized abuse.[50]

Zealous enforcement of "sus," it is worth noting, stood in
marked contrast to a decided absence of police action against
brazen racial attacks on Asian immigrants. This pattern was
exemplified by official indifference to the 1976 murder of
Gurdip Singh Chaggar in London Southall. Over the course
of the decade, moreover, racial violence toward Asians rose
sharply, especially assaults by NF skinheads. Between 1976
and 1978, over one hundred such attacks occurred in the
district of Tower Hamlets alone.[51] In incident after incident,
police failed to interview witnesses or make arrests, urging
victims to drop their cases for the sake of "good community
relations."[52] The result was that Bengalis living in London's
East End endured racial abuse as a "constant factor of everyday life" and no longer felt confident in the state protection.[53] This differential treatment typified the approach to
British race relations, with each ethnic or racial group seen
as presenting its own challenges to British society and requiring a different response. Thus, blacks were perceived as
criminals who needed to be kept off the streets, Asians were
criticized as overly sensitive and encouraged to toughen up.

Fueled by Thatcher's brutal austerity policies, the explosive situation between blacks and the police came to a head

during April 1981 in Brixton, the heart of London's Afro-Caribbean community. The immediate spark was an encounter between a bleeding young man, Michael Bailey, and law enforcement, in which police refusal to summon medical help drew Brixton residents onto the street. Less than a week before this episode, London Metropolitan Police had launched Operation Swamp '81, in which hundreds of plain-clothes policemen set up roadblocks in Brixton to stop and search anyone on the street. During the four-day operation, there were 943 stops, 118 arrests, and 75 charges, the majority of which were against black men and youth.[54] By the time of the Bailey incident, then, tensions were running high. Over the course of two nights, buildings were set on fire, police vehicles were torched, and three hundred policemen and sixty-five citizens were hurt. Between April and July, the violence spread first to other London districts, then outward to cities across England and Wales before returning to Brixton.

Forced to address the massive unrest, Thatcher appointed Lord Leslie Scarman to lead an inquiry into the riots' causes. The resulting report declared, "institutional racism does not exist in Britain: but racial disadvantage and its nasty associate, racial discrimination, have not been eliminated."[55] On the one hand, Scarman rejected the very idea that institutional racism among the police could have contributed to the uprisings. But he also urged decisive action to counteract "racial disadvantage," which could become an "endemic, ineradicable disease threatening the very survival of our society."[56] This assessment prompted Thatcher to allocate new resources to poor urban communities (where most ethnic minorities lived) that had been starved of funds for years. Specific targets included increased spending for the Urban Aid Programme from £202 million in 1981 to £338 million in 1984,[57] and a new Youth Training Scheme run by the Manpower Services Commission.[58] Under Thatcher's watch, the central government also made significant funds available for voluntary sector projects and tasked local governments with awarding and administering the money. Sir George Young, Conservative minister responsible for race relations justified the strategy: "We've got to back the good guys, the sensible, moderate, responsible leaders of ethnic groups. If they are seen to deliver, to get financial support from central government for urban projects, then that reinforces their standing and credibility in the community. If they don't deliver, people will turn to the militants."[59] Especially significant here is the fact that Thatcher framed these actions not as a state-sponsored multicultural policy, but rather as localized measures to facilitate urban renewal. The initiatives thus appeared as part of a piecemeal solution: allocating money to areas that had become unmistakably problematic.

It was also important that Thatcher's administration did not distribute the funds directly. Instead, she channeled monies through preexisting agencies (e.g., the Urban Aid Programme) and funding streams (e.g., Section 11 of the 1966 Local Government Act), administrated by local and city governments.[60] One of the great ironies of this approach was that the Labour Party thereby assumed a major role in determining how urban renewal actually played out.[61] Because the Labour Party's left wing was shut out of national politics during the Thatcher years, many of its ranks focused instead on local politics and controlled numerous municipal councils. A notable example can be found in the story of Ken Livingstone, the provocative, left-wing, thirty-six-year-old who became leader of the Greater London Council (GLC) in 1981. Livingstone used the GLC, flush with money earmarked for urban renewal, as the launching site for a citywide antiracism campaign, promising to eradicate

racial discrimination and fight prejudice.[62] The GLC established a general policy of municipal antiracism that became
the model for other progressive local authorities. Among
many initiatives, Livingstone set up regular consultations
with ethnic leaders, who helped identify projects worthy of
funding and served as de facto representatives of their communities.[63] This constituted a new approach for integrating
minorities into British society. He also pledged to transform the racial composition of the GLC workforce, a body
of more than twenty-two thousand people.[64] Livingstone's
efforts quickly made him a target of the tabloid press, which
routinely caricatured him as "barmy" and "loony" and denounced GLC policies as "crazy."[65] Thatcher's arms-length
stance toward race relations thus had the unexpected effect
of giving her political opponents the opportunity to push
central-government-funded programs in a more progressive
direction.

Significantly, it was precisely these localized programs,
especially the ones that relied on ethnic leaders to represent
their communities, that would later be described as the first
state-sponsored forms of "multiculturalism" in Britain. The
model involved not so much a radical break from the race
relations politics of the 1960s, but rather the injection of
sizeable funds—and the development of infrastructure for
distributing those funds—into an already existing way of
thinking about diversity. The first waves of British multiculturalism, in short, did not supplant the older notion of
separate, tightly bound racial or ethnic groups that required
active management. Instead, these initial efforts to manage
diversity accepted a balkanized view of race relations and
actually reinforced ethnic group identification by allocating
resources on the basis of those categories.

As we shall see, Thatcher's evolving efforts in these areas
went hand in glove with a highly racialized vision of national

boundaries—of who belonged to the nation and who did not. This vision is the subject of the next chapter. But for now, the crucial point is that Thatcher's innovations pushed the 1960s consensus to its limits, rendering it virtually unrecognizable: her policies were at once more draconian in the policing of minority populations and more extensive in the funding of urban renewal.

Pillarization

Britain was not alone in adopting policies that would later be described as state-supported multiculturalism. The Netherlands followed a similar approach in dealing with immigrants, one that emphasized stark differences between migrant groups and sought to manage those groups as independent collectivities in relation to mainstream society. For immigrants to be recognized as a population worth managing, however, Dutch leaders and policy makers needed first to accept them as permanent settlers who required integration. And on this score, the Netherlands (as well as all other Western European countries) lagged considerably behind Britain.

By the time of the 1973 downturn, the Netherlands was home to three major groups of immigrants: Indisch Dutch Eurasians, who held Dutch citizenship and were largely assimilated; Moluccans, who existed in a state of limbo on the edges of Dutch society; and guest workers, primarily from Turkey and Morocco, who were foreigners, though a significant number actually enjoyed permanent resident status. Neither the formerly colonized Moluccans nor the recruited guest workers were understood as a permanent part of Dutch society. The official line from government leaders was that the Netherlands was not a "country of immigration," with the influx over the previous twenty years merely a temporary expediency.

As economic slowdown gave way to recession, however, the Netherlands began to impose more stringent controls on the entry of new guest workers, even as its leaders expected those already on Dutch soil to go home. Between 1974 and 1977, the government encouraged the return migration of guest workers with a number of polices. These included a "departure bonus" and special training for any foreign worker who agreed to leave; payment for return transport; an allowance for departing migrants to receive unemployment payments and pensions even beyond their date of exit; and development schemes to aid the home countries.[66] These efforts, however, did not produce the desired results. In fact, the number of people from Mediterranean countries continued to climb throughout the decade, with roughly 140,000 in 1972, 196,000 in 1976, 244,000 in 1979, and 266,000 in 1980.[67] The bulk of these newcomers were spouses and children, who arrived as part of a provision for family reunion.

During the same period, the Netherlands experienced another significant wave of immigration—this time from its colonies of Suriname (in South America) and the Netherlands Antilles (in the Caribbean), which together made up the Dutch West Indies. In the immediate aftermath of World War II, the government had been preoccupied with the Dutch East Indies, specifically the process of decolonization in Indonesia and the resulting flow of immigrants (Eurasian and Moluccan) into the Netherlands. But it also began to renegotiate its relationship with the Dutch West Indies. A new Charter for the Kingdom of the Netherlands, signed in 1954, granted Suriname and the Netherlands Antilles virtual domestic autonomy, but left foreign affairs, defense, and the judiciary under the control of the central

government in The Hague. Importantly, the Charter established a single citizenship for the entire tripartite kingdom,
making inhabitants of the Dutch West Indies citizens with
free rights of entry, residence, and work in the Netherlands.[68] Soon thereafter, a small but steady stream of people from Suriname and the Netherlands Antilles began
to arrive as word spread about the economic boom in the
mother country.

Though the absolute number of arrivals was tiny, by the
early 1970s, Dutch authorities became concerned with the
demographic consequences of this colonial inheritance because people from Suriname and the Netherlands Antilles
were not subject to the same immigration controls as guest
workers or other foreigners. In 1972, Prime Minister Barend
Biesheuvel of the Protestant Anti-Revolutionary Party established a special commission to investigate immigration
from the Dutch West Indies. The committee floated the
idea of using visas to regulate this inflow, but its final report
admitted that it was unconstitutional to deny citizens access to the Netherlands. In search of a legal channel for preventing a "mass exodus" to the metropole, some politicians
suggested ending the quasi-colonial relationship between
the Netherlands, Suriname, and the Antilles as set out in the
1954 Charter.[69] Pursuing decolonization, in short, became
an alternative means of restricting immigration.

But the response to Dutch proposals for independence
in both Suriname and the Netherlands Antilles was decidedly mixed. The six small islands of the Netherlands Antilles refused the pressure to go it alone and remained within
the kingdom.[70] In Suriname, however, things were different:
in 1974, the newly elected prime minister, Henck Arron,
abruptly announced that his country wanted to become independent by the end of the following year. Without calling
a referendum, Dutch and Surinamese leaders embarked on

negotiations to cut ties. The Dutch delegation initially proposed halting Surinamese migration immediately and even
sought to strip Dutch citizenship from those already settled in the Netherlands. Facing massive resistance from the
Surinamese, it ultimately agreed to the free movement of
people between the two countries until 1980. But these debates created the impression that there would be no further
opportunity for Surinamese citizens to enter the Netherlands after the transition period had expired. Thus, at precisely the moment that the Dutch economy began to feel
the worst effects of the oil embargo, the number of Surinamese surged, with fifty thousand arrivals in advance of
independence in 1975 and another major influx of approximately thirty thousand before the halt of free movement
in 1980.[71]

During the first half of the 1970s, then, the Dutch government undertook two major initiatives designed to stem
the flow of non-Europeans, both of which produced the opposite effect. One might have expected these policy failures
to disabuse Dutch authorities of the illusion that guest
workers and colonial migrants were a temporary phenomenon. After all, the steady stream of new arrivals underscored
the extent to which immigrants wanted to enter the country and were becoming a permanent feature of Dutch society. Nevertheless, Dutch leaders continued to insist that the
Netherlands was not a country of immigration. One indication of the Dutch difficulty in admitting that their state had
become an immigration country was the language used to
describe newcomers. "Although the word immigrant exists
in Dutch," migration scholar Hans van Amersfoort has observed, "it was never used. The Eurasians were called 'repatriates,' the Surinamese 'overseas citizens,' and the Mediterranean labor migrants 'guest workers.'"[72] While the Indisch
Dutch had legitimate ties to the Netherlands, the terminology

suggests, non-European Surinamese and guest workers remained outsiders.

Ultimately, it was a series of terrorist acts carried out by Moluccans that finally impressed upon Dutch authorities the need for a new approach. In the 1970s, the Moluccan community, which had mostly faded from public consciousness, adopted a novel strategy to demand an independent homeland and to call attention to the deplorable situation of Moluccans in the Netherlands. Rather than continuing to hold demonstrations and signing petitions as their elders had done for the previous two decades, Moluccan young people—inspired by the Black Panthers and Palestinian Liberation Organization—turned to violence and force.[73] In August 1970, an armed group occupied the residence of the Indonesian ambassador, taking thirty-five hostages to protest the upcoming visit of Indonesian President Suharto. Five years later, in December 1975, Moluccan radicals orchestrated a string of attacks that shook the nation: first conspiring to kidnap the Dutch Queen Juliana (the plot was inadvertently foiled by a routine traffic stop); then seizing a train near the village of Wijster; and finally, occupying the Indonesian Consulate-General in Amsterdam. A coordinated action followed in 1977, which involved hijacking a train near De Punt and taking 110 students at the Bovensmilde primary school hostage. A final assault took place in 1978, when a self-described suicide commando occupied the Provincial Government Building in Assen.[74] These highly visible, violent acts galvanized both public fears and the attention of the country's leaders, who could no longer ignore the plight of the Moluccans.

The Moluccan violence prompted Dutch officials to shift approaches to the broader problem of immigration. The immediate goal, of course, was to end domestic terrorism. Authorities renounced their pledge (dating from the late 1940s) to support an independent Moluccan state, effectively re-moving any illusion that Moluccans might be able to return to an autonomous homeland. This renunciation deprived the rebels of a major justification for their actions. But it also signaled that the Moluccans, who had arrived as tem-porary migrants, were now a permanent minority group in the Netherlands. In 1976, Parliament passed the Facilities Act, which granted Moluccans the legal status of Dutch na-tionals with full entitlement to work, residence, and welfare services, although they still did not enjoy the right to vote or serve in the army.[75] Starting in 1978, moreover, the Dutch government launched a number of outreach initiatives on education and job skills training in order to help integrate Moluccans into Dutch society. That same year, Parliament acknowledged the need for an official plan to promote the integration of ethnic minorities, more generally, resulting in a new directorate within the Department of Home Af-fairs to develop and coordinate a minorities policy.[76]

This call for an official ethnic minorities policy signaled a major transformation in the Dutch approach to immi-grants. While authorities had previously offered an orien-tation program to help Indisch Dutch repatriates adjust to the Netherlands, they had provided no aid to Moluccans beyond housing.[77] Assuming that the Moluccans would re-turn to Southeast Asia within a few months, the govern-ment had not allowed them to work or provided Dutch lan-guage classes. These restrictions laid the groundwork for a disaffected minority population that, twenty-five years after its arrival, still lagged in educational and employment op-portunities. Similar patterns emerged in relation to sub-sequent labor migrants. While Dutch authorities took the lead in signing guest worker recruitment treaties, they left the responsibility of providing housing, training, medical in-surance, and other necessary facilities to the private companies that employed foreign laborers.[78] Charitable religious organizations stepped in to supplement these provisions, establishing recreation centers and organizing social work assistance.[79] But the predominant attitude among political leaders was that a formal integration policy was superfluous, since guest workers would eventually leave.

The establishment of the Minorities Policy Directorate in 1978 represented a major turning point. This agency was led by Social Democrat Henck Molleman, who had used the parliamentary debates on Moluccan terrorism in 1977 to argue for a "coherent set of measures concerning education, housing, employment, health and socio-cultural welfare, not just for Moluccans, but for all ethnic and cultural minorities."[80] Perhaps the most significant change to come out of these discussions among government authorities, policy makers, and academic researchers was the explicit acknowledgment that the Netherlands had become a "de facto country of immigration" and a "multi-ethnic society."[81] The statement, codified in the 1983 Memorandum on Minorities, officially addressed the growing contradiction between the expectation of temporary migration and the facts on the ground. The Memorandum set out three basic objectives. The first was to create conditions that would help minority groups emancipate themselves and participate in broader Dutch society, especially by promoting "mutual adaptation in a multicultural society" that offered equal opportunities for both natives and the foreign-born.[82] The second aim was to reduce the social and economic deprivation faced by ethnic minorities. The final goal was to prevent discrimination.[83]

Although official acknowledgment of ethnic minorities was novel, the actual policies recapitulated patterns that had been established for handling newcomers in the 1960s and 1970s. The Memorandum argued that immigrants should be encouraged to integrate into the Dutch economy, as well as society as a whole. It claimed that the best way for such integration to take place was through policies directed at entire groups. Dutch authorities thus continued to encourage immigrants to set up their own associations, which would serve as the primary vehicles for preserving their culture and representing their unique interests. Where previously policy makers had urged different groups to preserve their cultural identity in order to ease the process of reintegration upon their return home, now they exhorted immigrants to retain their culture as a source of strength for the arduous process of integrating into Dutch society. In addition, the state subsidized national advisory organizations to represent each immigrant group: the Dutch Center for Foreigners (guest workers), the Foundation of Surinamese Welfare Organizations, and the Consultation Body for Welfare of Moluccans.[84] These institutions facilitated a special mediating structure between Dutch authorities and immigrants, providing the state with clearly defined and separate interlocutors for all of the major ethnic communities.[85]

This strategy emerged organically from the country's traditional mode of social organization, known as "pillarization" (*verzuiling*). According to the original model, each religious (Protestant, Catholic, and Jewish) and ideological (socialist, liberal, humanist) community or "pillar" had its own set of institutions: schools, hospitals, social welfare agencies, trade unions, political parties, media outlets, voluntary associations, and leisure organizations. As a rule, the state did not interfere with the institutions of the "pillars," giving communities free reign to cultivate their particular identities and address their specific needs. The state's position, moreover, was unaligned: it was supposed to treat all communities in precisely the same ways; and its policies were to be religiously and socially neutral in order to be acceptable to all pillars. Unity and cohesion within this system of "institutionalized diversity" emerged through regular meetings of the pillars' elites—meetings designed to discuss issues of common concern and build coalitions for decisions affecting the whole.[86]

During the 1960s, Dutch society had moved away from pillarization (as a result of secularization, rising levels of education, and the student movement), but authorities reverted to this approach in their efforts to manage ethnic minorities. At a very basic level, this decision made sense because of the varied groups that composed immigrants in the Netherlands. Leaving aside the Indisch Dutch who were viewed as successfully assimilated by the 1960s, the Moluccans, Surinamese, Antilleans, and guest workers were markedly distinct communities, with each facing unique challenges around prejudice, legal standing, citizenship rights, and integration. A key advantage of pillarization, moreover, was that it seemed to depoliticize the issue of integration. Instead of debating specific integration initiatives in the political arena, they were resolved by "technocratic compromise." Ostensibly neutral experts, that is, handled the task of developing state policy, especially around employment, health, and education.[87] As head of the Minorities Policy Directorate, Molleman argued that this "rational approach" to immigrant integration, based on knowledge and expertise, required "broad political support" to work and "should be free of political conflicts or disagreements."[88]

The conflicts that Molleman had in mind here were not merely rhetorical. There had been sporadic clashes between native Dutch people and various immigrant groups dating back to the arrival of guest workers. Throughout the 1970s, there were attacks against individuals, such as that against a Turkish man who was deliberately thrown into a canal and drowned, as well as vandalism, assaults, and bombings.[89] In the political arena, the far-right Dutch People's Union and its offshoot, the Center Party (Centrumpartij, CP), gained support during this period as well. Running on an anti-immigration platform, the CP captured a seat in the Second Chamber (lower house) of Parliament in 1982, and both parties raised their share of votes in municipal elections that same year, winning between 1.7 and 2.4 percent in Amsterdam, Rotterdam, and The Hague.[90] Leaders from more mainstream parties thus supported the model of pillarization, fearing that immigrant issues could disrupt the delicately balanced coalition system and play into the hands of extremist parties willing to exploit popular racism.[91]

Meanwhile, Dutch authorities also addressed issues of border control and citizenship law, which they saw as crucial for integration initiatives to succeed. In this respect, the broader Dutch strategy for dealing with ethnic diversity mirrored the British dual approach to immigration and race relations. A 1979 Memorandum on Alien Policy called for further limits on immigration: it introduced visa requirements from countries with a "high immigration potential" (especially Turkey, Morocco, and Suriname); applied the rules for family reunion more strictly (particularly around pseudo-marriages); sanctioned employers that hired illegal immigrants; and abolished permanent labor permits for those who had worked five years.[92] Echoing British authorities, Dutch leaders claimed that integration initiatives could be effective only if further immigration was brought to a halt and borders sealed.

But the Dutch government also acknowledged that immigrants already settled in the Netherlands needed legal security and a political voice. In 1984, Parliament passed a new Dutch Nationality Act, replacing the law in effect since 1892. This bill granted automatic citizenship at birth to third-generation immigrants, whose parents and grandparents resided in the Netherlands. It gave the children of non-Dutch citizens, born and residing on Dutch soil, the ability to choose Dutch citizenship between the ages of eighteen and twenty-five. In addition, it allowed new immigrants to naturalize if they had resided in the Netherlands for at least five years, held permanent resident status, had a decent command of Dutch, did not constitute a threat to public order, and renounced their foreign nationality.[93] The following year, a separate constitutional amendment was passed granting non-Dutch legal residents the right to vote in municipal elections.[94]

Neither Dutch political leaders nor policy makers, however, described their approach to managing the highly distinct groups of immigrants as "multiculturalism." Indeed, the label was not adopted except in retrospect—as a way of explaining the failure of the ethnic minorities policy and delineating a new strategy of strong integration or assimilation. In this sense, the Dutch ethnic minorities policy bore a striking resemblance to the model of state multiculturalism developed in Britain. Both divided immigrants into ethnic minority groups. Both treated these groups as homogenous and separate. Both identified community representatives and enlisted them as interlocutors while encouraging ethnic minority groups to maintain separate identities. Both were also largely bipartisan strategies designed to keep the question of immigrants' place in British and Dutch society off the public political agenda.

Insertion

In France, by contrast, policy makers emphatically rejected the term "multiculturalism" as a general strategy for managing immigrant diversity. In fact, French political leaders, scholars, and intellectuals have repeatedly repudiated multiculturalism as a peculiarly "Anglo-Saxon" way of incorporating immigrants. Most specifically reject the formal recognition of ethnic differences as a threat to national identity and social cohesion.[95] Instead, they defend a uniquely French approach that requires political and cultural assimilation. Based on the country's venerable republican tradition, this model has emphasized assimilation as an individual process, rather than one mediated by immigrant communities as in the British or Dutch cases. In exchange for assimilation, this policy has offered full equality and citizenship through the possibility of naturalization. This prospect was extended to French colonial subjects under imperial rule, and was also proffered to postwar immigrants who settled in France.

The exigencies of dealing with ethnic differences on the ground, however, have never been so clear-cut. In actual practice, French authorities adopted many of the same strategies employed by the British for dealing with multiethnic society, especially as the country expanded labor migration in the 1960s. Like their counterparts in other Western European contexts, in the early 1970s French leaders worried about ever higher numbers of foreigners and began to pursue the now familiar two-pronged strategy of restricting further immigration while also seeking to alleviate domestic tensions.

French officials, as we have already seen, were primarily concerned with the size of the Algerian population. Initially, they tried to address the perceived "ethnic imbalance" by imposing new rules on residence and work permits. But in July 1974, with the support of President Valéry Giscard d'Estaing (l'Union pour la démocratie française, UDF) and the newly elected conservative government under Prime Minister Jacques Chirac (l'Union des Démocrates pour la République, UDR), authorities suspended labor migration from outside the European Economic Community. This

decision halted the flow of workers from Turkey and Yugoslavia, as well as the movement of people from the French
ex-colonies, including Algeria, Senegal, Mali, and Mauri-
tius.[96] While many industries and businesses protested this
change because of their reliance on foreign workers, French
political leaders—echoing their British counterparts—argued that immigration controls were absolutely necessary
in order to integrate the nearly four million foreigners already on French soil.[97] A "threshold of tolerance" (*seuil de
tolérance*) had been reached, they insisted, beyond which it
would be impossible to absorb additional immigrants.[98]

The halt of immigration went hand in hand with the establishment of a new government post, Secretary of State
for Foreign Workers (Secrétaire d'état aux travailleurs immigrés), now responsible for coordinating policies related to
immigrant laborers. Among the first tasks of the Secretary
of State was the suspension of family reunification, an extreme measure designed to cut off any remaining path to
legal migration. Although the French high court (le Conseil
d'État) ultimately struck down the ban as unconstitutional,
the action underscored the Giscard government's resolute
attempt to prevent the further influx of foreigners.

Meanwhile, the Secretary of State announced an extensive program to promote the incorporation of immigrants
and their families into French society—what some scholars
have called "insertion."[99] Authorities pledged to provide better housing, offered orientation and training programs, and,
most significantly, promoted the cultural differences of immigrants.[100] The idea of insertion had initially emerged as a
substitute for the more unilateral demand of assimilation,
which, after 1945, French leftists increasingly rejected for
its association with imperialist or fascist notions of ethnic
superiority. But the right also came to embrace an insertion
policy because encouraging non-European immigrants to

retain their own culture would prepare them for an eventual return home. Nurturing cultural differences, according
to the far right wing, would deter foreign workers from mixing with French society and thus make their deportation
easier.[101] In practice, insertion entailed a "loose collection of
narrowly targeted practices," which primarily focused on
basic welfare and social needs at the local level.[102] These policies relied on official statistics for income, criminality, and
educational achievement in order to determine which sectors (housing, employment, schools) required state attention and resources. The primary goal was to incorporate foreigners and immigrants into France's economic and social
fabric without insisting that they renounce their identities
in favor of French culture. Grassroots self-help associations,
trade unions, and cultural groups became important institutions for facilitating immigrant insertion.[103]

These measures did not emerge from thin air. They built
upon efforts initiated in the early 1960s, which themselves
had grown out of policies designed to monitor and manage
colonial Algerian workers in France during the Algerian
War. In 1956, the National Society for the Construction of
Housing for Algerian Workers (SONACOTRAL) had been
established to provide low-income accommodation for laborers from Algeria, typically situated in suburban rings
(*banlieues*) around the major cities, as part of the effort to
extricate them from the influence of the FLN in the *bidonvilles*. Similarly, the Social Action Fund (FAS) was formed
in 1958 to provide welfare aid to—and monitor—Algerian
workers on the mainland. The practical exigencies of dealing
with Algerian colonial workers thus pushed French authorities to treat Algerians as a distinct ethnic community—
one with its own needs, pressures, and problems. This approach, in turn, drew upon the late nineteenth-century notion of "associationism," an alternative to assimilation that

recognized that different cultural groups were in fact different and therefore had to pursue their own paths toward civilization and modernity.[104] Following Algerian independence, French policy makers simply changed the name of SONACOTRAL to National Society for the Construction of Housing for Workers or SONACOTRA, expanding its responsibilities to include the reception and housing of immigrants of all nationalities, and extended FAS's charge to cover the needs of all immigrant workers.[105]

At this juncture, it is worth noting the particularly fraught position occupied by Algerian workers in France. Migrants from Algeria, whether they came before or after independence, belonged to the same ethnic group; they were perceived by most French people as part of the same community of foreigners, bound by language, religion, and cultural traits. Yet this single group actually existed under two different legal regimes. Algerians who arrived before 1962 were colonial subjects with French nationality status and, after 1947, full citizenship rights. In contrast, Algerians who came after 1962 were foreign immigrants with few entitlements to speak of (although they could apply for naturalization and their French-born children received citizenship upon reaching the age of majority). One might have expected 1962 to provide a clean break between these legal regimes, but the Evian Accords guaranteed free movement between the two countries for five more years, and thus contributed to the significant expansion of the Algerian community in France. In the year of Algerian independence, there were about 350,000 Algerians living in France. That number had risen to 474,000 by 1968 and to 711,000 by 1975.[106] In practice this meant that the distinction between Algerians who were French citizens and those who were not was highly muddled.

At roughly the same moment, that is, the years when the Evian agreement was still allowing free movement between

France and Algeria, French officials—in pursuit of manpower for an expanding economy—signed a series of bilateral labor treaties to recruit temporary workers from Morocco, Tunisia, Mali, Senegal, Yugoslavia, and Turkey. Since their arrival overlapped with what was essentially guest worker recruitment, Algerians landing after 1962 were often assumed to be part of this new class of transient foreign laborers that was expected to go home soon. The fact that SONACOTRA and FAS merely enlarged their duties—rather than undergoing a major overhaul or radical reconceptualization—bespoke the seamless way in which Algerians (both citizens and noncitizens) slipped quickly and unremarkably into the far more insecure and problematic categories of foreign worker and immigrant.

Despite the radical shifts in Algerian legal status, policy makers' decision to pursue insertion meant that state strategies for managing Algerians remained largely consistent. In the colonial period, French authorities in Algeria had argued to their metropolitan counterparts that Algerian workers needed to retain their identity and culture as a way of protecting them from corrosive mainland influences. French officials thus actively supported Islamic religious practice as a means of social control, believing that Algerians who grew distant from Islam would invariably succumb to the urban temptations of alcoholism, moral laxity, and crime.[107] And after independence, it was the Algerian government that now sought to preserve these connections. The new state established the Fraternal Association of Algerians in Europe (Amicale des Algériens en Europe) to "nurture national identity and prevent the assimilation and acculturation of Algerians into French society."[108] The Algerian government's desire to cultivate a sense of national identity actually dovetailed with French policy makers' insertion approach, which sought to forestall foreign worker assimilation. The Secretary of State's initiatives emphasized giving immigrants the "freedom to preserve [their] linguistic, religious, and cultural identity."[109] To that end, French authorities created the National Office for the Cultural Promotion of Immigrants (ONPCI, l'Office national pour la promotion des cultures immigrées) in 1975 to create art exhibitions, television and radio broadcasts, and other cultural activities geared toward representing immigrant diversity. Such efforts were largely decentralized, but they brought together local immigrant organizations, grassroots self-help groups, metropolitan authorities, hostel associations, and business groups, as well as the *Amicales*.[110] These groups worked in tandem with FAS as the key agency through which the central government funded organizations related to the welfare of immigrants.[111]

Continuity was true at the ground level, too, where the experience of Algerians in France continued to be shaped by colonial dynamics and hierarchies. SONACOTRA, for example, hired many repatriated *pieds noirs* (European settlers in Algeria) and veterans of the colonial wars as directors of hostels for immigrant workers "because they were used to having foreigners under their command."[112] Algerians living in hostels were subject to strict discipline that recalled older colonial dynamics. This discipline included medical exams every six months, prohibitions on female visitors and political meetings, and random room checks by the hostel director.[113] A SONACOTRA study found that its hostel directors differentiated residents according to their nationality, salary, and professional situation, but they reserved the worst discrimination for North Africans.[114]

A major advantage of the insertion policies championed by Giscard and carried out under Secretary of State for Foreign Workers Paul Dijoud was their seemingly apolitical bent. Policies focused on basic socioeconomic problems such as housing, social security, and poverty. They were pitched at

the local level—away from the center of partisan politics—
and deployed by technocratic experts who relied on official
statistics about income, criminality, and educational achievement.[115] New initiatives tended to be announced through
governmental directives and implemented by agencies like
SONACOTRA, FAS, and ONPCI. Buried in the bowels of
the French bureaucracy, insertion policies received very
little attention from the public. This way of managing immigrants, as sociologist Adrian Favell has argued, "was a na-
kedly instrumental strategy of the state for dealing with a
social issue it did not wish to see explode."[116]

One area that could not escape public scrutiny, however,
was housing. In 1970, the tragic asphyxiation of five African
workers in the Paris neighborhood of Aubervilliers led to
a public outcry about the lack of decent living conditions.
Still, President Giscard d'Estaing steadfastly refused to commit major resources to the problem. The first Secretary of
State for Foreign Workers, André Postel-Vinay, resigned after just six weeks on the job (in July 1974) because his request to build additional accommodations for immigrants
received no financial backing from the state.[117] For five
years starting in 1975, fifteen thousand immigrants living
in SONACOTRA hostels throughout the country went on
strike, demanding lower rent, improved housing conditions,
an end to punitive hostel rules, and accommodation of
their religious needs.[118] At the height of the standoff in the
spring of 1976, key strike leaders were deported in the middle of the night, provoking major opposition from immigrant organizations. Both the French Communist Party and
Algerian *Amicales* also attempted to intervene on behalf of
the strikers.[119]

Hints of a more draconian approach to managing diversity emerged in 1977, when Lionel Stoléru became Secretary
of State for Foreign Workers. Stoléru refocused the office on

immigration control: his aim was not only to tighten the borders further, but to lower the numbers of immigrants on French soil. Specifically, he sought to replace foreign workers with French ones and repatriate Algerians. That year, the agency offered ten thousand francs to any migrant willing to return to his or her country of origin, with the larger goal of reducing the number of foreigners by one million within five years. Stoléru's policy was widely regarded as a failure: only 57,953 foreigners accepted the offer, and most of these were Spanish and Portuguese who were not considered a problem.[120] Undeterred, President Giscard d'Estaing mounted a massive 1979 campaign to repatriate half a million unregistered Algerians by force, but his initiative ground to a halt because of opposition by virtually all of the other major political parties, trade unions, churches, and Conseil d'État.[121]

When the Socialist François Mitterrand became president two years later, the expectation was for sweeping change after twenty years of conservative leadership. And indeed, Mitterrand and Prime Minister Pierre Mauroy quickly pushed for a major easing of immigration restrictions. While they reaffirmed the 1974 suspension of new immigration, they offered amnesty to illegal immigrants who could prove entry before 1 January 1981 and pledged to integrate all legal immigrants into French society.[122] They also succeeded in protecting certain categories of immigrants from deportation (including minors, people resident in France for more than fifteen years, and parents of a French child) and appointed immigrant representatives to the FAS administrative board.[123] Despite these progressive efforts, however, Mitterrand's amnesty program did not produce the desired outcome. Only about 131,000 people (of the expected 300,000) applied to regularize their legal status. And because amnesty was deemed a failure, Minister of the Interior Gaston Defferre reimposed strict visa requirements on all visitors from North Africa.[124]

At least on the surface, the Socialists continued to deal with different groups through the insertion approach established by their predecessors. One reason for this was left-wing sympathy for the "equality of different cultures" policy that agencies such as FAS and ONPCI promoted.[125] Mitterrand's government, in fact, extended insertion measures by creating "educational priority zones" (Zones d'Éducation Prioritaire, ZEP) to provide extra resources, staff, and experimental curricula for schools in areas with high levels of poverty and other social conditions deemed to be risk factors for scholastic success. This designation was widely recognized—although rarely acknowledged—as applying to areas with large concentrations of people from North and increasingly sub-Saharan Africa.[126] As such, it represented an effort to deal directly with concerns facing immigrant communities. In 1984, the Socialists also set up the National Council for Immigrant Populations, (CNPI, Conseil National des Populations Immigrées), an advisory body on all matters related to immigrants and their families.[127] These programs sought to incorporate foreigners by addressing their basic welfare, but without demanding full assimilation.

As Mitterrand's initiatives extended insertion in significant ways, they stretched this management strategy to its very limits. This stretching proceeded on two major fronts. His administration decided to repeal a 1939 law requiring immigrants to obtain permission from the Ministry of Interior to establish associations. But giving immigrants full privileges of association, in turn, produced a proliferation of groups organized to defend the rights and promote the cultures of a variety of immigrant communities.[128] Second, and in a seemingly unrelated effort, Mitterrand simultaneously

promoted new forms of French regional recognition, especially for business and administrative matters within the
state. This was a response to a burgeoning regionalist movement, crystallized most vividly in an ongoing fight between
the Gaullist UDR party and inhabitants of the Larzac region
in Provence over the decision to expand the local military
base.[129] Mitterrand declared to an audience in Brittany: "It
is to wound a people to its very core to limit it in its culture
and language. We proclaim the right to difference."[130] The
idea of the "right to difference" (*le droit à la différence*) had
initially been conceived "as a vehicle for increasing institutional autonomy" among the distinctive regions of France
(e.g., Brittany, Corsica, Provence), but Minister of Culture
Jack Lang now extended the concept to immigrants.[131] Here,
the logic of insertion, which had long acknowledged at a
practical level that immigrant needs varied by culture, was
pushed to its extreme conclusion. The policy of insertion
implied that the state could recognize cultural differences
without compromising the integrity of the nation. But for
the president and his ministers to acknowledge the right
to regional (and immigrant) differences raised what had
been a pragmatic management strategy to a vision of the
nation—one with major ideological implications: namely,
that France contained a multiplicity of cultures.

Together, these two initiatives dramatically altered the
public profile of immigrants in France. Armed with a more
secure legal standing for their organizations, younger second-
generation activists began to emerge as a vocal presence in
the public sphere. They drew attention to the failure of insertion efforts to combat poverty, under-resourced schools, and
unemployment. This immigrant politics had been primed,
no doubt, by the SONACOTRA strikes and Giscard d'Estaing's efforts to deport Algerians. Meanwhile, the idea of
the right to difference galvanized second-generation North

Africans, who adopted an inverted form of the French word for Arab (*Arabe*)—*beurs*—as the badge of a shared generational and cultural identity.[132] These groups joined forces in the highly publicized "March for Equality and Against Racism" that took place in October 1983. Young people of immigrant heritage, many of them *beurs*, marched from Marseille to Paris shouting slogans such as "Let us live equally with our differences." The larger goal here was not just to preserve and foster their cultural identities, but also to insist on the equality of those differences.[133] This activism seized on the Socialist vision of a pluralistic society and recast it as a claim on the state for equality without preconditions. In this way, behind-the-scenes insertion measures that discretely recognized cultural differences were transposed onto the public stage as a demand that French society both accept the presence of multiple cultures and grant them equal standing.

Immigrant activists, however, were not the only faction to claim the right to difference. Jean-Marie Le Pen and the far-right Front National, which was established in 1973 and rose to national prominence in the early 1980s, also seized upon this concept, transforming it from "a defense of diversity into a justification for French particularity."[134] In 1982, Le Pen declared: "We not only have the right but the duty to defend our national personality, and we too have our right to be different."[135] Immigrant groups that demanded recognition of their cultural differences, in this view, posed a threat to Frenchness itself. By asserting their right to difference, immigrants proved their failure to integrate, and perhaps more importantly, signaled that they could never be truly French: they were inassimilable.

For Le Pen, the government's technocratic approach papered over the heart of the matter: the relationship between national unity and cultural identity.[136] Insertion, he argued, granted immigrants "overly easy and unproblematic access to social rights and welfare,"[137] which was especially troublesome in the context of a national recession. Such policies cheapened French citizenship—a right, he insisted, that "should be based on loyalty to French territory, culture, and history," and therefore required "a strong cultural assimilation" as a precondition of "political incorporation."[138]

This combination of increasingly visible immigrant activism and Le Pen's provocations brought the problem of managing French diversity squarely into the realm of partisan politics, exactly the situation that mainstream politicians had taken great pains to avoid. In the run-up to the 1981 presidential election, significantly, Mitterrand and Giscard d'Estaing had privately agreed not to discuss immigration issues during their televised debate.[139] But the 1983 local election results in Paris and nearby Dreux, where candidates for the Front National gained seats on the town council, suggested that Le Pen had succeeded in politicizing the immigrant issue. The Front National's victories served to legitimate his rhetoric. Once Le Pen had skillfully seized on popular anxieties to link the immigrant issue with French national identity, the older insertion strategy no longer worked politically. These developments, in fact, would soon force the political center to seek a new framework for its policies, one that could respond to Le Pen's critiques about the tarnishing of French citizenship.[140]

Willful Neglect

The closest German equivalent to "race relations," "pillarization," and "insertion" was a vaguely defined "foreigner policy" (*Ausländerpolitik*). But a more accurate description here might be a policy of "willful neglect."[141] If Britain was an outlier among Western European countries for its early efforts to deal with demographic diversity, West Germany was an outlier in another direction: it was the last to confront the increasingly obvious settlement of foreign workers and develop national policies to meet their needs.

Like every other Western European state, the Federal Republic officially closed its borders to migrants in the wake of the OPEC-induced recession, issuing an *Anwerbestopp* (halt to the recruitment of foreign workers) in November 1973. For German leaders and policy makers, the suspension of guest worker recruitment indicated that the moment for return had come. But this message played differently among different groups of foreign laborers. Italians and other Europeans did not view the recruitment halt as a major policy change because they still enjoyed the right to work in Germany as citizens of EEC member states. A number of Italian laborers, for instance, left with the downturn, knowing that they could come back to Germany if and when they wanted. For workers from non-EEC countries and especially Turkey, where the economic prospects and political upheaval made return unappealing or even problematic, the suspension signaled not that it was time to depart, but rather that the doors to legal migration were closing. Instead of going home, many of these workers decided to stay and send for their families. It was during this period, in fact, that Turks began to overtake other national groups of foreign laborers. In 1970, the Federal Republic counted 469,200 Turks as residents, compared to 573,600 Italians and 514,500 Yugoslavians. A year later, the number of Turks had risen to 652,800, while those of other groups remained steady.[142] By the middle of the decade, Turks constituted the largest community of foreigners in West Germany, becoming, in the eyes of most Germans, the quintessential guest worker.

Yet even before the *Anwerbestopp* inadvertently produced an unwanted spike in foreign arrivals, German leaders and policy makers were well aware that guest worker behavior did not conform to their expectations. A 1969 study by the Federal Institute of Labor reported that half of the entire male foreign labor population had remained in residence for at least four years as of 1968, and 41 percent lived with their spouses in Germany. Around the same time, there were nearly 815,000 unemployed foreign citizens in the Federal Republic, a number that included laid-off workers, but more significantly, stay-at-home spouses and children.[143] What these statistics showed was that many guest workers were not leaving after the desired period of two to three years (or even after they lost their jobs), but instead were settling in Germany with their families.

Responding to these trends, the governments of some conservative-led states such as Bavaria proposed a five-year maximum stay for all foreigners. The Confederation of German Employers, (BDA, Bundesvereinigung der Deutschen Arbeitgeberverbände) even argued for reviving rotation and making it mandatory, so that firms could continue to recruit foreign workers but minimize their "social costs."[144] The latter suggestion, in particular, elicited considerable protest, with trade unions and guest worker advocacy groups rejecting what they described as "forced rotation" and calling on the federal government to improve the status and rights of foreign workers.[145] More progressive voices within Chancellor Willy Brandt's cabinet did, in fact, broach these issues. In 1972, Minister of the Interior Hans-Dietrich Genscher advanced a two-pronged policy that strongly echoed the "race relations" approach already taken in Britain and the emerging "insertion" measures under consideration in France. Genscher argued that the Federal Republic should curtail the recruitment of foreign workers because the country was fast approaching its "limits of receptiveness," but also challenged his colleagues in the Bundestag to develop a "real immigration policy" that offered guest workers who had already settled a meaningful "chance at integration in our country."[146]

From this perspective, Brandt's chosen course was less than satisfactory. Although the chancellor repeatedly refused to consider forced rotation and vowed that "no legal instruments would be used to enforce limits" on guest worker tenure,[147] he remained silent on the increasingly apparent signs of foreign workers' permanent settlement and did little to address their long-term welfare. When his coalition government announced an "Action Program" in June 1973, it emphasized new requirements for firms employing guest workers, including more stringent rules for housing and a recruitment tax to pay for language and job training.[148] It said nothing, however, about a broader strategy for integration.

Part of the federal government's lack of engagement was structural. Like other Western European countries that recruited foreign labor during the economic boom, the Federal Republic imported guest workers through the Ministry of Labor, whose primary focus was procuring manpower and optimizing productivity. The Labor Ministry's job was to identify suitable workers and regulate the number of foreigners in relation to the broader demands of the economy. Its liaison offices handled the bureaucratic tasks of fielding applications, screening applicants, conducting medical exams, and matching workers to specific types of labor and businesses.[149] To the extent that government officials registered any social component to recruitment, they generally off-loaded this responsibility to the companies that actually hired the foreign laborers. It was the responsibility of employing firms to arrange transportation for recruits to Germany, house them in hostels or dormitories, enlist German social workers to supervise them, and provide enough language and job training for the foreign recruits to do their work. But company interests drove these concerns, which meant that employers primarily addressed foreigners' working lives or their ability to manage their daily tasks efficiently.

As soon as the first guest workers arrived in the mid-1950s, religious welfare organizations (*Wohlfahrtsverbände*) stepped into the breach to aid new arrivals with non-work-related concerns. Caritas, the Catholic Church's charitable arm, and Diakonisches Werk, the Protestant equivalent, offered support to guest workers according to faith: Caritas ministered to Italians, Spaniards, and Portuguese, while Diakonisches Werk looked after Greeks. Starting in 1962, the Social Democratic Party (SPD) organization Arbeiterwohlfahrt attended to Muslim Turks, Yugoslavians, Tunisians, and Moroccans. All three associations established advice centers throughout the country to help workers navigate the German bureaucracy and facilitate social adaptation. They helped with translation services, German language classes, and legal rights counseling, offered assistance for the private housing market, and provided support for obtaining unemployment benefits or searching for a new job. The German Trade Union Federation (Deutsche Gewerkschaftsbund, DGB), the central organization for labor interests in the Federal Republic, also contributed to guest worker welfare. Initially, unions helped foreign recruits transition to a new work culture, and later they offered more broadly defined social services, including counseling and advice for the complicated process of renewing residence and work permits.[150] Along with the churches, then, unions were among the "earliest practitioners of integration."[151]

In other words, there was a strict (though largely unspoken) division of labor around guest worker management. Employers and nongovernmental associations engaged with the day-to-day needs and problems of foreign laborers, while the Labor Ministry confined its policy recommendations and initiatives to the economic sphere and especially the demands of the labor market. Over time, the Ministry of Labor realized that the manifold impacts of recruitment were extending far beyond its economic purview, yet it remained hemmed in by its original mandate. Significantly, when the department established a coordination committee for foreign workers to address the social consequences of labor recruitment in 1970, this group did little more than offer advice.[152]

The other key issue was ideological. Foreign laborers were recruited to the Federal Republic to supplement native manpower. Their presence was explained across the political spectrum as temporary and as based entirely on the needs of the economy. Since residence was never intended to be permanent, political leaders saw no need to facilitate integration on a broader scale and assumed that guest workers had no interest in such an endeavor. One can see these assumptions at work in the commentary of the Minister of Labor, Walter Arendt, who just a month after announcing the *Anwerbestopp*, reiterated the government's basic conception of the guest worker program: "The Federal Republic of Germany does not consider itself an immigration country in the classical sense. Our principal position is that people who come to our country to work should voluntarily return to their home countries after a time, and contribute to the further development of their country."[153]

Given these assumptions, it is not surprising that German leaders' initial strategy for dealing with the mounting evidence of long-term settlement was to encourage guest workers to simply leave "voluntarily." Policy makers pursued this strategy by rendering extensive stays more precarious. Between 1973 and 1975, Arendt announced a series of administrative changes that reduced the opportunities, status, and security of foreign laborers and their families. The Labor Ministry suspended automatic renewal of work permits and increased efforts to deport illegal workers. It declared a deadline for granting work permits to spouses and children from countries outside the EEC and decreed a reduction in child benefits for guest workers supporting children not living in West Germany. The department also designated certain urban neighborhoods as "overburdened" with foreigners and barred guest workers from moving into these "off-limits" districts.[154] But like the *Anwerbestopp*, these new policies failed to promote return and actually created another spike in migrations to reunify families. Counter to government hopes and expectations, both the deadline for work eligibility and the reduction in child benefits motivated many guest workers to send for their spouses and children.

Despite a policy approach that aimed at return, the three mainstream political parties did begin behind-the-scenes discussions on the question of integration in the mid-1970s. The Christian Democratic Union (CDU), for example, maintained the ultimate goal of repatriation, but in the meantime championed "social integration" as a strategy for achieving peaceful coexistence. This concept, a 1977 party statement explained, "does not mean assimilation which works toward making foreign workers and their families into Germans." Rather, the CDU defined social integration as a form of "preservation and support" of foreign workers and their families that would facilitate a seamless return to their home countries.[155] The liberal Free Democratic Party (FDP), by contrast, focused on offering unlimited residence permits. Guest workers, they argued, should have the chance to become unrestricted legal residents after three years of employment, provided they demonstrated recognizable efforts to become part of German society.[156] Meanwhile, the SPD viewed integration as a two-way process in which guest workers needed to familiarize themselves with German norms, but Germans needed to adjust to the permanent presence of foreigners and learn more about them.[157]

All three parties, it is worth noting, cast their positions on integration as "foreigner policy" (*Ausländerpolitik*). In other words, there was still no official acknowledgment that guest workers could be anything more than "foreigners" in national discourse, although these behind-the-scenes discussions at least registered self-consciousness of growing pressures on the ground. Most concrete policy recommendations focused on placing guest workers' legal status on a more secure footing. They offered neither a vision of what integration might look like in broader terms, nor provisions for helping guest workers achieve it. Integration, in short, was mostly left to the initiative of guest workers themselves and the civil associations (churches, social work agencies) that had traditionally served as their primary advocates.

By the second half of the 1970s, however, it was becoming harder and harder to ignore the concrete effects of having over a million guest workers and their families on West German soil. Foreign workers had been key participants in the wildcat strikes during the summer of 1973, taking on a more visible role in trade union politics. But even beyond the workplace, the larger cycle of family reunions compelled significant numbers of guest workers to move out of company-provided dormitories and seek private accommodations among native Germans. Working-class neighborhoods, where rents were more affordable, thus experienced a gradual but marked increase in foreign inhabitants throughout the decade.[158] Some urban districts registered proportions of migrant residents as high as 12 percent, which prompted authorities to seek new methods for preventing more guest workers from moving into those areas.

Family reunions also resulted in the arrival of significant numbers of foreign, mostly Turkish, school-aged children. With little warning, no planning, and few resources, German teachers and administrators struggled to educate a growing population of students who hardly knew the language and whose parents were unfamiliar with the German educational system.[159] Statistics confirmed the massive changes on the ground. In 1969, there were 364,000 migrant children under the age of sixteen; by 1974, that number had risen to 768,000; and by 1982, it had reached 1,183,203.[160]

These transformations—coupled with the lack of clear policy directives from federal officials—meant that the integration of guest workers and their families unfolded in an ad hoc manner. At the large Siemens Berlin facility, for example, the corporate daycare center became an important facilitator of day-to-day interactions. It hosted events to bring German and foreign children together, arranged social gatherings for their parents, and celebrated German and foreign holidays to promote cultural exchange.[161] School systems also became crucial engines for guest worker integration, bringing foreign children into direct contact with German peers and German authority figures, as well as socializing them to German institutions.[162] A case in point was the Berlin school system, which served as a central nexus of ad hoc integration, capping the number of foreigners at 20 percent in each classroom, but offering additional German and Turkish language instruction in smaller formats.[163]

Guest workers, of course, were not passive in this process. As Muslims from Turkey moved beyond their initial adjustments to work and life in the Federal Republic, they often looked for places to gather for prayer. Some companies supplied Muslim workers with a room on the factory site, but gradually guest workers sought spaces outside the workplace to congregate for religious activities. The arrival of families prompted a move away from improvised worship spaces, with communities now pushing to establish recognizable religious institutions that would allow more formal observance and offer support networks.[164] Initially, this involved moving from prayer rooms to larger makeshift venues that served as temporary mosques. The first purpose-built mosque was established by a group of Turkish guest workers in Duisburg in 1974.[165] Other signs of integration included the development of neighborhood gathering spots and efforts to reproduce older customs. In 1975, for example, the first Turkish-owned café opened, also in Duisburg, offering a place for Turkish men to meet and socialize.[166] And by the early 1980s, major West German metropolitan areas saw a burgeoning of small businesses owned by former guest workers: pizzerias, corner groceries, fruit and vegetable stands, travel agencies, and small street food shops (*Imbisse*).

Meanwhile, even as West German leaders remained reluctant to take an active hand in managing the changes that were afoot, the courts strengthened the residency rights of foreigners already settled in the country. In 1978, the Federal Constitutional Court ruled on the case of a construction worker from India who had come to Germany in 1961 for occupational training. His residence permit had been extended without question every year between 1967 and 1972. But after the worker applied and was turned down for naturalization in 1973, local authorities denied the routine renewal of his residence permit. They claimed that his intention to settle permanently in West Germany subverted state interests because the Federal Republic was not a country of immigration. Although the state administrative court upheld the local decision, the Federal Constitutional court reversed it, citing the principle of "legitimate expectations" (*Vertrauensschutz*). The higher court argued that earlier routine extensions of the Indian worker's permit had established a constitutionally guaranteed "reliance interest" in continued residence.[167] The decision marked an important watershed because it "solidified migrants' status as bearers of human rights and placed important limits on the state's ability to reverse immigration processes through deportation and the termination of residency rights."[168]

This ruling also buttressed Social Democratic Chancellor Helmut Schmidt's measures to make guest worker integration a centerpiece of his domestic agenda. That same year, his government shepherded through the Bundestag the Stabilization Statute (Verfestigungsregel), which established foreigners' right to unrestricted residence permits and outlined clear procedures for such applications. To bolster this process, Schmidt also established a new federal government post, Commissioner for Foreigners Affairs (Ausländerbeauftragte), whose entire mandate was to oversee national integration efforts.[169] By 1979, the newly appointed commissioner, Heinz Kühn, issued a major report that condemned in no uncertain terms the prevailing pattern of dealing with guest workers. The refusal to acknowledge the "social consequences" of the labor recruitment, Kühn charged, was "too much shaped by the priority of political, labor-market perspectives." The guest worker program had produced a situation "that is no longer reversible, and the majority of those affected are no longer 'guest workers' but rather immigrants."[170] In response, Kühn proposed improving access to education for the children of guest workers, streamlining naturalization procedures for second-generation foreigners, and granting local voting rights to settled immigrants.[171] Here, in 1979 was the first German state-sponsored program for the integration of guest workers.

The SPD's official recasting of foreign laborers as immigrants sent a clear message that a radical transformation was under way and thrust the issue into the realm of partisan politics. In the run-up to the 1983 federal elections just a few years later, the CDU reframed the SPD's integration efforts with a new term of their own: the "foreigner problem."[172] During a heated Bundestag debate in 1982, CDU representative Alfred Dregger charged that the SPD had "let things drift, repressed the problems, and shifted the burdens to others, especially the states and church organizations."[173] The subsequent CDU/CSU landslide victory of 1983 secured Helmut Kohl's leadership as chancellor, a position from which he quickly reasserted Germany's "principled opposition" to becoming an "immigration country."[174] In this way, SPD efforts to begin the process of actively managing West Germany's unmistakably multicultural society, were—at least temporarily—forestalled.

By the beginning of the 1980s, then, large populations of non-European immigrants had been a fact of life in much of Western Europe for well over two decades. The unmistakable growth of ethnic diversity had forced every major Western European country to grapple with the question of how to handle localized diversity and to begin to assess its national consequences. The specific policies pursued by Britain, the Netherlands, and France all initiated this process by insisting on strict limits: what has been described as the "threshold of tolerance." In each case, that is to say, they posited that the successful incorporation of the immigrants already settled in their countries depended entirely on the prevention of future immigration.

Within this framework, Britain and the Netherlands developed new strategies for managing diversity that harkened back to older models of cultural pluralism. Authorities treated ethnic minority groups as separate, homogeneous entities that were encouraged to preserve their own cultures. At the same time, each government strove to place existing immigrant communities in more stable positions. While British leaders attempted to legislate against racial discrimination, Dutch policy makers sought to provide a more secure legal status and political voice for recent arrivals.

French authorities, by contrast, did not entirely give up on the prospect of sending Algerian immigrants home. In fact, government officials followed an ad hoc strategy of addressing immigrant incorporation with bureaucratic instruments left over from the era of colonial migration. The "insertion" policies they put into place had the advantage of alleviating short-term social conflicts around housing, employment, and education, while also continuing to endorse the preservation of Algerian culture and supporting strong ties to Islam. But in so doing, they also pushed against stated national principles of republican universalism, treating immigrants less as individuals before the state than as members of a distinct group with particular social needs.

The most progressive West German SPD officials, meanwhile, flirted with the argument that their country had reached a "threshold of tolerance," even though the position also implied a new openness to a radical notion, namely, that guest workers had become permanent settlers. This notion, however, remained a minority position through the 1980s. Most clung to the belief that the Federal Republic was not a country of immigration and so guest workers would return home eventually. This conventional stance meant that practical initiatives to facilitate guest workers' adjustment and adaptation to West German society devolved almost entirely to nongovernmental associations, religious groups, and corporate triage efforts. The SPD's brief attempt to push beyond this model, it is worth noting, actually coincided with the Dutch development of an ethnic minorities policy. But where Dutch authorities followed through with elaborate programs for integrating different ethnic groups, the SPD measures were quickly aborted, cut short by the CDU's return to national power and its reassertion of older patterns.

The other key issue here is that most Western European countries initially tackled the question of immigrants almost entirely behind the scenes, without much public discussion of what was taking place or—in some cases—any acknowledgment of how radically their societies had changed. The overriding desire to avoid potentially explosive national debates motivated most of the mainstream political parties to work together to keep the management of immigrants out of public view and depoliticized. But this course ultimately set the scenes for a major backlash, as more conservative and far-right political forces propelled the problem of how to deal with new forms of social diversity onto center stage during the 1980s. Broader questions of "race" and national identity were about to explode across the continent.

CHAPTER THREE

Race, Nation, and Multicultural Society

During the 1970s, there were isolated moments when immigrants and foreign laborers attracted wider national attention. In 1970, for example, the asphyxiation deaths of five African workers in France provoked a public outcry about the deplorable housing conditions. Similarly, in Britain, the 1977 murder of Pakistani-born Altab Ali drew thousands onto the streets of London to demand an end to the racial violence committed by East End skinheads. But such episodes were typically occasioned by an individual tragedy, one whose reach could largely be contained by addressing a localized problem. Over the next decade, however, something changed. Not only did questions about the place of non-Europeans surface more frequently in public debate; increasingly, these questions became intensely politicized, transcending the early contexts of labor migration. As the 1980s wore on, major controversies around immigrants shook country after country, ultimately roiling much of the continent. This was the pivotal moment when a much more open and polarizing struggle over diversity first emerged in postwar Europe.

Consider a series of well-known incidents. In 1978, leader of the British Conservative Party Margaret Thatcher granted an interview to Granada TV's *World in Action* in which she defended ordinary Britons who felt their nation was being "swamped" by alien immigrants. In 1982, during the West German federal election cycle, Chancellor Helmut Kohl vociferously condemned the opposition's recent efforts to integrate guest workers, arguing that Turks, in particular, were too different from Germans to be absorbed into the Federal Republic. In 1986, conservative French Prime Minister Jacques Chirac sought to reform the nationality law, convening a special Commission on Nationality to investigate what it meant "to be French now and in the future."[1] Finally and most notoriously, in 1989, novelist Salman Rushdie published *The Satanic Verses*, his controversial novel that fueled protests against its depiction of the Prophet Muhammad, which, in turn, catalyzed stern public statements about the proper way to be British.

These incidents each produced explosive national debates, with some—the Rushdie affair, in particular—resonating well beyond their initial contexts. Previously, policy makers had cloaked their management strategies in abstract, often bureaucratic language that helped them keep the actual policies concealed from public view. Over the course of the 1980s, by contrast, newly empowered conservatives began to adopt a very different politics of immigration. The British Tories, the French Gaullist party, the Rally for the Republic (Rassemblement pour la République, RPR), and the West German Christian Democratic Union all developed new ways of talking about non-European settlers that focused more explicitly on questions of cultural difference. These strategies, it is important to note, carefully avoided the older, biologically inflected notions of race that had led to the demise of Enoch Powell. As political weapons, however, they served a similar set of functions, routinely characterizing entire groups of immigrants as unfit for—or even incapable of—integration because of the intractability of their cultures. In this way, the 1980s witnessed the rise of what scholars have subsequently come to describe as the "new racism"—a system of racial- ized thinking in which culture supplanted biology as the key marker of incommensurable difference. For our purposes, though, this broader shift in the political landscape raises a number of questions. How, exactly, did the new ideas about culture and national belonging come to be introduced into political discourse at a moment when it was still largely taboo to talk about racial differences—at least in the older ways? How did Islam become so central to this process—a novel means of explaining the impossibility of integration in every one of the major Western European powers?

This is the first in a pair of chapters that traces the back- lash against European multiculturalism even before it was fully launched, a backlash facilitated by new kinds of lan- guages, logics, and narratives. The process that began in this period laid the groundwork for the broader conclusion that particular groups of immigrants were simply incompatible with "Western values," or European ways of life. If we are to make sense of this conclusion, however, we first need to understand the larger process by which certain immigrant cultures came to be demonized, politicized, and policed dur- ing the 1980s. As we shall see, the political retrenchment af- ter 9/11 was merely the final stage of a much longer cycle that began at the very dawn of the European Union.

Cultural Nationalism in Place of Racism

When Margaret Thatcher appeared on *World in Action* in January 1978, she was facing the prospect of a general election. Interviewer Gordon Burns used this expectation to inquire about a "possible new get-tough Tory policy over immigration." Thatcher prefaced her reply by citing Home Office numbers that projected "four million people of the New Commonwealth or Pakistan" in Britain by the end of the century. She then declared: "Now, that is an awful lot and I think it means that people are really rather afraid that this country might be rather swamped by people with a different culture. The British character has done so much for democracy, for law and done so much throughout the world that if there is any fear that it might be swamped, people are going to react and be rather hostile to those coming in."[2] Her choice of words here would continue to resonate. Several months later, during a call-in show on BBC Radio 4, Thatcher was challenged by a black listener to withdraw or apologize for her portrait of a Britain increasingly "swamped" by non-white immigrants.[3] She refused.

On the face of it, Thatcher's claim that the high numbers of new arrivals might make British people feel "rather swamped" simply recapitulated what many of her predecessors in both political parties had long maintained—namely, that ordinary Britons had a limited capacity to absorb New Commonwealth immigrants. Yet in both the television appearance and the radio defense of her initial comments, Thatcher introduced two subtle and crucial new twists. The first came in the interview with Burns during a part of the conversation that has mostly been forgotten. When pressed about whether the Conservatives would make immigration an election issue (as opposed to a matter of backroom policy making), Thatcher answered in the affirmative, signaling a break with nearly fifteen years of bipartisan consensus. She justified this politicization by pointing to the growth of the far-right National Front party, whose success she attributed to its willingness to talk about immigration. "If we do not want people to go to extremes," Thatcher explained, "we ourselves must talk about this problem and we must show that we are prepared to deal with it."[4] The Tories, in other words, had an obligation to introduce immigration as a matter of public debate or else cede the issue to right-wing extremists.

Thatcher's second shift was less immediately clear. After justifying the Conservatives' plan to restrict immigration even further, she continued: "We are a British nation with British characteristics. Every country can take some small minorities and in many ways they add to the richness and variety of this country. The moment the minority threatens to become a big one, people get frightened."[5] This statement appeared to flesh out the implicit logic of a limited absorption capacity, differentiating between scales of demographic change—some acceptable, others dangerous. But Thatcher was also drawing a distinction between conceptions of the nation—one with specifically "British characteristics," and another imperiled by "people with a different culture." In her later radio defense, she elaborated on the change wrought by large-scale immigration: "Some people do feel swamped if streets they have lived in for the whole of their lives are really now quite, quite different."[6] The point was not just to reiterate thresholds of tolerance, but also to draw a line between the British people, endowed with British character, and those marked as bearers of "alien" cultures who were rendering British streets unrecognizable. The latter, she implied, were not really part of Britain, and too many of them threatened to eclipse the core.

This effort to define fundamental differences between the British people and those who hailed from the Commonwealth became a hallmark of Thatcher's leadership strategy, but it was not entirely new.[7] As we have seen, the Conservative politician Enoch Powell had painted a version of this portrait a decade earlier. His infamous 1968 Rivers of Blood speech was a dystopian depiction of immigrants swamping traditionally white Britain, too. "The black man," he had warned, "will have the whip hand over the white man" in Britain, predicting a radical inversion of traditional hierarchies (white over black, master over slave) that would lead to national decline.[8] Six months later, in a lesser-known follow-up address at Eastbourne, Powell more clearly articulated his racial thinking: "The West Indian or Indian does not by being born in England, become an Englishman. In law he becomes a United Kingdom citizen by birth; in fact he is a West Indian or Asian still."[9] In this view, long-term residence, place of birth, and even legal status could not alter one's essential character. National belonging, he suggested, was transmitted as birthright or cultural inheritance. If there was no possibility of assimilation, Powell asked, why allow Britain and its national identity to be overrun by West Indians and Asians? Why not send them home where they really belonged?

For a brief moment in the late 1960s, these unapologetically racial views brought immigration out of the shadows of House of Commons debate and onto the national stage. They tapped into deep prejudices and racial resentments, striking a chord among certain sectors of the British public and making Powell the era's most popular Tory politician. In 1968, however, they also got Powell drummed out of the Shadow Cabinet by his Conservative colleagues, many of whom viewed his speeches as "embarrassing, immoral and even illegal."[10] Leading politicians across the political spectrum believed Powell had gone "well beyond the bounds of acceptable conduct."[11]

But what exactly made Powell's position so problematic? And more to the point, why did his 1968 statements lead to political disgrace, while Thatcher's comments a decade later did not? To answer these questions, we need to consider the longer trajectory of European and British understandings of racial difference. Before World War II, the idea of separate racial groups, as well as racialized distinctions of inferiority, had been understood as common sense throughout the West. Although scholars began to question the assumptions of biological racism in the 1920s and 1930s,[12] few if any would have described Powell's views as "well beyond the bounds" of acceptability. In many ways, it was the war against the Nazi German state that unsettled these assumptions about racial difference. An early report issued by the United Nations Educational, Scientific and Cultural Organization (UNESCO) explained: "The great and terrible war was made possible by the denial of democratic principles of the dignity, equality and mutual respect for men, and by the propagation in their place, through ignorance and prejudice, of the doctrine of inequality of men and races."[13] More specifically, the Nazis' exclusion of entire groups of people from the nation on the basis of putatively "racial" traits revealed the frightening potential of this concept and the abhorrent repercussions of its misuse. Most immediately, Nazi programs to exterminate entire racial groups deemed undesirable created universal moral revulsion. These crimes also increasingly led to the widespread repudiation of scientific racism—and in the European context, the category of race itself.[14]

The discrediting of race and racism took several forms in the immediate postwar period. The Nuremberg War Crimes Trials (1945–46) revealed to the world the extent of the atrocities committed under the Nazi regime, and the International Military Tribunal—convened by the victorious Allies—prosecuted Nazi leaders for "crimes against humanity." In 1948, moreover, the United Nations (UN) began outlining a doctrine of human rights, emphatically declaring that the principles of dignity, equality, and self-determination applied to all peoples "without distinction of any kind."[15] This newly launched organization also developed educational programs to prevent discrimination and protect minorities, charging UNESCO with the "dissemination of scientific facts designed to bring about the disappearance of that which is commonly called race prejudice."[16] The process involved assembling an international committee of social and biological scientists to collect scholarly views on the idea of race and formulate an "authoritative declaration on the race problem."[17] And in 1950, the UNESCO committee's statement on race rejected racism as

> a particularly vicious and mean expression of the caste spirit. It involves belief in the innate and absolute superiority of an arbitrarily defined human group over other equally arbitrarily defined groups. . . . Concern for human dignity demands that all citizens be equal before the law, and that they share equally in the advantages assured them by law, no matter what their physical or intellectual differences may be. . . . The conscience of all mankind demands that this be true for all peoples of the earth. It matters little, therefore, whether the diversity of men's gifts be the result of biological or of cultural factors.[18]

Whereas prewar authorities had often divided the world between "civilized, racially superior peoples subject to the rule of law and uncivilized, inferior subjects governed by . . . paternalism and force," UNESCO now championed a postwar equality based on individuals' membership in a shared human community.[19] The 1950 statement concluded: "For all practical social purposes 'race' is not so much a biological phenomenon as a social myth."[20]

In the aftermath of the Second World War, then, race and racism were increasingly discredited, at least at the level of international politics.[21] The overall effect of the Nuremberg trials and UN initiatives was to create a kind of unspoken consensus around the renunciation of the concept of race. To a surprising extent, political leaders and prominent figures actively shied away from referring to race or racial distinctions, at least in public. This taboo was especially strong in Western Europe. As the heir to the Third Reich, Germany faced enormous pressure to repudiate the Nazi racial project. The Allied occupiers, in fact, emphasized Germany's rejection of Nazi racism as an integral element of the democratizing process, with all four powers pursuing de-Nazification initiatives in their zones.[22] As a result, the language of race was largely eliminated from German public discourse, and this was doubly true in West Germany, which assumed the burden of successor state to the Nazi regime when it gained sovereignty in 1949.[23]

The broader pattern was repeated in the Netherlands, where a "code of silence" on racial difference, the concept of race, and even the word "race" became the norm in Dutch politics and academia.[24] In France, as well, where leaders initially preferred to stress the nation's victimization at the hands of the Nazis and studiously avoided the topic of French complicity with the Vichy regime, the anthropologist Claude Lévi-Strauss argued that the concepts of race and racism should be replaced by the ideas of ethnicity, culture, and xenophobia. His 1952 book *Race and History* largely rendered race an "illegitimate category in French intellectual life."[25]

In Britain, meanwhile, revelations about the Third Reich's race-based crimes acted as a powerful check on both public references to race and vulgar expressions of racialist thinking. Although there was plenty of hand-wringing behind the scenes about the effects of "a large coloured community" after the 1948 arrival of the passenger liner, the *Empire Windrush*, the British political establishment notably refrained from pursuing immigration restriction at this early date.[26] Government ministers feared the "controversy and embarrassment that would arise if immigration controls were introduced against British subjects." "Suspicions of racism so soon after a world war partly waged against the racial genocide of the Hitler regime," they worried, would serve to discredit the nation.[27]

However, the language of race was never fully expunged from the British public sphere, in contrast to other Western European countries. Signs reading "No Coloureds," "Europeans Only," or "No Blacks, No Dogs, No Irish" were widely visible in many areas of the country, used primarily to deter blacks and other New Commonwealth immigrants from applying for lodging. Many pubs and restaurants operated with unofficial "color bars," refusing to serve nonwhite clients. These everyday forms of discrimination—along with the violent attacks against West Indian immigrants in Nottingham and Notting Hill in 1958—made it difficult to pretend that racism did not exist in postwar British society. Still, by and large, British authorities dismissed this sort of racism as "a form of false consciousness, as 'wrong' ideas" on the part of ignorant Britons.[28]

But even among the political elite, eschewing race was far from absolute. A key example can be found in the Labour Party's effort to legislate against discrimination through the Race Relations Act of 1965. The idea of "race relations," according to sociologist Michael Banton, presumed that "each individual could be assigned to a race, and that relations between persons of different races were necessarily different from relations between persons of the same race."[29] Using this language in the bill's name (even though "race relations" was not referenced in the text of the law itself) inadvertently legitimized the concept of race by enshrining it in political discourse. It also cast the issue of immigration in specifically racialized terms. By "legislating for race relations"—rather than "against racism"—the government framed the problem "in terms of 'colour,' in terms of 'them.'"[30] Managing race relations was necessary, the law suggested, because the presence of blacks in a white-majority society inevitably produced conflict. Thus the very instrument that was supposed to prevent immigrants from being treated as second-class citizens instead underscored their differences from mainstream British society.

Somewhat paradoxically, the fact that race remained part of the public lexicon also seemed to facilitate the recognition and condemnation of full-throated racism. When Peter Griffiths's campaign used a blatantly racist slur in the 1964 Smethwick election, the press corps directly questioned the candidate and forced him to take a stand.[31] After Griffiths's stunning victory, Labour Prime Minister Harold Wilson publicly denounced the political upstart's racist campaign and vowed that he "would serve his term as a parliamentary leper."[32]

The political fallout from Enoch Powell's 1968 Rivers of Blood speech was even more extreme. What was ultimately most problematic for British leaders about Powell's declarations was not simply that they invoked race or distinct racial groups, but rather that they married this language to an apocalyptic sense of national decline.[33] "Those whom the Gods wish to destroy, they first make mad," warned Powell. "We must be mad, literally mad, as a nation to be permitting the annual inflow of some 50,000 dependents, who are for the most part the material of the future growth of the immigrant-descended population. It is like watching a nation busily engaged in heaping its own funeral pyre."[34] By linking racial difference to a broader national threat, Powell licensed the public utterance of deeper prejudices, open expressions of racism that the British political elite had worked very hard to keep under wraps.

A decade later, Thatcher repackaged Powell's transgressive ideas of racial difference into a more positive argument about cultural and national belonging. "We are a British nation with British characteristics," she asserted in her Granada TV interview. Here, the nation served as the natural repository not of a homogeneous racial group, but of a particular "culture" and "character" whose demographic foundations were implied rather than stated. It was only reasonable, Thatcher insisted, that ordinary Britons wanted to defend their way of life against immigrants who followed alien traditions and customs. In this view, policies such as the 1981 British Nationality Act, which further constrained the boundaries of citizenship and closed loopholes for immigration, were understandable measures that any nation would take to protect its historical integrity. By emphasizing the importance of a unified national community bound by a shared culture, she offered a novel way of speaking about immigration that did not sound openly xenophobic or racist.[35]

These efforts were tightly linked with a simultaneous project to restore British self-assurance and pride, which had suffered major blows after 1945. Throughout the 1960s, Britain endured a succession of national independence movements that reduced its great empire to little more than the territory of the British Isles. On the continent, moreover, British leaders rebuffed economic integration efforts spearheaded by the French and Germans only to find themselves desperate to join the EEC once the domestic economy flagged. By the early 1970s, the country's demotion to a second-tier power in the Cold War order was upstaged by even more urgent concerns. Protracted struggles with the Irish Republican Army resulted in terror threats and bombings across the country. Meanwhile, the economic downturn triggered by the oil crisis brought the British government into repeated standoffs with labor unions, forced an embarrassing bailout by the International Monetary Fund, and culminated in the nation's virtual paralysis during the so-called Winter of Discontent (1978–79).

Thatcher's response to these developments, arguably, was the 1982 Falklands War, a ten-week conflict over the British overseas territory off the coast of Argentina. When Argentina invaded and occupied the islands in a bid to establish sovereignty, Thatcher dispatched a naval fleet to protect the Falkland inhabitants—descendants of nineteenth-century British settlers—and reassert British control. At a conservative rally in Cheltenham in July of that year, Thatcher explained what had been won in the battle:

> When we started out, there were the waverers and the fainthearts. The people who thought that Britain could no longer seize the initiative for herself. The people who thought we could no longer do the great things which we once did. Those who believed that our decline was irreversible—that we could never again be what we were. . . .
>
> What has indeed happened is that now once again Britain is not prepared to be pushed around. We have ceased to be a nation in retreat. We have instead a new-found confidence—born in the economic battles at home and tested and found true 8,000 miles away. That confidence comes from the re-discovery of ourselves, and grows with the recovery of our self-respect.[36]

Britain's "new-found confidence" and "self-respect," in short, involved reclaiming Britain's imperial legacy. But who, exactly, was worth such sacrifices? Although Thatcher didn't reference immigration or race relations in this context, other conservative commentators made the connection explicitly. Associate editor of the *Sunday Telegraph* Peregrine Worsthorne minced no words when he observed: "If the Falkland Islanders were British citizens with black or brown skins, spoke with strange accents or worshipped different Gods it is doubtful whether the Royal Navy and Marines would today be fighting for their liberation."[37] The Falklands War, then, not only gave British morale a shot in the arm, it underscored a very particular vision of national belonging, one that encompassed anyone of British stock even if they resided eight thousand miles away.

These attempts to shore up borders and bolster national pride had an important domestic complement: efforts to mark the alien elements already inside the nation and cast them as the "enemy within." A crucial and recurrent feature of this boundary drawing was criminality. As sociologist Paul Gilroy has noted, the law was increasingly used in this context to tie national belonging to particular rules and patterns of behavior.[38] By identifying certain groups of citizens as prone to breaking the law, it became possible to portray them as a threat to national "unity." Already in 1958 in the aftermath of the Nottingham and Notting Hill riots, a link between Afro-Caribbeans and criminal behavior was starting to be forged. In popular discourse, the clashes were typically described as a "black" disturbance, even though authorities acknowledged the violence had in fact been instigated by whites.

This connection was further amplified in the 1970s with the moral panics around "mugging" and urban disorder. In the early part of the decade, mounting public concerns about young blacks involved in street crime had prompted Edward Heath's Conservative government to investigate the interactions between police and ethnic minorities. The resulting report actually admitted that "coloured immigrants are no more involved in crime than others; nor are they generally more concerned in violence, prostitution and drugs. The West Indian crime rate is much the same as that of the indigenous population."[39] Nonetheless, the report warned that West Indian youth were increasingly "resentful of society" and claimed that they expressed their frustration against the police. It blamed the "nature of West Indian family discipline" as well as tough competition for jobs and housing for this dynamic.[40]

By mid-decade, a growing perception that law and order was breaking down fueled a deep sense of national crisis.[41] Initial police efforts to tackle the rising crime rate had focused on preventing specific types of illegality. Mugging, as we have seen, came to be viewed almost exclusively as a black offense, prompting authorities to regard neighborhoods where Afro-Caribbeans had settled as "criminal areas." Law enforcement, in turn, shifted to an area-based approach: any inhabitant of a high-crime district could be treated as a criminal by invoking the "sus" law.[42] This strategy amounted to racial profiling, even though it avoided the older languages of racism. Police automatically assumed that blacks were engaged in criminal behavior, not because of an inherently violent nature but rather because of dysfunctional family culture.

Driving the perception of crisis were media images of immigrants collectively engaging in "street violence." These included increasingly routine, low-level skirmishes between young people and police, as well as acts of political protest. In 1977, the far-right National Front (NF) members marched through London's Lewisham district to publicize their view of "multi-racial society" as "wrong" and "evil," and display their desire to "destroy it."[43] The rally drew several thousand anti-NF counterdemonstrators—black and white, immigrant and native—coordinated by the All Lewisham Campaign against Racism and Fascism (ALCARAF). The standoff escalated into violent clashes among the NF, anti-racism activists, and hundreds of police officers on the scene to protect the NF marchers. Two years later, a similar NF provocation in the London neighborhood of Southall produced much the same outcome and, far worse, resulted in the death of the Anti-Nazi League activist Blair Peach. But the mainstream press made little effort to differentiate between patently illegal acts and organized forms of social dissent, dubbing all street violence criminal and blaming the clashes on blacks' antagonism toward law enforcement.[44] Such representations confirmed and even fanned the growing belief that violence, criminal behavior, and distrust of authority had something to do with what made immigrants—and especially West Indians—culturally distinct.[45] This increasingly reflexive criminalization of blacks drew on established patterns of racialized thinking that were now mobilized to new and powerful effects.

When anti-police violence erupted in Brixton in 1981, commentators seized the occasion to underscore the threat of this menace to the nation. On 11 July, the *Financial Times* published an article titled "Outbreak of an Alien Disease": "Like an epidemic of some alien disease, to which the body politic has no immunity, street riots have erupted in different parts of England during the past ten days. There have been plenty of outbreaks of mob violence in Britain in the past.... But never before has there been an outbreak so widespread, so sudden and so threatening to the social order in what ... has always been regarded as one of the world's most law-abiding and peaceful countries."[46] Introduced by "alien" cells, this cancer-like violence was cast as antithetical to the British "law-abiding" culture and character. Especially troubling here was the fact that the "outbreak" had metastasized well beyond immigrant districts such as Brixton or even culturally mixed London to "different parts of England." The "sudden" spread of this "alien disease," the *Financial Times* concluded, posed a mortal danger to Britain's very "social order." The basic well-being of the nation was at stake.

What was taking shape in British immigration and race relations politics under Thatcher's watch, then, was a clear delineation of who was and was not included in the national imaginary. This ideological process did not rely on a rejection of particular groups based on racial characteristics, or even an explicit call to keep Britain white, strategies that might have been criticized as racist. Instead, it emphasized that the specific *cultures* of immigrants and their descendants were incompatible with British culture, and more importantly, that they posed a danger to the British way of life. In this respect, national belonging became the new terrain on which questions of diversity and multicultural society played out. The message here was quite clear: people with "alien" cultures were increasingly understood as swamping the nation from without and destroying its social order from within. And as the external borders were made more impenetrable, attention increasingly turned to the demarcation of internal others. Those groups that had made Britain into a multicultural society were now, at least at the level of public rhetoric, largely excluded from the nation. At this point, though, the "enemy within" was almost exclusively associated with blacks of West Indian heritage.

Making the Nation Respectable

In West Germany, the possibility that guest workers might be viewed as immigrants was only just being broached in the late 1970s, with the introduction of Chancellor Helmut Schmidt's integration initiatives. This represented the first moment in which a public discussion of the Federal Republic as a multicultural society might have been possible. But Schmidt's efforts were largely swept aside with the Social Democratic Party's political setbacks in 1982. First conservative Helmut Kohl became chancellor of the Federal Republic in October, the result of a no-confidence vote against the Social Democrat Schmidt. Then the newly energized CDU confirmed this power shift with a major electoral victory in 1983. Kohl quickly charted a different path from his predecessor. He focused on the work of national recovery after a tumultuous period marred by the abrupt halt of the economic boom and the aftereffects of the splintered 1968 student movement. Starting in the early 1970s, grassroots campaigns for nuclear disarmament, environmentalism, and women's equality had taken to the streets, and throughout the decade, the radicalized youth of the Red Army Faction orchestrated a series of robberies, kidnappings, and hijackings that shocked the nation, hoping to provoke the state into a full display of what they saw as its latent authoritarianism.

Among the new chancellor's first acts was the announcement of two monumental projects that marked a concerted attempt to promote West German nationalism. The House of History (Haus der Geschichte), to be located in Bonn, would tell the nation's postwar history, beginning in 1949 with the establishment of the Federal Republic.[47] The German Historical Museum (Deutsches Historisches Museum) would be located in Berlin and provide broader treatments of national culture so that younger citizens could glean a sense of "whence we come, who we are as Germans, where we stand, and where we are going."[48] In both cases, the goal was to offer positive narratives of German belonging that would inspire pride—rather than guilt or shame—in the nation's history.

However, efforts to resuscitate national identity, culture, or history were anything but simple given Germany's National

Socialist past. A museum project that conveyed the entire sweep of German history necessarily raised crucial questions about the place of National Socialism, the singularity of Nazi crimes, and the extent to which Germans could legitimately see themselves as victims of the war. Kohl seemed to offer an answer to these questions in 1985, when he invited US President Ronald Reagan to lay a wreath at the Bitburg military cemetery to commemorate the fortieth anniversary of Germany's unconditional surrender. But when it became known that SS soldiers had also been interred there, controversy quickly erupted, with some commentators calling for Reagan to skip the ceremony. The US president ultimately made good on this symbolic act of reconciliation, defending his participation as a tribute to the beginning of peace rather than to the war or its dead. From Kohl's perspective, though, the primary object of this commemoration was to signal "Germany's long-earned return to normalcy."[49] Precisely because the Federal Republic had achieved four decades of democratic stability, Kohl insisted, the country deserved the right to honor its war dead like any other democratic nation.[50]

This claim that West Germany was now like any other democratic nation soon provoked additional lines of debate. In response to leftist critics who argued that the Nazi past could not simply be buried and glossed over as the SS soldiers at the Bitburg ceremony had been, conservative historian Ernst Nolte published an article in the *Frankfurter Allgemeine Zeitung* titled "The Past That Will Not Pass Away." Here, Nolte argued that the "race murder" carried out by the Nazis was a direct response to the "class murder" perpetrated by the Bolsheviks.[51] Nazi genocide, he suggested, must be understood in relation to other genocides, rather than designated as a singular event. In response, philosopher Jürgen Habermas accused Nolte and other "neoconservative" historians of trying to revive a "conventional" national identity as an ersatz religion for the sake of ideological cohesion.[52] This testy exchange precipitated what became known as the *Historikerstreit*, a heated public debate among the country's leading historians and philosophers, including at least one scholar involved in Kohl's German Historical Museum project. The *Historikerstreit* represented a key moment of "national self-interrogation about historical responsibility and national consciousness." It seemed to confirm that most West German intellectuals, especially those on the left who were part of the 1968 generation, still rejected overt displays of nationalist feeling and insisted on continuing to work through the nation's troubled past.[53]

Nevertheless, conservative political leaders persisted in pushing for a return to normalcy. In January 1987, Franz Josef Strauß, head of the Christian Socialist Union (CSU) and the second most powerful politician in the Federal Republic, delivered a speech expanding this position:

> It's high time we emerged from the shadow of the Third Reich . . . and become a normal nation again. . . . To idolize the nation is catastrophic and disastrous; but to deny the nation, to deny one's national identity, to destroy our national identity, to refuse to return to it, to a purified national consciousness, is just as disastrous. . . . German history can't be reduced to the twelve years of Adolf Hitler or even to the years 1914–45. German history can't be presented as an endless chain of mistakes and crimes, and our youth thereby robbed of the chance to recover some genuine backbone among our people and toward the outside world.[54]

For Strauß, the Third Reich's "mistakes and crimes" were an exceptional moment in German history rather than its defining epoch. Only by putting the Nazi period in its proper place—in a longer historical trajectory—could the Federal Republic "become a normal nation again." In this way, rehabilitating German history became a means of restoring national identity, so that Germans might feel "proud" once more.[55]

These conservative efforts to revive German pride were only one component of an emerging narrative of national belonging. The other key piece involved delineating which peoples and cultures actually constituted the German nation. On this score, the CDU/CSU vociferously challenged the new direction in "foreigner politics" undertaken by Social Democrats. In the late 1970s, as we have seen, SPD chancellor Schmidt had begun to address the West German government's entrenched pattern of willfully marginalizing guest workers by insisting that their presence was only temporary. The CDU/CSU responded by deliberately politicizing every policy component of the "foreigner problem." Their proposals included reviving rotation, offering financial incentives for repatriation, and withholding German citizenship. At the same time, it offered a broader statement on the place of guest workers in the Federal Republic. On behalf of the CDU/CSU, caucus head Alfred Dregger addressed the Bundestag on this issue in 1982: "It is always false to disregard human nature and people's ways of thinking when making political decisions. People, not only Germans, place value on preserving their national identity in principle. This permits the acceptance of only a limited number of foreigners."[56] Echoing Thatcher's earlier statements on immigration to Britain, Dregger drew on "human nature" to explain why too many "foreigners" in Germany posed a threat to national identity. Certain groups, he argued, presented more difficulties than others. Those from the German-speaking regions of the South Tyrol, Austria, and Switzerland fit into this vision of a cohesive culture easily. Other Europeans such as Italians, Spaniards, and Portuguese, who shared common Christian cultural roots, also posed few integration problems. Turks as well as people from Africa and Asia, however, possessed cultures so different that accommodation was almost impossible. "The Turkish people," elaborated Dregger,

> were not shaped by Christianity, rather by Islam—another high culture, and I stress, high culture. The fact that the state founded by Ataturk in 1918 is secular and understands itself as European changes nothing, anymore than the fact that our state is also secular rather than the earlier Holy Roman Empire. Even in its more secular form, the cultural impulses of Christian and Islamic high culture have a lasting effect on our peoples. This contributes, in addition to a pronounced national pride of the Turks, to the fact that they are not assimilable. They want to remain what they are, namely Turks. And we should respect this.[57]

This claim of incompatibility, Dregger emphasized, had nothing to do with racial prejudice or discrimination. Instead, it was a matter of essential cultural differences steeped in venerable histories and deep traditions. Turkish culture, Dregger pointedly stressed, constituted "another high culture"—neither inferior nor superior to its German counterpart. The two were simply different. But what was especially significant was Dregger's explicit identification of religion as the crucial element that rendered Turkish culture an impossible fit within German society.

In many respects, Dregger's speech took its cues from Thatcher's efforts at national boundary drawing in Britain. He acknowledged tipping points and natural German worries about being overwhelmed by people from different cultures. Yet Dregger pushed the process even further by pointedly naming Islam as the key issue: it was the incommensurable feature of Turkish culture and the reason why Turks could never become German. This marked the very first moment that religion was used to define an entire national group within European political discourse. The fact that this shift first occurred in Germany is not especially surprising; Turks were the largest group of "foreigners" in the Federal Republic, whereas in the United Kingdom there were many non-European immigrant groups with multiple religions.

Given West Germany's status as heir to the Third Reich, it was crucial that this exercise in defining national belonging steer clear of explicit pronouncements of racial difference. We have seen that most European states repudiated the biological conception of race in the wake of the Holocaust, but these issues were always more complicated in Germany. Initially, the Allies made disavowing state-sponsored racism a precondition of democratization. Each of the four occupying powers rapidly instituted measures to de-Nazify society by removing Nazi Party members from positions of power and influence in the cultural sphere, press, economy, judiciary, and politics. With the hardening of Cold War lines and the formal division of Germany in 1949, the United States and Britain pushed to solidify the Federal Republic's position within the Western alliance of liberal democratic nations, a response to the German Democratic Republic's membership in the communist Soviet bloc. Still, American leaders such as US High Commissioner in Germany John McCloy made clear that acceptance by the Western alliance required the Federal Republic to reject the Nazi racial project and accept full responsibility for the Holocaust.

Yet, even as West Germans underwent the process of denazification, they absorbed a new set of lessons about the relation between race and democracy from their American occupiers. Firsthand witnesses to the US Army's practice of racial segregation, West Germans learned that some types of race thinking—namely, prejudice and discrimination against blacks—were not incompatible with "democratic forms and values."[58] Military occupation reinforced ideas of white supremacy across American and German cultures, thereby encouraging West Germans to reframe their conceptions of difference through a white/black lens. In this way, West German society developed a complex and malleable understanding of race and difference. Although "race" (in German, *Rasse*) was widely understood as a tarnished category that could no longer be openly invoked, this taboo did not carry over to the race-based ideas of black and white applied to Afro-German children of African American GIs and German women, children who became the object of social concern during the 1950s and 1960s.[59]

By the late 1960s, a new wrinkle in West German attitudes toward the Nazi past and its racial ideology began to emerge. The generation born immediately after the war—the so-called 1968ers—was reaching adulthood and started raising doubts about the extent of West Germany's democratizing process. Serious public consideration of the National Socialist past had begun in the late 1950s, prompted first by the Auschwitz trials in Frankfurt and then by the Adolph Eichmann trial in Jerusalem. These debates were intensified in the 1960s by young leftists who wanted to purge postwar society of what they viewed as fascism's lingering effects. As 1968ers came of age, many found the perfunctory descriptions of the Nazi era in their schoolbooks dissatisfying. These young people posed pointed questions to their parents, asking about specific actions (or inactions) during the Third Reich. The most radical openly "condemned [the older] generation for its complicity with Nazism and its conspicuous silence about the Nazi period."[60] For those who adopted the politics of the New Left, in particular, postwar democracy seemed hollow because the majority of West Germans had never acknowledged any personal implication in the Nazi regime. Instead, the elder generation had turned quickly to rebuilding society, fighting communism, and single-mindedly pursuing economic prosperity, tasks that young leftists believed had taken the place of a real grappling with the country's shameful Nazi past.[61] As this younger generation matured and assumed a more prominent public voice, its New Left members energetically worked to strengthen the West German taboo against explicit Nazi symbols, language, and assumptions. By the late 1970s, the 1968ers' commitment to "overcoming the past" (*Vergangenheitsbewältigung*) produced a highly attuned public sensitivity to any utterance that condoned National Socialism or smacked of its racial ideology.

Alarms went off, for instance, in relation to the Heidelberg Circle, a fringe group of right-wing university professors who decried the "infiltration of the German *Volk* by the immigration of millions of foreigners" and called for the establishment of an organization devoted to the protection of the German people. According to an early 1982 article in the weekly newspaper *Die Zeit*, leftist student groups from Munich found an unpublished copy of the extremist group's mission statement and leaked it to the press.[62] Both *Die Zeit* and the left-leaning daily *Frankfurter Rundschau* published this statement, which they dubbed the Heidelberg Manifesto, as well as multiple articles that energetically condemned the document for inciting nationalism and racism.[63]

But this heightened vigilance against any public expression associated with Nazi racialist thought did not regularly extend to the broader phenomenon of xenophobia. In its 1 January 1982 issue, *Die Zeit* announced that "a threshold of tolerance had been reached," saying that the belief held by many Germans that the arriving relatives of guest workers were exploiting their country now threatened to become a full-blown "hatred of foreigners."[64] A second major recession in the late 1970s had fueled the growing antipathy, and the simultaneous spike in the number of asylum seekers further inflamed the public.[65] "All of a sudden," observed the reporter, "everyone is talking about the fact that we could be flooded and crushed in our own country by foreign guest workers and their families, by false—and even real—asylum seekers."[66] In April of the same year, *Die Zeit* reported that half of all West Germans felt *ausländerfeindlich*, or hostile toward foreigners.[67] While the sharp rise in xenophobia was a worrisome development, prompting significant coverage by the press, this trend did not elicit the same kind of outright and unequivocal condemnation as the Heidelberg Manifesto.

Given the country's heavy historical burden, we might have expected the Federal Republic—among Western European states—to be the most open to the possibility of a truly heterogeneous, multicultural population. In theory, at least, it might follow that rejection of Nazism would entail a rejection of the basic premises of a racially pure and decidedly homogeneous nation. West German officials were keen to show the world a transformed attitude and eagerly pointed to the guest worker program as evidence of the nation's new openness to internationalism. In 1964, Labor Minister Theodor Blank declared that guest worker recruitment facilitated "the merging together of Europe and the rapprochement between persons of highly diverse backgrounds and cultures in the spirit of friendship."[68] Yet importing guest workers in the context of economic rebuilding and expansion did not radically alter the basic terms of society. Guest workers were insistently understood as a transient and foreign presence, not as permanent additions to the West German social body. In this respect, pursing the guest worker program continued to complicate—and undercut—German authorities' self-congratulations for their international openness as a post-Nazi nation. Indeed, the postwar celebrations of internationalism never came close to posing a threat to the core idea of West Germany as a non-immigrant, homogeneous society.

By the 1980s, however, disavowal had given way to more explicit forms of cultural retrenchment as growing numbers of West Germans openly admitted hostility to the presence of foreigners. This retrenchment operated in at least two distinctive registers, which, in turn, elicited notably different responses in the public sphere. During the early 1980s, the vigorous policing of Nazi-like expressions of racism (or potential Nazi behavior) in contexts like the Heidelberg Manifesto could coexist with open expressions of intolerance toward guest worker populations who stubbornly remained in the Federal Republic. Precisely because anti-Nazi vigilance offered proof of a society that had transcended its Nazi past, West Germans could be more open about their uneasiness with the permanent presence of Turkish workers and their families. Hostility toward "foreigners," in this view, was categorically different from a return to Nazi intolerance—a conventional form of xenophobia that regularly surfaced in many other Western democracies, rather than a more distinctive German racism associated with Nazi ideology.

It's especially significant, therefore, that the CDU/CSU efforts to articulate more acceptable forms of boundary drawing and national differentiation adopted new justifications—that is, culture rather than biology. Explaining to fellow Bundestag members why Turkish guest workers ought to go home, Christian Democrat Dregger emphasized the distinctive imprint of Islam on Turkish culture. Islam, he claimed, was a fundamentally different tradition that operated according to its own logic. In fact, it was the very strength and persistence of Islamic culture that produced the dilemma for West German society: Turkish "ghettos" created pockets of enduring minority difference within an equally strong and unchanging majority culture. The uneasy coexistence of people who belonged to two unyielding cultures and lived in isolated enclaves was becoming untenable, Dregger insisted. The only solution was for Turks to return to their natural and historical home.

To be sure, this conception of culture betrayed an underlying sense of essential, unchanging difference often associated with more explicit ideas of race. Islam had so deeply imprinted the Turkish character, noted Dregger, that it even defied Turkey's own self-definition as a *European* and *secular* state. But these racist echoes remained hidden because of the reliance on the language of culture and the issue of religion to argue for Turkish incompatibility. In this way, Christian Democrats took seriously the fears and concerns expressed in opinion polls and documents like the Heidelberg Manifesto, while shifting the ground on which nationalist arguments about German belonging could be constructed. Cultural difference, rather than racial purity in the older Nazi sense of blood and biology, became the new, more acceptable way of explaining who belonged to German society and who did not.

And with the CDU electoral victory in 1983, previous Social Democratic efforts to develop serious federal-level policy initiatives to integrate de facto immigrants largely ceased. Although Kohl maintained the post of commissioner for foreigner affairs, the emphasis of his "foreigner policy" returned to "consolidation" efforts, that is, measures to further restrict and even reduce the numbers of foreigners in the Federal Republic. These included reconsideration

of a "humane" rotation policy, a push to offer financial incentives for repatriation, and a repudiation of the right of
foreigners to become German citizens. For the next fifteen
years of Kohl's leadership, federal policy reverted to its old
mantra: Germany is not a country of immigration.

Resurgence of Republicanism

Just as in Britain and West Germany, the contours of national identity became a central topic of public discussion in
France during the 1980s. In all three countries, national revitalization projects emerged as a response to anti-immigrant
anxieties inflamed by the far right. In Britain and Germany,
this was an effort launched by mainstream conservative parties that sought to replace overtly racialist arguments with
socially acceptable debates about national belonging. In
France, however, the politics were somewhat more complicated. Where Britain's Powell and West Germany's Heidelberg Circle were openly castigated and pushed to the political margins, France's Jean-Marie Le Pen gained considerable
traction in the voting booth. The electoral success of his
party, the Front National (FN), forced both the mainstream
right and the mainstream left to engage with explicitly exclusionary visions that had demonstrable public appeal.[69]

Initially, the French political establishment had dismissed
the FN as a far-right fringe movement and refused to take
it seriously. Launched in 1972, the party struggled to find a
coherent message and failed to receive even one percent of
the vote in its first few national election cycles. In the early
1980s, the party began to advance an anti-immigration platform with provocative statements like "two million unemployed is two million immigrants too many."[70] As we have
seen, Le Pen also reinterpreted regionalist and immigrant

calls for the "right to difference" as a demand for national preference. In his view, France had the right to exclude foreigners deemed inassimilable because they imperiled the nation and degraded French citizenship.[71] While young *beurs* and the second generation of French immigrant families employed the slogan to appeal for an expansive nation that embraced multiple cultures, Le Pen used the phrase to argue for an increasingly circumscribed national vision that preserved the French right to be French. The FN thus justified its anti-immigration platform as a defense of French national identity.

To a certain extent, the FN seemed worth ignoring through the early 1980s because it made no effort to disguise its racist views. Le Pen denounced the corrupting influence of North African and Islamic culture and described Algerian immigrants as an invading presence that threatened to "mak[e] the French nation disappear before the next twenty years" had passed.[72] Another FN leader warned, "western civilization is in peril. The white race risks submersion by the third world, and shouldn't one defend oneself?"[73] These positions rejected the mixture of races as socially and politically untenable and cast Algerian people as so fundamentally different that integration was impossible. The continuing presence of inassimilable immigrants (many of whom, although the FN did not acknowledge this, were actually citizens) directly endangered the health of the French nation.

In March 1983, however, Le Pen was elected as local ward councilman of Paris's twentieth *arrondissement*. Six months later, the FN gained four seats on the newly right-wing town council of Dreux.[74] As Le Pen began to establish a political foothold, the left vehemently lambasted him as a transparent bigot, while a number of eminent Catholic bishops condemned him for stirring up racist sentiment.[75] Still, the FN enjoyed electoral success. The party made major inroads

with the 1984 European elections, winning 10.95 percent
of the national vote and sending ten deputies (including
Le Pen) to the European Parliament in Strasbourg. In the
national legislative elections two years later, the FN scored
a resounding victory with nearly 10 percent of the vote, giving them thirty-five seats in the National Assembly.[76] This
support, in turn, forced Le Pen's opponents to engage the
question of immigrant integration much more squarely on
his terms.

Especially striking in these debates was the extent to which
the political mainstream—both right and left—accepted the
basic premise of Le Pen's critique: namely, that immigrants
posed a threat to the national community. For the right, this
was not such a big stretch, since many conservative authorities had worried behind the scenes for decades about the
growing numbers of Algerian workers. Although former
president Giscard D'Estaing maintained that France must
accept those foreigners who "wished" to integrate, he also
argued that "the central problem of immigration is the
question of the menaced identity of French society."[77] The
widely circulated conservative publication *Figaro Magazine*
devoted its 26 October 1985 issue to the demographic future
of France. The front cover asked provocatively, "Will we be
French in thirty years?" Inside, readers were enjoined to "save
this dossier on immigration. You will find here, revealed
for the first time, the secret numbers that, in thirty years to
come, will put in peril our national identity and determine
the destiny of our civilization."[78] On the left, meanwhile, Socialist Prime Minister Laurent Fabius conceded in 1984 that
the positions of the right extremists were "false answers to
real questions."[79]

But why would the Socialists concede that Le Pen's exco-
riations of immigrant compatibility were "real"? Just a few
years earlier, after all, the party had championed the "right

to difference" and, in 1985, it reintroduced a measure from its 1981 campaign supporting the right of foreign residents to vote in municipal elections.[80] While Socialist Minister for Social Affairs and National Solidarity Georgina Dufoix admitted that immigration posed a "challenge to French society on all levels," she also insisted that French identity was strong enough to embrace the contributions of immigrants.[81]

Part of the willingness to accept Le Pen's framing may have had something to do with the coming of age of second-generation immigrants, who were born or at least raised and educated in France. Most of these young people had grown up in the *banlieues*, suburbs on the outskirts of major metropolitan areas with large housing blocks built in the 1960s to accommodate returning *pieds-noirs*, Algerians relocated from the *bidonvilles*, and newly imported foreign workers. By the late 1970s, these areas had high rates of unemployment and poverty and a lack of educational opportunity. Long ignored by the public, they provoked national attention in 1981, when a series of clashes took place between immigrant youth and the police in housing projects around Lyon.[82] These revolts, combined with the growing activism of *beurs* and other young people of immigrant origin, raised questions about the efficacy of integration. Much more than their parents, this generation had been educated in the French system and was schooled in the civic values of the nation. In different ways, however, both the Lyon riots and increasingly visible demands for the "right to difference" suggested that immigrant youth—despite their French citizenship—had failed to assimilate.

This was precisely the issue that Le Pen targeted. Emboldened by the FN's strong electoral showing in 1984, he now proposed eliminating the principle of jus soli—which granted automatic citizenship based on one's birth on French soil—and replacing it with a formal naturalization procedure that would require immigrants to *demonstrate* assimilation into the French national community.[83] This desire to reform the French nationality code was not unique to the radical right. In the 1970s, immigrant and leftist activists had criticized the automatic granting of citizenship to second-generation immigrants as a form of state-imposed assimilation.[84] State authorities, in turn, had toyed with revising the nationality code on several occasions, but these behind-the-scenes discussions focused on bureaucratic technicalities. By the mid-1980s, the question of citizenship was increasingly attached to highly politicized debates about the terms of integration and the boundaries of national identity.

At first glance, such fights over the nationality code appeared to be a straightforward clash between traditional political opponents. In the spring of 1985, the mainstream right largely endorsed Le Pen's proposal to eliminate jus soli and any automatic bestowal of citizenship. The RPR-UDF platform for the 1986 elections, for example, asserted that French citizenship "must be demanded (by the candidate) and accepted (by the state), and its acquisition ought not result from purely automatic mechanisms."[85] This new procedure was needed, claimed many conservatives, because second-generation immigrants—especially French Algerians—treated nationality as a fungible commodity, benefitting from "paper marriages" or dual nationality, which proved that they were not French "at heart."[86] Forcing immigrants to choose French citizenship, the RPR-UDF platform argued, the reform would "strengthen" the nation, making the citizenry "more confident in its identity."[87] Even mainstream conservative politicians Michel Noir (RPR) and Bernard Stasi (UDF), who normally would have repudiated any proposal linked to the far right, agreed that active choice could serve as a kind of "moral contract" between the French and those immigrants who desired to "share the values of the national community."[88]

Leftists unequivocally rejected this vision and condemned the reform as part of the right's broader package of anti-immigration policies. Socialist President Mitterrand specifically decried the elimination of jus soli, arguing that it was the key provision that made French citizenship uniquely inclusive. Leftist critics accused reform supporters of corrupting the "classical universal idea of French citizenship," which had extended (and guaranteed) citizen status to all born inside the nation's borders. They denounced the reformers' new conception of citizenship as "perversely un-French," "nativist," and "reactionary."[89] The right's narrow vision of the national community, they argued, was the real danger to the nation.

After the RPR-UDF coalition won a legislative majority in 1986, Prime Minister Jacques Chirac spearheaded the political process of changing the nationality code. But his efforts ground to a halt in the winter of 1987, stymied by the inertia of bureaucrats struggling to formulate new administrative practices; a negative ruling by the Conseil d'État, which said the reform went counter to the republican tradition; and highly public protests organized by antiracism groups such as SOS Racisme, France-Plus, and the League of Human Rights.[90] The final push against Chirac's efforts came in December, when students began to mobilize against the revision of the nationality code as part of larger demonstrations against educational reforms. The police beating and subsequent death of a French Algerian student at a rally helped to fuse the two movements. The nationality reform is "an encouragement to racism and exclusion," declared student activists. "We reaffirm our solidarity with all foreign students menaced by expulsion."[91]

Chirac's decision to withdraw his initiative from legislative consideration appeared to be a decisive defeat for the right, certainly for the radical right and its explicitly exclusionary definition of citizenship. But Chirac did not simply abandon this issue, instead pursuing his goal of reform through a more conciliatory approach. As Justice Minister Albin Chalandon explained, the aim now was to use revisions of the nationality code to "enhance the sentiment of belonging to the nation, without giving it any character of an instrument of exclusion against foreigners."[92]

In June 1987, Chirac convened a Nationality Commission (Commission de la Nationalité) to provide a "comprehensive reflection on the basis of social integration and national unity in France." The task here was to create a "large national consensus" that might serve as the basis for "any modification of the nationality law."[93] This nonpartisan, independent committee of experts met for six months and produced a two-volume report with recommendations.[94] Commissioners studied existing law, consulted with relevant government ministries, took "field trips" to local police stations (where nationality applications were filed), and debated possible proposals. Most importantly, perhaps, they held public hearings, where over one hundred prominent public figures (including immigrant association leaders, teachers, politicians, religious representatives, journalists, and intellectuals) were asked for their opinions about immigration and integration.[95] Every session except the final two was broadcast live on television and radio, facilitating an unprecedented public discussion about the place of immigrants in the French national community.

While the initial debates about the nationality code had focused on eliminating the territorial basis for French citizenship, those led by the Nationality Commission zeroed in on definitions of the nation itself. Precisely because the

Commission was understood as an independent group, it avoided some of the burdens associated with both the right's restrictive immigration politics and the left's (putatively) uncritical celebration of cultural differences. This freedom enabled the Commission to mount a strong defense of national identity on the basis of a radically circumscribed vision of pluralism. In his notes about the work of the committee, Commissioner Pierre Catala, professor of law, affirmed that "French nationality law is at the service of the French nation, ... its continuity implies a rejection of a multicultural society and the maintenance of a community of culture. Such an affirmation in no way implies the closing of France to exterior contribution ... it leads simply to control of the migratory flux ... to favor its integration, and to consecrate this by the attribution or acquisition of the nationality."[96] In this way, the Commission reframed previous divisions between right and left. What it sought to foster was not a choice between an exclusive national identity or blind acceptance of "multicultural society," but rather the fusion of a strong national identity with numerous immigrant populations.

The key to this fusion, according to the Commission, was "national integration." Historically, this term had referred to the process of transforming regional minorities with linguistic and cultural particularities (e.g., Breton, Corsican, Occitan) into modern citizens with a common set of characteristics—or, as historian Eugen Weber famously put it, turning "peasants into Frenchmen."[97] An earlier version of this model (with strong assimilationist overtones) had been applied to colonized peoples, requiring them to give up certain cultural differences (especially religion) in exchange for French citizenship. In presenting the Commission's report, chairman Marceau Long asserted that France, "inheritor of a secular, cultural and political centralization ... was occupied by the instinct to transform [its] foreigners into French

citizens, speaking *the same language*, sharing the *same* culture and patriotic *values*, participating in the national life
like the others, *even if they retain in the private order their
religious and cultural loyalties*."[98] In this case, Long explained,
the Commission self-consciously moved away from strict
assimilationism by gesturing toward limited tolerance for
alternate "loyalties" of religion or culture in "private." But,
crucially, these particularities were understood to be sub-
sumed under French identity.

To be effective, Commissioners maintained, integration
required unbending adherence to a common language, culture, and civic values. Integration, they insisted, could not
be "nourished by a weakening of the national identity. The
French 'creuset' can only play its role if the French identity
exercises a strong attraction, and for that, it is still necessary
that it be firm."[99] This firmness was especially urgent, since
many of the traditional institutions of integration—school,
the military, and unions—were no longer as effective as they
had been in the past. A "weakening" of the "national tradition," the final report concluded, "constitutes a real danger to
the national future."[100]

Significantly, the Commission's report zeroed in on Algerian immigrants and Islam as the crucial challenge to French
national identity. "The Islamic question," it declared, "[c]an
be cited as a future test case for the affirmation of such an
identity and for a policy of integration. The integration of
an Islamic element into the French national community implies an acceptance by Muslims in France of the rules and
the law of a republican and, above all, secular state. For Islam
this represents a real upheaval. The French state . . . cannot
renege on this demand."[101] Here again, it was Islam that figured as the central problem, a cultural force that required its
followers to put loyalty to the religious community above
loyalty to the national community. For the Commission, the

"French national community" enshrined the universal ideal of equality of mankind before the law. Equality within a "republican state" relied on secularism (*laïcité*) to prevent the encroachment of religious affiliations (or other competing loyalties) and instill civic values. It also required stripping individuals of any affiliation (biological, historical, economic, social, religious, cultural) that would distinguish one citizen from another.[102] It was only as abstract individuals, divested of all particularity, that citizens could be treated equally.

A crucial dimension of this integration process, the Commission asserted, was the individual's active decision to acquire citizenship. Declaring one's desire to be French harkened back to older ideals (first conjured by the nineteenth-century historian Ernest Renan) of the nation as a daily plebiscite.[103] National identity, in this schema, was a deliberate act of political will. As sociologist and Commission member Dominique Schnapper put it, "one is French through the practice of language, through the learning of a culture, through the wish to participate in an economic and political life."[104] The element of choice was something on which both left and right participants in the proceedings agreed. Testifying before the Commission, the left-leaning philosopher Alain Finkielkraut declared: "In reversing the automatic acquisition [of nationality] to a voluntarist act, one would be faithful to the elective tradition that made the nation a pact, a secular association."[105] Representatives from Alain Juppé's conservative Club 89 concurred that it is "necessary" that the foreign-born and children of immigrants "opt for our nationality; it is for them to decide that they are linked to our country."[106] Casting citizenship as a volitional process provided room for the left to counter ethnic definitions of the nation, while allowing the right to insist on basic thresholds for national integration.

The work of the Nationality Commission was clearly designed to create the impression of a wide-ranging public

debate about French identity as well as the policy components of integration. Yet as political scientist Miriam Feldblum has argued, it functioned more like a "political specta-
cle" through which the Commission carefully constructed
a consensus on the definition of French belonging.[107] This
consensus resuscitated ideas from France's venerable republican tradition that had long been dormant—at least in relation to immigrants, for whom, as we have seen, the behind-
the-scenes pragmatics of integration between the 1950s and
1970s had been far more flexible. Invoking an older notion
of republican piety, the Commission raised universalism
over particularism, politics over culture, and individuals over
groups as the first principles of the French nation. The best
way to approach the challenges of entrenched diversity, the
Commission concluded, was to insist that immigrants accept this series of republican zero-sum choices.

Immigrant representatives called to speak at the Commission's hearings, it is important to note, largely endorsed
this republican universalist program. One prominent voice
was Harlem Désir, leader of the antiracist organization SOS
Racisme. This association had previously served as a touchstone for the *beur* movement and embraced the "right to
difference."[108] But after Le Pen co-opted the slogan, SOS Racisme began championing the "right to resemblance," a subtle
departure that stressed equal access to and inclusion within
a common set of republican values. In his testimony before
the Commission, Désir explained that "integration" is best
understood as "the refusal of this perversion of the right
to difference, which institutes different laws for people of
different origins.... The Republic is just the possibility for
men and women of different origins, different cultures to
live according to common values, to adhere to principles of
common laws, to be submitted to the same responsibilities with, in counterpart, the same rights."[109] Speaking on

behalf of France-Plus, an organization working to involve the Franco-Maghrebi population in the political process, Arezki Dahmani concurred: "Our values, these are the values of the French revolution. Our values are the values of secularity. Our values are the values of democracy."[110] Notably absent from the hearings were *beur* organizations that had called for the "right to difference" and wanted to recast French citizenship in a more pluralist mode that might allow the preservation of religious and cultural differences.

Ultimately, then, the conclusions of the Commission were not so much the product of open debate as the consolidation of a specific political project, one that sought to thread the needle between the far right's desire for an ethnically homogeneous France and the left's tolerance of heterogeneous inclusion.[111] But the real accomplishment here went beyond just forging a political consensus. It was the construction of a commonsense understanding of national identity, now legitimized through the founding myth of the French Republic. By casting its politics as an articulation of republican universalism, the Commission naturalized its view of integration, rendering it virtually unimpeachable and thus unchallengeable. But despite the universalist claims, this conception of the nation did not live up to its promises of inclusion irrespective of race, color, or creed. Riots in the *banlieues* or *beur* demands for a more expansive French identity, for example, were now read as failures to integrate properly. Immigrants' refusal to give up their cultural differences—or at least to relegate them to the private sphere—became grounds for exclusion from the national imaginary (if not the nation itself). Above all, this understanding of French belonging now targeted most non-European, non-Christian residents as particular problems for the nation.

To put it another way, just as in Britain and West Germany, the French reinvigoration of national identity during the 1980s came as a response to the growing anxieties about immigrants previously voiced mostly by the far right. In the British and West German cases, mainstream conservatives used national rehabilitation projects to draw boundaries between those who belonged and those who didn't. Such arguments did not go uncontested by leftist critics, but they dominated public discourse because the Tories and Christian Democrats remained in power for well over a decade. French efforts at national revitalization, by contrast, were more of a collective political project. Responding to the radical right's provocations, French leaders from across the political spectrum were drawn into public debates about national identity. Invoking the country's republican tradition, Chirac's Nationality Commission successfully consolidated a vision of Frenchness that appeared to be inclusive of cultural differences, but actually insisted on absolute assimilation. In all three cases, then, the new narratives of national belonging functioned as a way to draw stricter limits as to who was eligible for integration and under what conditions such a process might take place. British and West German conservatives avoided accusations of anti-immigrant racism by framing their arguments in terms of cultural differences, even as they cast immigrant cultures as monolithic, isolated, and immutable. French leaders, by contrast, forestalled the very possibility of cultural pluralism by cloaking a much more rigid definition of national identity with the founding principles of the Republic itself.

The Rushdie Affair and the Struggle over Multiculturalism

Although this wave of conservative retrenchment was clearly political (and often politicized) through the 1980s, it rarely provoked national upheaval. But in February 1989, an event occurred that reverberated through Western Europe on a wider and more visible scale—one that seemed to pit immigrants and their distinctive values against the national reconstruction work that had been taking place over the decade. This event precipitated a broad-based political crisis in Britain and heralded the onset of more aggressive public debates in other European states as well. It began when the Indian-born British author Salman Rushdie published his fourth novel, *The Satanic Verses*, in the fall of 1988. At this point, Rushdie was a major light of the British literary scene, although his work had often courted controversy. His second novel, *Midnight's Children*, had been awarded the prestigious Booker Prize, but it angered Indian Prime Minister Indira Gandhi for depicting her putative neglect of her husband—so much so that she sued Rushdie for libel in the British courts. A third work of fiction, *Shame*, took aim at Benazir Bhutto and was aggressively suppressed in Pakistan.

Almost immediately, *The Satanic Verses* won critical acclaim in Britain: it was short-listed for the Booker Prize and received the Whitbread Award for fiction. Yet many Muslim readers found the novel deeply offensive. Several chapters unfold as a series of dream sequences that refashion parts of the early history of Islam and feature Muhammad and his wives. In Rushdie's retelling, Muhammad appears as "Mahound," an epithet coined by medieval Christian crusaders to suggest "a lustful and profligate false prophet and idolator."[112] Some of the scenes that depict Muhammad and his wives are arguably pornographic: at one point, prostitutes in a brothel pose as Muhammad's wives; at another, the recently widowed Prophet indulges in a promiscuous sex binge. Rushdie, in other words, had few qualms about taking imaginative aim at Islam's most sacred figure, the role model for millions of believers. And for many of those believers, even the less pious ones, Rushdie's portrayal of Muhammad seemed like a cruel attack—if not on themselves, then on their community.

Hints of trouble surfaced first in India. Before Penguin Press had even released the book, it received a warning from its editorial consultant in India that the novel would upset many Muslims and could provoke unrest across the subcontinent.[113] Upon learning of the book's impending appearance in September 1988, two Muslim members of the Indian Parliament began a successful campaign to ban the novel in India.[114] When the book appeared in Britain a month later, a handful of British Muslim community leaders initiated a behind-the-scenes campaign asking Penguin to withdraw the novel, have Rushdie issue a public apology, and donate the book's proceeds to date to an agreed-upon Muslim charity. The initial assumption here was that the publishers were simply ignorant about Islam and did not grasp the offensiveness of certain passages.[115] Penguin, however, refused to budge, prompting British Muslim opponents of the book to turn to the government for redress. As a first step, they wrote to Prime Minister Thatcher asking that the novel be banned under Britain's blasphemy law, which, they argued, should extend beyond Christian faiths to include all of the country's constitutive religions. From there, members of the Muslim community lobbied local Labour MPs and organized mass demonstrations in London and Bolton. During a third major rally, this one in the Midlands city of Bradford (home to Britain's largest Muslim community), the book was burned. At this point, it is important to note, the protests against Rushdie's novel were relatively circumscribed, confined to the Indian subcontinent and a few localities in Britain. Most Muslims, in fact, were hardly aware of the controversy, and there was little anti-Rushdie sentiment in the Arab world, in Turkey, or among Muslim immigrant communities in other parts of Europe.

On 14 February 1989, however, the tenor of the situation abruptly changed, as Iran's Ayatollah Khomeini issued an Islamic legal ruling, or *fatwa*, which sentenced Rushdie and his publishers to death and called on the Muslim faithful to serve as their executioners. Rushdie was forced into hiding soon after, and he remained underground for nearly a decade. In 1990 a London bookstore was firebombed. Over the next three years, Rushdie's Japanese translator was knifed to death, his Italian translator was beaten and stabbed, and his Norwegian publisher was shot.[116] But even before this violence, the fatwa recast the controversy from a set of localized disputes into a conflict between a global "nation of Islam" and the laws of non-Islamic communities around the world.[117] Khomeini's edict treated all Muslims as accountable to Islamic law, regardless of religious commitment or national legal status. As Kenan Malik has explained, this was a highly unorthodox and unprecedented move—traditionally, Sharia law had applied only to states under Islamic authority.[118] In dramatic fashion, the fatwa underscored the transnational community to which even Muslims living in non-Islamic states belonged. However, despite their anger over the novel, most British Muslim leaders sought to contain the broader controversy by denouncing Khomeini's death sentence. Even a self-described Islamist like Kalim Siddiqui, co-founder of the Tehran-funded Muslim Institute and a public supporter of the fatwa, advised British Muslims to abide by British law and not commit murder.[119] Initially, then, support for or opposition to Rushdie was not a test of British or Muslim identification.

For British Muslims who objected to Rushdie's novel, the basic claim was this: as citizens of Britain, Muslim immigrants had every right to expect the laws of their land to safeguard their religion from defamation—just as it protected Christianity for the majority population. British Muslims simply asked for the law to grant them equal protection, and they made this demand through democratic practices such as letter-writing campaigns, the lobbying of elected officials, and public protests. What they asked for, in short, was due deference for their supposedly alien traditions, and they did so using the language of Western liberalism and widely recognized forms of democratic politics. But in making their claims on these terms, opponents of the book found themselves becoming the targets of a much larger set of debates about British culture as a very specific "way of life."

Ten days after Khomeini issued the fatwa, Tory Home Secretary Douglas Hurd delivered a speech titled "On Race Relations and the Rule of Law" to a gathering of Muslims at the Birmingham Central Mosque. While acknowledging that Muslims "no doubt felt their faith had been insulted," he admonished them to refrain from violence or the threat of violence.[120] Hurd further emphasized the importance of proper integration for ethnic minorities, which, in this case, was demonstrated by respect for the rule of law, freedom of speech, and tolerance of alternative viewpoints. Five months later, Home Office Minister of State John Patten issued an open letter to Britain's Muslim community in the *Times* and followed it with a more pointed statement titled "On Being British." At each turn, these authorities stressed the need for "anxious" and "insulted" Muslims to adhere to the essential characteristics of Britishness.[121]

Given Patten's admission that the "great majority of Muslims in this country" had "handled" their outrage at Rushdie in a "responsible way," it seems worth asking why he and other political leaders felt the need publicly to lecture an entire immigrant community on the proper way to be British.[122] Indeed, as anthropologist Talal Asad has noted, many groups—from fascists to antiracists, students to trade unionists, feminists to gay activists—had taken to the streets in various forms of angry protest before. But neither protests, nor race riots, indeed, not even the Irish Republican Army's planting of bombs on British soil had prompted government representatives to reprove these groups for behaving in an "un-British" manner.[123] Here, the order of events is crucially important. During the fall and early part of the winter, prior to the fatwa, the domestic campaign against Rushdie's novel had not attracted much attention from either the British government or the national press. In fact, it was largely out of frustration at the lack of political and journalistic response that Bradford Muslim leaders decided to burn Rushdie's book. But this form of public protest took on new meaning after Khomeini's fatwa, when any form of public anger directed at Rushdie became one more piece of evidence proving the rage, intolerance, and illiberal nature of Islam.[124] Such protests also dramatically transformed the place of Asian Muslims within British immigration politics. Where Afro-Caribbeans had long been seen as injecting an alien criminal element into a law-abiding society, Asian Muslims now became the face of the "immigrant problem," suspected of introducing religious fundamentalism and violence into a tolerant liberal polity.

In his initial letter to the Muslim community, Patten asserted that, moving forward, the "single most important guiding principle" was that minorities "should be part of the mainstream of British life."[125] While he assured his readers that "no one would expect or indeed want British Muslims . . . to lay aside their faith, traditions or heritage," he insisted on "full participation in our society by Muslim and other ethnic minority groups" and rejected any hint of "separation or segregation."[126] But his message went beyond simply encouraging older forms of cultural integration. "Being British," he now insisted, had to do with "those things which . . . we have in common. Our democracy and our laws, the English language, and the history that has shaped modern Britain." At the center of British culture, he asserted, was "freedom": the "freedom to choose one's faith, to choose one's political allegiance, to speak and write freely, to meet, argue and demonstrate, to play a part in shaping events."[127] These principles were undergirded by tolerance and obligation. As Patten explained, "there is plenty of room for diversity, precisely because our traditions are those of tolerance." But rights, he cautioned, come with obligations: above all, the obligation to respect the rights of others.

British critics on both sides of the political spectrum welcomed these sorts of statements. In a 23 July 1989 piece titled "Ground Rules for the British Way of Life," the center-right editorial board for the *Sunday Times* endorsed Patten's interventions as "a long overdue reassessment of the nature of British citizenship."[128] Similarly, a 1990 seminar on the Rushdie affair organized by the left-leaning Commission for Racial Equality in conjunction with the more moderate liberal Runnymede Trust pushed for "dialogue and discourse in pursuit of common values and meanings to which the United Kingdom must commit itself if it is to survive as a multi-faith democracy—multi-cultural, multi-racial, multi-lingual and politically pluralist, yet not balkanized."[129] Across much of the political spectrum, in other words, British commentators insisted that shared fundamental values were crucial for social cohesion and, in fact, constituted the necessary basis for British citizenship itself.

As the response to the Rushdie affair reverberated in the national media, critical voices began to coalesce more specifically around the value of free speech. Patten had identified freedom as the heart of British values and principles, invoking speech protections as the reason why *The Satanic Verses* could not be banned.[130] The point was echoed by the conservative *Economist*, which named free speech as the core "principle upon which democracy is based,"[131] and the liberal *New Statesman & Society*, which singled out the right of public expression as "the most essential freedom of democratic society."[132] A consensus thus emerged around freedom of speech as the very foundation of British culture. But this consensus also increasingly functioned as the proverbial line in the sand, the singular principle that marked the limits of liberal tolerance. As the *Economist* crowed, "religion has something to teach the rational secular world; some principles should be defended without recourse to a blurry halfway house."[133] The intractability typically associated with religious belief, that is, ought to be applied to the tenets of liberalism.

This defense of free speech as the bastion of Britishness, in turn, began to dovetail with existing attitudes toward diversity. In 1989, for example, the self-described "left humanist feminist" author Fay Weldon ventured a redefinition of British culture through a broader critique of multiculturalism. "Our attempt at multiculturalism has failed," she declared. "The Rushdie affair demonstrates it."[134] Instead, Weldon championed a "uni-culturalist policy" that harkened back to older visions of the American melting pot. This approach, she explained, "weld[s] its new peoples, from every race, from every nation, every belief, into a whole: let the child do what it wants at home; here in the school the one flag is saluted, the one God worshipped, the one nation acknowledged."[135] Because of its critical function, however, the school could brook no compromise: it must acknowledge one flag, one God, and one nation at every turn. Weldon's emphasis on schools, it's worth noting, was a pointed endorsement of the recently passed 1988 Education Reform Act, which mandated that all school religious assemblies be "broadly Christian" in character.[136] Weldon thus sought to replace "our agreeable and passive over-tolerance of everything and anything," with a much stricter adherence to core British values.[137] In this way, the Rushdie debates simultaneously became the vehicle for some of the first highly public critiques of "multiculturalism" in Western Europe, as well as the first public use of the term as a way to point to attitudes and policies that had overindulged immigrants' cultural differences (and, along the way, inadvertently fostered illiberal values).

There were, to be sure, a handful of voices that challenged the dominant view. Deputy leader of the Labour Party Roy Hattersley, for instance, offered a rebuttal to Patten's July statements in the liberal daily, *Independent*:

> The principle is clear enough. Salman Rushdie's rights as an author are absolute and ought to be inalienable. A free society does not ban books. Nor does it allow writers and publishers to be blackmailed or intimidated. The death threats are intolerable whether they are seriously meant or the rhetoric of hysteria. . . . Every group within our society must obey the law. But support for that principle is not the same as insisting that "they" must behave like "us." The doctrine of assimilation is arrogant and patronising. . . . In a free society the Muslim community must be allowed to do what it likes to do as long as the choice it makes is not damaging to the community as a whole.[138]

In this view, significantly, the "inalienable" right of free speech and respect for the rule of law were actually compatible with, rather than not antagonistic to support for cultural differences. Hattersley's position, however, provoked a cascade of attacks by commentators, who denounced it as a "craven appeasement of dangerous forces."[139] The liberal journalist Edward Pearce, for example, declared: "The Hattersley faction of the Labour party has taken up a position at once illiberal, repressive and abjectly deferential to a bunch of Islamic clergy firmly planted in the 15th century."[140] Here, British Muslim activists were conflated with medieval "Islamic clergy," and any support for religious differences (more specifically, any effort to see the controversy from the perspective of Rushdie's opponents) was deemed "illiberal" and "repressive" by association. Pearce, in fact, dismissed the Labour deputy's defense of the Muslim community as shameless and unprincipled groveling, a calculated attempt to retain the backing of his predominantly Muslim constituency in Birmingham.

By the early 1990s, then, the Rushdie affair had served to reframe the debate about immigrants and their place in British society, crystallizing the combination of race, nation, and culture in new and powerful ways. Even as Muslim immigrants availed themselves of democratic practices and liberal modes of argument to press their own concerns, British authorities and public figures across the political spectrum responded with efforts to reassert "core" values and "traditional" principles. At the center of the British way of life, most insisted, was "freedom"—and especially freedom of speech. Postcolonial Muslim immigrants who sought to ban or censor Rushdie's novel contravened this fundamental principle—and they did so in the name of a religion now marked as patently intolerant.

By casting the debate in terms of "liberal values," moreover, British commentators subtly but effectively placed the immigrant critics who defended their religious traditions outside the bounds of British culture. That such critics would ban or burn Rushdie's book only proved their failure to assimilate. British authorities thus drew a line around the nation without having to resort to the older modes of racialist thinking that had discredited zealots like Enoch Powell. It was Muslim immigrants' religion and culture, in this view, that prevented them from conforming to the basic tenets of Western liberalism. And in this sense, the British response to the Rushdie affair continued the work begun by Thatcher to establish new forms of cultural nationalism. If crime-prone West Indians had constituted the primary threat of the early 1980s, Muslims were firmly established as the central problem by the early 1990s.

As we have seen, politics in Germany and France were pushing in similar directions. In West Germany, this process took the form of novel arguments that Turkish culture and its religious components were better situated in their proper contexts—that is, in Turkey rather than Germany. In France, by contrast, the arguments proceeded through a re-energized republicanism that professed to embrace cultural tolerance as long as each new wave of immigrants agreed to leave its cultures behind. It is not particularly surprising, then, that the Rushdie affair was never simply confined to British soil. In France, less than two weeks after Khomeini issued his fatwa, fifteen hundred Muslims took to the streets of Paris in a demonstration against Rushdie's book.[141] *Le Monde* suggested that the rally was orchestrated by the Voice of Islam (one of a number of "fundamentalist associations" operating in France) and blamed "external forces" in Algeria or Saudi Arabia for attempting to exert influence over Muslim immigrants.[142] A *New York Times* article expressed skepticism about these conclusions, however, reporting that French television footage (shown repeatedly over several days) relied on "close-up camera work" to make the "small-ish crowd" look like "a fanatic Islamic fifth column."[143] The next week, SOS Racisme organized a counterdemonstration of roughly the same size to defend Rushdie and stand against fundamentalist extremism, but this action did not receive nearly as much media attention. Instead, the widely covered anti-Rushdie protests prompted French leaders to caution both French Muslims and foreigners against murder and violence.

In West Germany, the Rushdie affair did not catalyze large protests, but it did lead a number of critics to consider the episode's domestic implications. Within a matter of weeks, progressive commentator and respected political scientist Claus Leggewie published in the left-liberal weekly *Deutsche Volkszeitung* an essay that used the conflict over *The Satanic Verses* as an occasion to weigh the pros and cons of "multiculturalism" itself. Leggewie argued that Khomeini's edict created a confrontation between "the universally declared right to the freedom of speech" and the more particularistic "worldwide claim of an Islamic sect to protect and spread the true teaching."[144] This confrontation, he asserted, underscored the central dilemmas of European diversity—namely, how to adjudicate the inevitable conflicts between cultural differences and determine the parameters for democratic accommodation. In Germany, however, these discussions were not yet possible because Turkish guest workers and their families remained "foreigners," excluded from formal citizenship. For Leggewie, the Rushdie affair thus held a very specific lesson: the need to give migrants a meaningful stake in civil society in order to forestall a turn to religious extremism. Conservative critic Dankwart Guratzsch, by contrast, drew a much more straightforward—and typical—conclusion from the events in Britain: namely, that they revealed the basic "intolerance" at the heart of Islam. This intolerance, he insisted, acted as "a deathly frost on the blossoming dreams of a 'multicultural society,'" raising new doubts about Muslims' ability to coexist in a democratic polity.[145]

In all of these ways, the Rushdie affair introduced a number of important wrinkles to the national conversations on postwar immigration. For many Western Europeans, this was the moment when Muslim immigrants with diverse national origins merged into a single, distinctive category. This was also the moment when Islam was first identified as unbending, an intolerant religion that explained Muslim immigrants' failure to properly integrate. One might argue, in fact, that this was the pivotal juncture when Islam itself came to be seen as a central threat to "liberal values," not just in Britain, but across all the major Western European powers.

The specific timing of these shifts seems especially noteworthy. The late 1980s, after all, are also generally recognized as a watershed moment in the creation of the "New Europe." This was the period when Western European states began to take concrete steps toward formal economic and political integration; the Polish Round Table Agreement was concluded; the borders between Hungary and Austria were reopened; the Berlin Wall fell; and the Velvet Revolution unfolded in Czechoslovakia. Together, these developments seemed to mark the putative "end of history," demonstrating the superiority of capitalist democracies in the West to other social and political systems. Historians have typically treated these events as part of the denouement of the Cold War and the rise of the European Union. For our purposes, however, it is important to register that this consolidation of a particular constellation of "Western" identities also took place in relation to volatile debates around immigration. In retrospect, the close proximity of these political shifts is striking: as the process of integration raised urgent questions about what precisely bound European states together, a new source of public anxiety began to surface that would only grow in the coming decades. Once again, the danger was formulated in relation to a bipolar system, but now it was cast as the defense of "freedoms" against pernicious forms of religious intolerance.

If we are to fully understand how these novel forms of Western self-identification operated, though, we need to turn our attention to questions of gender and sexuality in the context of French republicanism. Indeed, even before the Rushdie affair had begun to dissipate in Britain, another, very different furor around the putatively dangerous effects of "Muslim culture" was about to explode in France.

CHAPTER FOUR

Muslim Women, Sexual Democracy, and the Defense of Freedom

On 18 September 1989 (roughly seven months after the Rushdie affair began), sisters Leila and Fatima Achaboun were sent home from the Collège Gabriel Havez, a public middle school in the town of Creil near Paris, for refusing to take off their headscarves (*foulards*) in the classroom. Three days later, a third student, Samira Saidani was also dismissed for covering her head. Although pupils had previously been permitted to wear headscarves, the school's administrative council now declared that these coverings were no longer allowed. When the girls declined to comply with the new rule, school principal Ernest Chénière suspended them, on the grounds that headscarves infringed on "the laïcité and neutrality of the public school."[1] Several rounds of negotiation ensued, involving the school administration, parents, and a local Tunisian cultural association. The girls returned to school on 10 October after a compromise was reached: they would be permitted to wear headscarves on school grounds, but not in the classroom. Ten days later, however, the girls were dismissed a second time for violating the compromise. Soon, what had started as a local conflict escalated into a national controversy, with newspapers from around the country, government leaders, and public figures all weighing in. On the 25th of October, the National Assembly even convened a meeting—broadcast on national television—to determine how to address the questions raised by the Creil girls' insistence on wearing headscarves in the classroom.[2]

Less clear is how these familiar events of 1989 fit within the broader history of postwar immigration. As I have already begun to suggest, this was the third time in less than five years that a major national debate had exploded over the relationship of immigrants to the demands of French citizenship. In this case, the controversy emerged not in a vacuum, but in the wake of Prime Minister Jacques Chirac's efforts to revise the nationality code. This, in turn, soon led to the months-long public conversation about citizenship and its requirements conducted by the Nationality Commission in 1987. The headscarf affair in Creil echoed many of the broader issues from these earlier episodes, but it gave the public debates a much more specific object of scrutiny. Rather than considering abstract questions of how immigrant differences might mesh with newly resurgent ideas about French citizenship, public attention now centered on whether Muslim girls should be compelled to uncover their heads in public schools.

The Creil controversy also dovetailed with events in Britain in a number of important ways. Just as British officials interpreted Muslim calls to ban Rushdie's novel as violating a key value enshrined in British culture, French authorities viewed the Muslim girls' insistence on wearing the *foulard* as a challenge to the very terms of French citizenship. In both cases, local efforts to claim legitimacy for religious traditions were perceived as indications of cultural intractability, an unwillingness to compromise and assimilate in reasonable ways. The French *affaire du foulard*, in other words, seemed to confirm a growing set of Western European suspicions about the very nature of Islam, suspicions that now cut across lines of nationality as well as categories of civil liberties—freedom of speech replaced here by the putative secularism of French schools.

Yet the events in Creil also pushed these arguments in new directions, marking the first widely resonant occasion when Muslim gender relations surfaced as an explicit problem. Much of the French discussion, in fact, zeroed in on the deeper meanings of this piece of cloth, with commentators of all political persuasions agreeing that it was a symbol of female subjugation. In this way, the treatment of women under Islam became an issue around which both conservative defenders of a homogeneous Europe and left-leaning feminists could unite. Whereas the revivals of nationalism, policing of national boundaries, and discourses around criminality had been hallmarks of the right, "saving Muslim women" now became a crucial rallying cry across the political spectrum. Over time, this prevailing concern with vulnerable women came to include homosexuals as well, consolidating into a broader conviction that Islam itself was fundamentally at odds with what some have recently described as the sexual democracy of Western society.

In many respects, this recasting of Muslim cultural practices as both pernicious and intractable marked the culmination of a much longer process. During the 1950s and 1960s, older, biological conceptions of "race" had been discredited in the aftermath of the Holocaust and largely banished from

European politics. For Enoch Powell, violating this taboo was enough to derail his political career. By the late 1970s, however, racialized thinking began surfacing in new guises, especially as part of the British anti-mugging campaigns that increasingly demonized the behavior of nonwhite immigrants and former colonials as criminal. In this context, the critiques of immigrant behavior often coalesced along clear lines of color and nationality, but without using the tainted languages of biological racism. By the late 1980s, these novel modes of social differentiation (which defined groups in relation to cultural rather than genetic traits) had become increasingly common, part of a "new racism" that could be mobilized for a wide variety of political purposes: from Margaret Thatcher's early pronouncements on the "swamping" of British culture to CDU officials commenting on the incommensurability of Turkish traditions with German ways of life.

It was not until the Rushdie and headscarf affairs of 1989, however, that the new forms of racialized thinking fully crystallized around questions of religion and the intractability of Muslim culture. This emerging consensus often treated Islam in much the same ways that earlier forms of racial science had presented phenotype and physiognomy—that is, as an inherited, unchanging boundary between groups of people. Indeed, if the Rushdie affair marked the moment when narrower and more rigid conceptions of Islam began to consolidate a different kind of racialist thinking in relation to religion, France's multiple headscarf affairs served as the crucial counterpoint in relation to gender. What began to emerge after 1989 was a mutually reinforcing pair of cultural logics that pushed toward much the same conclusion: namely, that Islam was incompatible with Western values and incapable of adaptation.

Headscarves Become a National Problem

When principal Chénière expelled the three French Muslim girls in September 1989, his decision was part of a larger effort to establish a stricter educational environment in the *collège*. The lower secondary school was known as a difficult place to teach. It was located in a poor neighborhood of the industrial city of Creil, a district that had been targeted by the state as an Educational Priority Zone (Zones d'Education Prioritaire, ZEP). This district drew the bulk of its students from the Plateau Rouher, a high-rise public housing project in one of the city's most disadvantaged areas. Foreign nationals, moreover, composed roughly 55 percent of the student body, with about two-thirds of those from North Africa and, especially, Morocco.[3]

For several years before the headscarf conflict of 1989, Chénière had repeatedly clashed with local community groups over what he saw as their encroachment on school matters. The Georges-Brassens cultural center, for instance, ran an after-school tutoring program that the principal regarded as exerting "outside interference" in the school. Another organization, the Association of Children's Houses of the Château de Laversine, a boarding house for poor children run by the Jewish division of the French Boy Scouts, also attracted his ire. Around twenty Gabriel Havez students lived there and took its bus back and forth to school. These pupils formed what the principal viewed as a "Jewish clique" within the *collège*, a form of self-segregation that conflicted with the ideal of a "secular school."[4] Chénière was particularly frustrated with the Laversine Jewish contingent because they regularly skipped classes on the Sabbath (Saturday is a school day in France), as well as on Friday afternoons during the winter, when early sundown meant that the Sabbath began before school was dismissed. His decision to enforce school regulations more strictly, then, was a response to "a particular genre of rule-breaking behavior—violations of *laïcité*."[5]

The French notion of *laïcité* (or secularism, as it is typically translated) insists on the separation of church from state, not so much to ensure equal protection of an individual's religious beliefs (as in the United States), but to secure an individual's full allegiance to the state by counteracting religious prejudice.[6] A cornerstone of republican ideology, *laïcité* was first envisioned as a crucial instrument for securing the universal promise of equality, with the secular ethic seen as "the means of educating the free and tolerant citizens required by the new democratic order."[7] Historically, public schools had played a crucial role in this process: schools constituted the critical civil institution, the place where pupils left behind "the dogmas and traditionalisms of family, regional and religious life" and joined the "world of progress, justice, toleration and liberty."[8] Education was to be the arena in which religious prejudices would be contained, distinctions would be eliminated, and children of diverse backgrounds would be taught a common civic identity.[9]

This core function was challenged both by the Laversine Jews' regular absences and the Muslim girls' refusal to take off their headscarves. As a result, Chénière and the school administration sought to reassert the priority of secularism by demanding "discretion in regard to external cultural signs" on the part of the Muslim girls and regular attendance by the Jewish students.[10] These were the particular circumstances in which the three girls were suspended. The Laversine Jews also continued to break the rules—in fact, they did not even appear for classes until ten days after the start of the school year. But, as Chénière admitted, he had targeted the Muslim girls because he could actually enforce school policy in their case, whereas he could not forcibly drag twenty absent Jewish pupils to school.[11]

Once the Creil girls' expulsions became a national controversy, however, the complexity of the local situation was largely drowned out by other concerns. On 5 October, the socialist magazine *Le Nouvel Observateur* ran a cover story on "Muslims, Jews, Christians: Fanaticism, The Religious Menace." The article emphasized broader problems posed to national integration by any kind of religious fanaticism, but it also prominently featured a photograph of a girl wearing a black chador, a style of veiling specifically associated with Iran. This image drew readers' attention to the specific "religious menace" of Islam and implicitly linked the French headscarf dispute to Iranian Islamic practice—and thus to the Rushdie affair. Two weeks later, the right-wing news weekly *L'Express* published a report, "The Secular School in Danger: The Strategy of Fundamentalists," while the conservative *Le Point* featured an article titled "Fundamentalists, the Limits of Tolerance."[12] All of these pieces suggested that headscarves were not simply a marker of religious particularism on display in an inappropriate place, but rather a sign of overly "aggressive" religious observance.[13] The media thus played on French fears of possible encroachment by Islamic fundamentalism in the wake of the 1979 Iranian Revolution and the eleven-month-long American hostage crisis.

Government officials and public intellectuals, in contrast, focused on the issue of secularism. Many critics decried the wearing of headscarves as "an intrusion of religion into the sacred secular space of the schoolroom, the crucible in which French citizens are formed."[14] For example, Jean-Pierre Chevènement, Socialist Minister of Defense (and former Minister of Education), advocated secularism without compromise: headscarves should be prohibited, he asserted, because they were a form of proselytizing that threatened France's republican identity. Five leading leftist intellectuals, Elisabeth Badinter, Régis Debray, Alain Finkelkraut, Elisabeth de Fontenay, and Catherine Kintzler, offered a collective statement on the question in *Le Nouvel Observateur*, warning: "The foundation of the Republic is the school. . . . That is why the destruction of the school will lead to the fall of the Republic."[15] Conservatives also endorsed an increasingly strict interpretation of secularism, insisting that religious neutrality should reign in the classroom and that all differences had to be banned. UDF representative Hervé de Charette, for instance, argued "the task of education is to instill recognition of the other, but also to promote integration of different cultures thanks to a unification of personal conduct."[16] In this sense, he concluded, it was necessary as a matter of national policy to prohibit religiously symbolic clothing from schools.

By framing the headscarf debate in these ways, French commentators effectively undercut any effort on the part of the Creil girls (or the French Muslim community more generally) to stake their own public claims to some degree of free expression. As the controversy began to gain momentum, at least a few immigrant activists praised the schoolgirls for demanding public recognition of their viewpoints and accommodation for their ethnic-religious differences.[17] But they were fighting a cultural battle that went to the very core of French identity. According to the logic of secularism, public demonstrations of religious affiliation defied a fundamental tenet of French citizenship. In order for the state to fulfill its ideal of treating citizens as equals, citizens had to put aside their particularities and differences because the state could treat them equally only as identical, abstracted individuals. The secularist framework thus pushed the debate toward the question of whether headscarves should be banned from schools and precluded any serious consideration of how French identity itself might be broadened or even redefined in light of the extensive demographic shifts that had transpired over many decades.

Significantly, even authorities who took a more practical and flexible approach to the crisis did not question the deeper logic of secularism. Socialist Minister of Education Lionel Jospin unequivocally affirmed the secular educational system, stating that children should "not come to school with any sign affirming a religious distinction or difference."[18] Yet he also insisted that excluding the girls would only isolate them from the very institution charged with socializing them to secular values. As a pragmatic solution, he therefore supported limited toleration of headscarves. Socialist Prime Minister Michel Rocard advanced a similar position, while insisting that such limited toleration was not intended as an embrace of cultural and religious diversity. "A multi-confessional school is not a secular school," he declared during a debate in the National Assembly. "Our school is secular; it will not be multi-confessional."[19] In terms of specific policy guidelines, the government urged local school officials to try to persuade their pupils to comply with the parameters of secularism. But if their efforts failed, it discouraged those same officials from expelling students who insisted on wearing scarves.

In the meantime, Jospin requested that the Conseil d'État consider the matter from a constitutional perspective. The Conseil ruled that wearing a Muslim headscarf did not in itself violate the secular education system, provided it did not pose "a threat to the establishment's order or to the normal functioning of teaching," or "by its ostentatious or demanding nature, constitute an act of pressure, provocation, [or] proselytism."[20] In the end, the Conseil suggested that the question of when secularism required absolute neutrality had to be decided on a case-by-case basis.[21] This relatively open-ended approach gave school administrators a good deal of latitude to interpret and enforce secularism as they saw fit. But while the council's ruling brought the Creil controversy to its localized denouement, it also left the door open for continuing conflicts in other contexts.

Crisis indeed erupted again in 1994, following parliamentary elections that ushered in a conservative coalition under Prime Minister Édouard Balladur (RPR). That September, new Minister of Education François Bayrou issued an administrative circular banishing "ostentatious" signs of religious affiliation in all public schools. Addressing the Conseil d'État's caveats from 1989, he argued that the actual behavior of the students did not matter because "certain signs" were by definition "transparent acts of proselytizing."[22] While Bayrou studiously avoided naming the headscarf per se, he drew a distinction between "discreet signs manifesting personal commitment to beliefs" and "ostentatious signs, which constitute in *themselves* elements of proselytism or discrimination."[23]

This decree lent support to school administrators who wanted to ban the headscarf entirely, prompting the expulsion of sixty-nine girls from various locations around the country.[24] It also reignited the media firestorm around headscarves, providing yet another opportunity to rehearse many of the same arguments first advanced in 1989. Challenged in the courts by some of the suspended girls, Bayrou's decree was overturned at the lower levels and then sent back to the Conseil d'État. The council, in turn, argued that the meaning of certain signs could not be divorced from the intentions of those carrying or wearing them and reaffirmed its earlier decision to allow school administrators the latitude to decipher the actions of their students.[25] Meanwhile, Minister of Social Affairs Simone Veil appointed Hanifa Chérifi, an immigrant from Algeria, to serve as official mediator for headscarf problems. This approach seemed to mitigate the confrontations, with the number of disputes dropping from around twenty-four hundred in 1994 to one thousand in 1996 and only about a hundred girls wearing headscarves to class.[26] But as with the 1989 resolution, it did nothing to settle the fundamental conflict between a militantly secular conception of Frenchness (which required that differences remain invisible) and an ethnic minority population that sought to express its cultural differences through forms of public display.

The third major explosion of this issue came in 2003, when Minister of the Interior Nicolas Sarkozy instituted a new policy requiring Muslim women to pose bareheaded for official identity photographs. The requirement quickly reignited the question of headscarves in the schools, leading Socialist deputy Jack Lang to propose a bill in the National Assembly that would ban signs of any religious affiliation in public educational institutions. President Chirac responded by appointing a commission on *laïcité*, headed by the moderately conservative parliamentary deputy Bernard Stasi, to explore whether such a law would be feasible. Just as with the Nationality Commission, this group devoted six long months to interviewing numerous representatives from different social groups, including religious leaders, politicians, school teachers and administrators, as well as representatives of equal rights organizations and immigrant associations.

The Stasi Commission's report, "Secularism and Republic," confirmed the principle of *laïcité* as a fundamental component of French national identity and advocated the prohibition of all "conspicuous" signs of religious attachment. But it also recommended state measures to recognize the variety of religions practiced by the country's now long-resident immigrant groups. These included adding history and philosophy of religion courses to the educational curriculum; establishing a national school for Islamic studies; creating Muslim chaplaincies in hospitals and prisons; providing special consideration for religious dietary restrictions; and making Yom Kippur and Aïd-El-Kébir national holidays.[27] Such policy changes, the Commission suggested, were necessary in order to help Muslims feel more included in French society and to demonstrate that the headscarf ban was not simply a narrow attack on Islam alone.

Chirac, however, accepted just one of these recommendations: the ban on headscarves in public institutions. This prohibition, which was passed by the National Assembly in 2004, sought to end the fifteen-year conflict over headscarves by providing a clear and decisive ruling. Technically, it applied to all articles of clothing that "conspicuously" displayed religious attachment, including yarmulkes and Sikh turbans. But it was generally understood as targeting headscarves and Muslim women.[28] As a stand-alone measure, "without the softening effect of the other recommendations," the ban effectively ended the possibility of future compromise: the choice was "either Islam or the republic."[29]

With the prospect of legal prohibition now on the horizon, public debate increasingly turned to the question of what exactly the *foulard* symbolized and why so many Muslim girls insisted on wearing it. The crux of the matter was whether the headscarf could be understood as a "legitimate expression of individual conscience" that deserved "protection under liberal secular law."[30] *Laïcité* dictated that religion was a private matter and had no place in a national culture historically defined as secular. This stance, however, required individuals to divide themselves between private beliefs and public commitments. Some of the girls involved in the ongoing disputes argued against such compartmentalization, asserting that the headscarf was simply "part of myself."[31] But their position made no sense within the parameters of official French identity. Critics thus concluded that the girls were either "delusional (overcome by irrational sentiments), dishonest (acting as agents of political Islam), or, most likely, forced by (male) family members into acts they would otherwise refuse."[32] By this logic, wearing the headscarf did not represent a choice at all.

Moving forward, the crucial question became the inherent meaning of the headscarf itself. Commissioner Bernard Stasi asserted that "the veil stands for the alienation of women."[33] A commentator for the centrist newspaper *France-Soir* declared, "it's not right that women are veiled in France when here they are very liberated," suggesting that the mere practice of covering the head indicated both restriction of unwitting victims and symbolic rejection of Western modernity.[34] Even the antiracism group SOS Racisme joined advocates of the ban on the grounds that the headscarf oppressed women.[35] The feminist philosopher Badinter, too, pronounced the headscarf "a terrible symbol of submission," adding that "if we allow women to wear headscarves in state schools, then the republic and French democracy have made clear their religious tolerance but they have given up on any equality of the sexes in our country."[36] At issue here, or so these arguments asserted, was the place of Muslim women not only within French republicanism, but also within their own religious tradition. Islam, in this view, deemed women inferior to men and marked this inferiority by forcing women to cover their heads. As historian Joan Scott has put it, those who endorsed the ban reasoned that "one could not tolerate the expression of religiosity that was itself inherently intolerant and oppressive."[37]

Meanwhile, the ban's opponents focused on national integration efforts, even as they shared many of the assumptions held by the other side. The sociologists Françoise Gaspard and Farhad Khosrokhavar, for example, put it this way: "If one accepts the postulate that the royal road to liberation is through education, then to reject girls with veils . . . is to penalize them . . . by denying them the possibility of becoming modern."[38] In this view, the putative linkage between Islam and female subjugation was a given, and for precisely this reason, banning headscarf-wearing girls would short-circuit the very process of integration that education made possible. A group of academics that included philosophers Étienne Balibar and Pierre Tévanian, and sociologists Catherine Lévy and Saïd Bouamama, along with Gaspard, issued another version of this viewpoint in the center-left newspaper *Libération*. "It is by welcoming [the Muslim girl] at the secular school," they argued, "that we can help her to free herself and give her the means to her autonomy; it is in sending her away that we condemn her to oppression."[39]

Women and the Civilizing Mission

This pattern of using another culture's treatment of women to gauge its level of "civilization" was hardly new, of course.[40] Indeed, for much of the eighteenth and nineteenth centuries, Europeans had similarly justified their colonialist and imperialist exploits by asserting the moral superiority of a "modern" West over a "traditional" East. This logic, as legal scholar Leti Volpp has pointed out, "was premised in part on perceptions of non-Western women as oppressed subjects."[41] In his monumental history of British India from 1817, for instance, the utilitarian thinker James Mill employed "the position accorded to women" as a key criterion for judging the level of Hindu civilization.[42] He asserted that Hindu women were in "a state of dependence more strict and humiliating than that which is ordained for the weaker sex." "Nothing," he declared, "can exceed the habit-ual contempt which Hindus entertain for their women. . . . They are held in extreme degradation."[43] For Mill, this "ex-treme degradation" was particularly apparent in the "cruel" ritual of *sati* or widow burning. Both Sanskrit scriptures and Hindu legislators, he explained, sanctioned the "barba-rous sacrifice" made by women throwing themselves on the "funeral piles" of their husbands rather than the alternative of "leading a life of chastity, of piety, and mortification."[44] As historian Lata Mani has demonstrated, however, the effect of such British colonial commentary on *sati* was to make an "exceptional and caste-specific practice" into a "potent signi-fier of the oppression of all Indian women, and thereby of the degradation of India as a whole."[45] This impulse to save "native" women, moreover, was never the prerogative solely of British men. Starting in the 1860s, British feminists also took up the cause of Indian women, a project that offered female reformers a concrete way to contribute to the civiliz-ing mission and justify their work in the empire.[46] In this respect, rhetoric about the "helplessness and backwardness" of Indian women's condition not only bolstered a broader sense of British cultural superiority, but also served as a ra-tionale for the British imperial presence in India even for those committed to reformist politics back home.[47]

British officials highlighted the problem of "native" women in other parts of the empire, as well. For example, Lord Cromer, Britain's first Consul-General of Egypt, viewed women's op-pression under Islam as a sign that the entire cultural tradition was corrupt and a failure. "The degradation of women in the East," he asserted, "is a canker that begins its destructive work in early childhood, and has eaten into the whole system of Is-lam."[48] As historian Leila Ahmed explains, "Veiling—to West-ern eyes, the most visible marker of the differentness and infe-riority of Islamic societies—became the symbol now of both the oppression of women . . . and the backwardness of Islam, and it became the open target of colonial attack and the spearhead of the assault on Muslim societies."[49] Behind the condemnations of these strange religious cultures was an implicit comparison with Christianity: the English (and Europeans more generally) elevated women because Christianity taught respect for the lesser sex, whereas the degraded religious traditions of Muslims and Hindus led to the hiding, segregating, and even killing of women.[50]

In the French empire, indigenous women did not become an explicit part of the imperial project until the later decades of the nineteenth century.[51] But there, too, they served as a crucial touchstone for efforts at cultural assessment and comparison. In his 1860s study of Arab women, the French military general Eugène Daumas declared: "it seems to me that in all the countries of the world the condition of woman allows us to evaluate the social state of a people, their mores and level of civilization. . . . It is extremely important, particularly for our domination of Algeria, to know where we stand on such a controversial subject, given the fact that women are viewed so differently."[52] Here, Daumas explicitly linked the "condition" of Algerian women to the French "domination of Algeria," thereby establishing indigenous women as an important object of inquiry. Knowing the Arab woman, he suggested, would facilitate the conquest and subjugation of Algeria.

One key strategy of the imperial project was to make Algerian women objects of cultural improvement. Like her English counterparts, the late nineteenth-century French feminist Hubertine Auclert championed the emancipation of Algerian women, whom she saw as the "degraded victims of child-marriage, veiling, seclusion, polygamy, repudiation and 'feudal' patriarchy."[53] Similarly, during the interwar period, Marie Bugéja, the wife of a retired chief administrator in French Algeria, took seriously the proposition that indigenous Algerians needed civilizing, and called for the education of Algerian girls. She argued for the improvement of Muslim women's status "for the greater good of the Muslim home and for France above all," seeking to wean Algerian women from their backward cultures by providing them the tools of liberation.[54]

Several decades later, in the context of the Algerian War for Independence, the Martinican psychiatrist Frantz Fanon observed that colonial administrators and social workers made it their mission to "defend" the Algerian woman, whom they saw as "humiliated, sequestered, [and] cloistered" by "medieval and barbaric" Algerian men.[55] Their assumption, echoing earlier attitudes, was that the treatment of Algerian women reflected the retrograde nature of native culture. The French, Fanon suggested, sought to rescue these women as a first step toward mastering Algeria itself. According to historian Neil MacMaster, after 1956 the Fifth Bureau (the psychological warfare branch) of the French Army in Algeria actually targeted Algerian women as part of its revolutionary warfare strategy. The goal was to "modernize Algerian women, to liberate them from what was perceived to be the ignorance and benighted horrors of Muslim patriarchy and seclusion, and to transform them via a European model of womanhood."[56] The most spectacular evidence of this strategy was the mass unveiling ceremony that took place on 18 May 1958. The event featured an Algerian woman, who spoke to a crowd of over a hundred thousand from the balcony of the General Government in Algiers: "We are aware of how far our traditional dress, our reclusive existence, are factors that separate us from our French sisters of a different religion to ours," she declared in French. "We wish to engage fully in the route to modernity and to profit from the exciting epoch which Algeria is currently traversing to accelerate our progress."[57]

Switching to Arabic, she urged her "sisters" to remove their veils, "the barrier between two communities."[58] In the context of the Algerian War, emancipating Muslim women had become a tool to separate Algerian women from their traditional culture and win them over to continued French rule.

This longer historical pattern of evaluating civilizational advancement in terms of gender norms forces us to be quite specific about the nature of contemporary discourse. Earlier assessments, as we have seen, took place in the context of imperial projects, part of the attempt to both justify Western conquest and strip indigenous traditions of their social and political force. These efforts, moreover, were pervasive across multiple Western empires. European colonizers judged as inferior the status of women in almost every colonial culture and religious tradition that they encountered, from Muslims in Algeria to Hindus in India.

From Migrant Women to Muslim Women

The more recent focus on women's status emerged, by contrast, in the heart of a demographically transformed Western Europe struggling to come to terms with internal diversity. Under these conditions, gender norms perceived as patriarchal by Europeans served to crystallize the fundamental differences of would-be citizens not yet defined as fully integrated (or in some cases, capable of integration). Here, too, however, the pattern was pervasive, extending across multiple Western European contexts and long-settled Muslim immigrant communities from places as varied as Turkey, Morocco, Pakistan, Bangladesh, Algeria, Senegal, and other sub-Saharan African countries.

Yet it is crucial to stress that the initial influxes of nonwhite and non-European migrants did not immediately provoke

public anxiety around Islamic practices in any of these European contexts. For much of the 1950s, 1960s, and 1970s,
labor-hungry European states received people from geo-
graphically diverse locales without making religion an explicit issue—neither as a matter of politics, nor even in more
specific relation to Muslim women. While many workers
in France were Muslims from Algeria whose numbers grew
rapidly during and after decolonization, the French immigrant labor force also included Muslims from the ex-
colonies of Senegal and Mali, as well as Christians from
Italy, Spain, and Portugal.[59] Colonial subjects from the Caribbean (largely Christian) were the first to arrive in Britain,
followed by former colonials hailing from India (predominantly Hindu and Sikh), and from Pakistan and Bangladesh
(mostly Muslim). Guest workers recruited by Germany came
from Catholic Italy, Portugal, and Spain; Christian Orthodox Greece; Muslim Turkey; and Yugoslavia, which encompassed all three faiths. The Netherlands likewise employed
laborers from Italy, Spain, Yugoslavia, Turkey, and Morocco,
and absorbed ex-colonials from Indonesia and Suriname as
well. In none of these national contexts was there a sense
that the figure of the Muslim would come to dominate the
European imagination, or that Islam itself would be identified as a major obstacle to the integration of immigrants.

Part of this pattern had to do with the basic dynamics of
postwar labor migration. For many Western European states,
the majority of foreign workers were initially men who either were single or left their families at home. They came to
Europe as unskilled or semiskilled laborers to work in phys-
ically taxing industries such as construction, mining, metal-
lurgy, and automobile manufacturing. But as the waves of
migration continued, the demographics shifted. In 1950s
France, for example, government officials began to encourage Algerian women to join their spouses, in the hope that

more domesticated Algerian male laborers would be less susceptible to the appeal of anticolonial radicalism.[60] In the 1960s, new kinds of West German industries—textiles, food, and electronics—accelerated the labor recruitment by explicitly recruiting foreign female workers. As migrant laborers prolonged their stays through the 1970s, moreover, they often sent for their spouses and children. These family reunions dramatically swelled the foreign population and raised a host of new concerns, including housing, living conditions, stay-at-home spouses, and education.

It was in the context of these changing demographics that policy makers and social workers began to focus on migrant women. French authorities, for instance, quickly identified Algerian women as the "key to solving the Algerian problem" (here defined as the social marginality of Algerian laborers, which made them easier targets for the FLN).[61] Welfare providers aimed to introduce Algerian women to "modern life" so that they might create appealing and stable households for their male counterparts. But social service agents also "believed they were liberating women from the bonds of a culture that confined them to the home and required them to be veiled and completely submissive to the male head of household."[62]

In this sense, administrators, social workers, and volunteer teachers who staffed this welfare network in the 1950s shared with their earlier colonial counterparts certain assumptions about Algerian women's putatively backward status. The *Cahiers nord-africains*, a respected journal about Algerians intended for local welfare providers, explained that Algerians were "Orientals with a patriarchal mentality" and that Muslim women were "treated as inferior" and "suffer[ed] under matrimonial law."[63] Nevertheless, the *Cahiers* experts insisted that "Algerians' deficiencies stemmed from a lack of 'education' and not some kind of inherent quality."

"No hereditary obstacle," they insisted, prevented Algerian integration.[64] At this point, *Cahiers* framed the cause of "backwardness" primarily through cultural practice. Islam as religion or belief system was not yet the central framework through which the customs of veiling or segregation were understood.

In West Germany, the conditions of foreign women emerged as a major area of research and policy making roughly two decades later, prompted by a belated official acknowledgment that guest workers had become de facto immigrants. The earliest scholarly studies focused on nonworking women: the wives of guest workers who stayed at home and looked after the children. These studies often lumped different migrant groups from the Mediterranean together, observing that women from Italy, Greece, Yugoslavia, and Turkey all experienced similar sorts of gendered spatial segregation. As one report explained, most female migrants from Southern Europe tended to interact with the German world through their husbands and did not leave the house unaccompanied.[65]

Soon, however, social workers, teachers, and counselors quickly narrowed their focus to Turks. In fact, it was at this point in the late 1970s that a mass-market literature on Turkish women geared to feminist welfare providers began to appear. In popular works such as the 1978 *Die verkauften Bräute* (The Sold Brides), the authors expressed discomfort with the sight of Turkish women walking "two steps behind their husbands," or the sense that these female migrants had "relinquish[ed] the particular domain of women—shopping for food and clothes—to their husbands or children."[66] Such divergent gender norms raised the crucial question of whether Turkish women measured up to "emancipated demands" of Western culture in their "own ways of life."[67] At certain moments, the authors' tone grew more strident. They declared that Islam "discriminates strongly" against women and exerts a pervasive influence on Turkish women's lives, especially through its laws of marriage and divorce. "Firmly fitted within the patriarchal family," the authors announced, "the trajectory of women's lives is completely predetermined. Decisions are first made for them by the father; after the wedding, by the husband. They have little influence on the choice of marriage partner. Their role in the household is characterized by unconditional subordination to the husband and head of the household. Their social place within the family and in the village is defined by their sons."[68] Islamic law and custom, in short, left little room for individual female agency. But even as feminists and social workers sought to extricate Turks from customs and practices they deemed illiberal, they still held out the possibility of cultural reform.

Immigrant women also became a recurring object of public concern in postwar Britain. In the earliest versions of this process, previous colonial encounters had framed British understandings of South Asian women, with *purdah* (female seclusion, both physical separation of the sexes and women covering their bodies) and *sati* (self-immolation by widows) serving as "emblematic means of signifying the presumed religious differences" inherent in their womanhood.[69] In the postwar context, though, state policy and public interest focused on the broader category of "Asian" women, as opposed to their specific national origins in India, Pakistan, or Bangladesh. This category effectively collapsed the differences between Hindus and Muslims by foregrounding such practices as "tradition," "the home," and "arranged marriages"—which were presumed to be common to both groups.[70] "The most familiar image of the Asian woman," according to Pratibha Parmar, was "a passive woman walking

three steps behind her domineering and sometimes brutal 'lord and master.'"[71] Education policy debates described
the "Asian woman" in multiple, sometimes contradictory
ways: she was the "symbol and chief bearer of the admi-
rably strong, tightly-knit family"; the "oppressed subject of
traditional Asian patriarchal practices"; and a "problem," because of her "failure to learn the language and customs
which might allow a smoother integration" into "the British way of life."[72] Despite these seemingly obvious contra-
dictions, officials could group Asian women together because of their guiding assumption that the more relevant
social contrasts among immigrant groups were between
Asians and Afro-Caribbeans.[73] The sheer variety of immigrant groups from the former empire thus cut against the impulse to equate female oppression with a singular religious
tradition.

While academics, social service providers, and community volunteers were already concerned about immigrant
women, Western European feminist organizations did not
explicitly take up these issues until the mid-1980s. In part,
this was because European women's movements of the late
1960s and early 1970s (including the more radical French
Mouvement de libération des femmes and British Women's
Liberation Movement) emerged as a response to women's
experience of being marginalized within male-dominated
student activist circles. Their central goal was thus to define
a politics and feminist theory that challenged patriarchy
and women's subordination in a set of contexts that had little connection with immigrant lives.[74] Many of these early
feminist organizations tended to assume that all women
experienced subjugation in the same ways: the experiences
of a universal woman (assumed to be Western and white)
served as the basis for critique and political intervention.

In practice, of course, these organizational feminists were never completely separable from the social workers, welfare providers, and educators who constituted the front line of immigrant support. Indeed, many who aided ethnic minority and guest worker populations counted themselves as feminists and were part of the broader women's movement. And in these contexts, many service providers undoubtedly understood their work with immigrants as part of an effort to fight for and improve the lives of women more generally. Nevertheless, at the level of political platforms and theoretical debates, the specific experiences and perspectives of ethnic minorities were largely absent from European feminism through the 1980s.

One exception to this pattern was West German feminist publisher Alice Schwarzer, whose writing on Muslim women brought together several competing—even contradictory—perspectives. Schwarzer traveled to Iran and in a series of articles for *Emma*, a popular women's magazine among German feminists, described the key role played by women in overthrowing Shah Reza Pahlavi's regime. Yet she ended her admiring account with a caution about injustices being perpetrated on women by the Islamic faithful (men), underscoring her skepticism about Islam as a uniformly patriarchal religion. Prompted by a young female revolutionary's parting words of "Allah is great," Schwarzer concluded: "And I know that she will be deceived by Allah's disciples. Because Farideh and her sisters were good enough to die for freedom. But they will not be good enough to live in freedom."[75] Here, Schwarzer interpreted the customary words of farewell as blind devotion to Islam (a mistake roughly equivalent to reading the common Bavarian greeting *Grüß Gott*—literally, "greet God"—as strict adherence to Christianity). From this, she concluded that Muslim women, more

generally, did not grasp the fundamental incompatibility of their religious traditions with female emancipation.
Schwarzer's views were especially important because they
offered one of the very few early sources of information
about Muslim women for many West German feminists
who served immigrant communities, despite the fact that
Schwarzer herself was not actually engaged with Turkish
women in the German context.

Even before white feminists took issue with Islam, ethnic
minority and immigrant women took issue with white feminism. By the early 1980s, European women of color themselves were becoming more vocal in pointing out blind spots
within West European feminism. White feminists, they argued, failed to acknowledge the unique struggles of women
of color because they did not grasp that patriarchy had differential effects depending on race and ethnicity. In a ground-
breaking essay titled "White Women Listen!," the black British feminist Hazel Carby condemned "feminist ideology"
for recapitulating the assumption that Asian women needed
"liberation" into the more "'progressive' social mores and
customs of the metropolitan West."[76] Similarly, in 1984, German feminist academics and their migrant women counterparts organized a joint congress to discuss the situation of
women in relation to xenophobia. The meeting, according
to a report by Fatemeh Serdani, criticized "everyday racism
in practice"—for example, "the arrogance of many European
women and a few feminists," who often viewed "a foreign
woman as an 'exotic,' or a 'poor, pitiful oppressed woman.'"[77]
Meanwhile, ethnic minority activists in France castigated
feminist theorists for insisting that the primary relation of
domination was that between the sexes, thereby elevating
sexual subordination above all other forms of oppression.[78]
This expansion of debate put pressure on European feminists to rethink their most basic assumptions about whom

the women's movement ought to serve, what its priorities should be, and how the "common interests of sisterhood" might be more effectively recognized.[79]

In many ways, however, the French headscarf affairs short-circuited this growing set of exchanges between immigrant women and European feminists. Indeed, their larger effect was to reduce an increasingly complicated and nuanced discussion about immigrant women to hand wringing about an abstracted Islamic patriarchy. Coming directly on the heels of the heated controversy over Salman Rushdie's *The Satanic Verses*, the conflict over headscarves drew unprecedented attention to Muslims as the most visible (and putatively, most troublesome) minority group across France, Britain, and Germany. The two episodes underscored the fact that Muslims made up a significant portion of the first waves of postwar labor migrants and were disproportionately represented among refugees of the 1970s—including East African Asians, Palestinians, and Iranians. Initially, these new arrivals had been identified in public discourse according to their legal status—that is, as former colonial subjects, as foreigners, as guest workers, or later as refugees. Once European host countries began to acknowledge the long-term presence of immigrants, these transplants came to be thought of in terms of their national or ethnic culture—as "Algerians," "Moroccans," "Asians," and "Turks." With the onset of the Rushdie and headscarf affairs in 1989, however, these previously distinctive national groups were recast as part of an ethno-religious monolith.[80]

The larger process of collapsing migrant women with Muslim women, moreover, expanded well beyond France in the course of about a decade. In Germany, Muslim gender relations became a topic of national concern in 1997, when Fereshta Ludin, an Afghani-born German citizen who had recently completed her teacher training certification, was denied a permanent position in the Baden-Württemberg public school system because she insisted on wearing a headscarf while she taught. The State Minister of Culture, Youth, and Sports, Annette Schavan justified this decision by making the point that the Koran does not explicitly require women to cover their heads. Since the headscarf was not a religious obligation, she argued, it was therefore "inherently a *political* symbol" that "infringe[d] on a student's freedom *from* religious participation."[81] Ludin, in turn, quickly sued, arguing that she wore the headscarf for personal reasons of religious custom with no intention of proselytizing for Islam.

Ludin's case was different from the French affairs in several key respects. First, in contrast to the strict separation of church and state in France, Baden-Württemberg identified itself as upholding Christian ideals. The problem, then, was not that Ludin was injecting religion into the secular space of the classroom, but that it was the wrong kind of religion. Denying Ludin a teaching position thus rested on "her inability to represent a state rooted in Christian values."[82] Second, the German controversy involved a teacher—rather than students—who wanted to cover her head. In this case, then, the issue turned first on Ludin's role as a representative of the state, and second on whether an authority figure whose attire was perceived as conveying gender inequality could effectively teach children German constitutional principles (which included equality between the sexes). Three lower courts considered Ludin's case, and each upheld the state's position. In 2003, however, the Federal Constitutional Court sided with Ludin, arguing that individual German states had not yet formulated laws on the question of religious expression in the classroom.[83] Still, the court suggested that a nondiscriminatory law banning the headscarf could be constitutional if properly formulated—which immediately prompted Baden-Württemberg and Hesse to pass such prohibitions.[84]

These differences aside, what is striking about the French and German headscarf debates is the way that ideas about gender, Islam, and integration converged in both. Just as in France, German commentators equated Muslim women covering their heads with patriarchal domination. The SPD politician Ulrich Maurer, for instance, pronounced "the Muslim woman wearing a headscarf to be the embodiment of the cultural opposite of emancipation."[85] Most self-identified German feminists likewise condemned the headscarf, explaining: "The feminist position sees the headscarf as a symbol of women's subordination and the inequality between men and women."[86] These critics assumed that Muslim women were "passive victims of an unchangeable Islamic culture,"[87] and many were thus willing to endorse state intervention to root out such a form of female subjugation.

Even those who supported Ludin and the right of Muslim women to cover their heads recapitulated this view of Islam. The legal scholar Sabine Berghahn argued that Muslim women might be unequal to Muslim men in their private sphere, but they ought not to be denied opportunities in the public sphere regulated by the German state.[88] Berghahn thus accepted the notion that Islam promotes inequality between the sexes, proposing "public freedom as the remedy for private oppression." In this respect, Germans who advocated tolerance of the headscarf echoed their French counterparts, viewing German culture as a means to "modernize" and "emancipate" Muslim immigrants.[89] These assumptions about the treatment of immigrant women ultimately pushed toward the conclusion that Muslim culture is "oppressive to a degree that German culture is not."[90] In so doing, they also began to authorize a very specific political posture toward

Muslim—and in most cases Turkish—immigrants: namely, that giving up Islamic culture was the necessary prerequisite to successful integration.

Headscarves were a volatile issue in Britain as well, but the British controversy took a somewhat different turn than those in France and Germany. For one thing, in Britain the issue did not erupt until 2006, nearly seventeen years after the first French episode and nine years after the German dispute. For another, it was prompted not by a specific incident in a public space, but rather by the publication of an op-ed piece by former Minister of Foreign Affairs Jack Straw. In this article, Straw discussed his personal discomfort with Muslim women wearing the niqab (or face veil), which he perceived as a "visible statement of separation" between the white and Asian communities.[91] In this case, moreover, Straw's target was the niqab, a more extreme form of covering that included the entire body and face, rather than the headscarf, which covered only the hair, ears, and neck. Significantly, Straw maintained the "right of any woman to wear a headscarf" and admitted that wearing a full veil "br[oke] no laws."[92]

In the British context, then, the central issue was not so much the challenge posed by Muslim head coverings to national principles of secularism or gender equality, but rather their putative threat to British social cohesion. Straw and his defenders repeatedly pointed to the niqab as a manifestation of "community separateness" and "parallel lives" that precluded the possibility of multiethnic interaction.[93] This form of veiling, according to anthropologist Sevgı Kılıç, signaled to British critics that immigrants constituted a community at once distinct, different, and unwilling to "accept the norms of the dominant, host community."[94] On one key point, however, the British debates converged very clearly with those in other European contexts: namely, that Muslim women who wore the niqab evinced a culturally demonstrable unwillingness to integrate.

Secular Muslim Women

Significantly, the same year that the French Stasi Commission and the German Constitutional Court weighed in on headscarves in public institutions, another set of voices began to intervene in what was fast becoming a Europe-wide discussion of Muslim gender relations. The first of these emerged in France during the spring of 2003, as the provocatively named association Neither Whores Nor Submissives (Ni Putes Ni Soumises, NPNS). Their opening move was a five-week "March of Women against the Ghetto and for Equality" that crisscrossed the country to highlight the condition of women in the blighted French *banlieues*. This demonstration culminated in the presentation of a petition to the prime minister in Paris on International Women's Day (8 May). The group's message was twofold. On the one hand, it sought to criticize the "strict control of women's bodies and sexuality" within immigrant communities in France. At the same time, its members also wanted to challenge the media's portrayal of Muslim and Arab women as submissive, docile, and complicit in their own oppression."[95]

What especially stood out about NPNS was its co-founder and president from 2003 to 2007, Fadela Amara—one of a number of self-identified "secular Muslim women" (*les musulmanes laïques*), Muslim women whose public championing of secularism made them increasingly visible in cultural politics.[96] Amara's father had come from Algeria to work in 1955, and she grew up in a housing project on the outskirts of Clermont-Ferrand, the heart of industrial France. As a second-generation Algerian immigrant, Amara was a product of secular education: she had been taught republican values and was well versed in the rights and responsibilities of French citizenship. Like many of her peers, her initiation into political activism had been the 1983 March of the Beurs youth movement. As a young activist, she supported the right of girls to wear headscarves and remain in school.[97] But by the time Amara orchestrated the NPNS march in 2003, her position had come full circle. Believing now that many girls were pressured to wear headscarves by "religious obscurantists" operating in the neighborhoods, she endorsed calls to ban covering altogether, even though she still counted herself a practicing Muslim.[98] Here, then, was a strong, self-assured, and highly visible Algerian Muslim woman who offered an appealing alternative to the image of the passive, silent, and shrouded victims at the center of the national debate.

Along with her leading role in NPNS, Amara built her public profile through a best-selling autobiography that appeared toward the end of 2003.[99] The book's vantage point, significantly, was the *banlieues*. Amara chronicled her childhood in this difficult environment, recounting numerous personal experiences of racism and social marginalization. She also offered a general portrait of the declining living conditions, which, she suggested, exacerbated both gender tensions and generational relations. Poverty and racism, she argued, "generated an incredible rage" within young men who compensated for "their feelings of powerlessness by exercising mastery over the only domain they c[ould] control, namely, women in the housing projects."[100] This was a more complicated take on Muslim gender relations because it linked the oppressive treatment of women to the psychological effects of living in low-income high rises in isolated suburbs.

Given her background, one might have expected Amara to condemn both the long-running neglect of the *banlieues* and the emerging republican litmus tests that effectively excluded immigrants—many of them legal citizens—from French society. Instead, she firmly embraced French republicanism and its insistence on assimilation. Even as Amara acknowledged rampant "discrimination, exclusion, and racism," she insisted that "deep down I knew with certainty that this was not France. My own France ... is the France of the Enlightenment, the France of the republic, the France of Marianne.... In short, the France of liberty, equality, and fraternity."[101] While Amara drew attention to the difficulties faced by Arab and North African women in impoverished neighborhoods, she also affirmed the republic's core principles of secularism and universalism. Any redress for inequality and discrimination would thus need to come within existing political languages and institutions.

In other accounts, Amara drew on family stories to flesh out a picture of gender dynamics in the *banlieues*. She described her father as "living with the legacy of a patriarchal society," which in turn led him to insist on a gendered division of labor: men providing for the family, women raising children and maintaining the household. There was thus no question in Amara's family of her mother finding employment outside the home. Nonetheless, Amara insisted that her father did not apply these standards to his female children because he understood that "society ha[d] evolved." She was also very clear that her father suffered gross exploitation as an Algerian worker, a predicament she underscored by recounting his astonishment upon learning that his wife would receive state retirement payments for raising children in France: "I worked like crazy my whole life and I'm entitled to nothing at all, so why does she have the right to retirement?"[102] Because her father had been a construction worker who was often paid under the table, he lacked an official employment record that would allow him to claim retirement benefits. Here again, Amara was very sensitive to structural differences particular to different types of Muslim immigrants.

In her work as a full-time community activist during the 1990s, moreover, Amara honed her unique approach to women's issues. Above all, she wanted to address the effects of ethnic discrimination, social exclusion, and economic deprivation on women in the *banlieues*. Yet she framed this project in consistently "universalist" terms, emphasizing equality and cooperation among the sexes. More specifically, she enlisted both men and women to help organize and participate in her events. This strategy was a direct rebuttal of some mainstream feminist organizations in France, which had long argued for gender specificity and women-only safe spaces.[103] Meanwhile, Amara's close involvement with communities in the *banlieues* alerted her to the growing power of extremist Islamist groups. She was especially critical of their recruitment tactics, the way they extended their reach in the projects by offering seemingly innocuous social welfare services (i.e., cultural activities, language classes, religious education) while simultaneously inculcating "religious precepts that ha[d] nothing to do with the tolerant Islam practiced by the great majority of Muslims in France."[104] In response, she condemned the "reactionary" codes of morality imposed by Islamists on women and called on the French state to take action.[105] In this way, her firsthand experiences in the suburban "ghettoes" shaped Amara's agenda for NPNS: combating both violence against women and the rising tide of Islamic fundamentalism.

The state, it is important to note, responded by funding several major initiatives that the original NPNS petition had demanded. These included creating a manual for middle and high school youth, *Guide to Respect*, which emphasized equality between the sexes as the governing principle for intimate relationships and family; a counseling and resource center in Paris to serve as the NPNS headquarters; and an annual series of educational events to raise awareness of women's issues. In 2007, the United Nations officially recognized the organization, a sign of the international respect that the movement had garnered.[106] That same year, newly elected French president Nicolas Sarkozy tapped Amara as minister of urban policy, an indication that her combination of republican values and women's activism resonated widely.

Yet Amara's position within Sarkozy's right-wing government cut in two new and consequential directions. For many observers, the choice of Amara was a calculated, even cynical, effort by Sarkozy to appear more open to diversity. In the wake of massive riots by immigrant youth in *banlieues* across the country two years earlier, Sarkozy had visited affected areas near Argenteuil as interior minister and pledged to a bystander, "We will rid you of this scum."[107] His comments made national headlines and were blamed for inciting further violence. They also suggested a tough, law-and-order approach to these issues, a readiness to characterize the young immigrants at the center of the conflicts as "subhuman," "criminal," and "worthless."[108] Choosing Amara, then, was both bold and shrewd. Among other things, it was a way for Sarkozy to acknowledge the growing suburban crisis, while insisting that any solution remain within a framework of republican values—and strict integration. And in the process, he would score political points by appointing a minister who was from the very same ghettos.

For other observers, however, Amara's acceptance of the appointment was a betrayal of NPNS's leftist roots and the more complex understanding of suburban disadvantage that had initially shaped her ways of seeing. Her decision to join the Sarkozy government, in other words, seemed to make her part of the larger political apparatus that treated gender equality and adherence to Islam as mutually exclusive, a zero-sum choice between citizenship and religiosity.

It was in this capacity that Amara became the most visible among a growing cohort of immigrant women in France whom anthropologist Mayanthi Fernando has dubbed "secular Muslim women."[109] Loubna Méliane, another French Algerian immigrant and co-founder of NPNS, adopted a similar personae, likewise framing the republican values of secularism, liberty, equality, and tolerance as largely incompatible with Islam. She, too, drew on her family history to justify speaking on behalf of Muslim women (in general) and parlayed her position into an official role as a member of the national council of the Socialist Party. Similarly, Chahdortt Djavann, an Iranian dissident who fled to Paris after the 1979 revolution, claimed authority to represent the plight of Muslim women based on her own experiences in Iran. She characterized the Islamic veil as a form of "psychological, sexual, and social mutilation" that denied women their "humanity."[110]

Around 2005, the pattern began to extend to Germany, with Turkish female activists such as sociologist Necla Kelek and lawyer Seyran Ateş condemning Islam for subjugating women and championing Western emancipation as the way to achieve gender equality. The most vocal and well-known figure of this type, however, was the Somali-Dutch pundit Ayaan Hirsi Ali, who burst onto the Dutch political scene in 2003, after being elected as a member of Parliament for the conservative-liberal People's Party for Freedom and Democracy (VVD). The next year, her visibility skyrocketed once again—this time due to her collaboration with Theo van Gogh on the 2004 film *Submission*, which provoked the filmmaker's murder by a Moroccan-Dutch Muslim extremist. At precisely the moment when the problem of "victimized Muslim women" became the most potent symbol of Islam's incompatibility with liberal values, then, the "secular Muslim woman" became a mainstay in the politics of immigration.

The pattern was strikingly similar in each of these cases. At the most basic level, these spokeswomen seemed to confirm the claims made by white Europeans about the oppressive treatment of women under Islam. Each of them published best-selling autobiographies, offering authentic, authoritative testimony of their personal subjugation. In this sense, they all functioned as native ethnographers providing firsthand evidence of the presumed horrors of Islamic patriarchy. Not surprisingly, French critics who advocated banning the *foulard* routinely invoked the writings of Amara, Méliane, and Chahdortt to bolster their arguments. Likewise, Germans who fought against Ludin's right to wear a headscarf frequently referred to the testimony of Kelek and Ateş for support. Feminist Alice Schwarzer, in fact, praised Kelek and Ateş, along with Hirsi Ali, for "risking their lives" to speak out against Islam. "We owe them everything," she declared, "for their courage in breaking the law of silence."[111]

But as figures that claimed to reveal the ugly truth about Islam, these women modeled a particular trajectory of integration. On the one hand, they confirmed European critics' worst suspicions that Islam was irreconcilable with Western liberal values. On the other hand, they presented themselves as "having cast off the chains of Islamic tradition and embraced the . . . values of liberty, equality, and tolerance."[112] Or as Amara put it in her autobiography, hers was the "true" France of the Enlightenment, of the republic, of Marianne.[113] Not to be outdone, Hirsi Ali's provocative book, *The Caged Virgin*, offered a full-throated "emancipation proclamation for women and Islam," arguing that Islam needed to undergo the same kind of enlightenment process as European societies in the eighteenth century.[114] Amara, Hirsi Ali, and their fellow "secular Muslim" sisters thus served as examples of precisely the sort of successful integration many French and other European authorities had envisioned a decade or two earlier, a process that relied on disavowing Islam in public life. The most vivid representation of this contrast came in the televised French debates about the headscarf. In a nationwide broadcast, secular Muslim women sat with exposed hair and arms across from Muslim women in headscarves and modest clothing. The tableau presented openly secular Muslims as the symbolic counterweight to publicly pious Muslim women (here figured as a sign of integration's failure).[115] Secular Muslim women, that is to say, provided at least two different, but equally crucial, forms of political proof: first, that integration on the terms set out by Europeans was possible; and, second, that Europeans were capable of embracing difference. These women, in short, were the powerful exceptions that proved the rule of Islam's incompatibility with European norms.

Sexual Democracy, or Democracy Writ Large

But the politics around Muslim women did not just serve to confirm the failure of immigrants to assimilate. In France, Germany, and the Netherlands (although less so in Britain), this mode of sexual politics also became one of the early twenty-first century's most powerful symbolic instruments for constituting a positive national or shared European identity. If headscarves, veils, burqas, and niqabs signified the subordinate status of women vis-à-vis men in Islam, sexual freedom and equality between the sexes—"sexual democracy," in short—served to define what it meant to be French, German, and Dutch. Nowhere did the sexual component of national belonging emerge so clearly as in the debates around the introduction of citizenship tests in Germany and the Netherlands. In 2005, the German states of Baden-Württemberg and Hesse proposed their own versions of the federal citizenship test that included questions about matters of conscience. Widely understood as directed toward candidates from Muslim-majority countries, this line of questioning aimed at ascertaining the applicant's views on forced marriage, homosexuality, and women's rights. These efforts ultimately failed, but proposed questions included "Do you find it acceptable for a man to lock up his wife or daughter in order to prevent her from shaming him in public?" "Would you have difficulty with a woman in authority?" and "What would you do if your son announced that he was homosexual and wanted to live with his boyfriend?" To qualify for German citizenship, applicants would have had to endorse not only gender equality but also certain views around sexual tolerance.[116] They would have done so, however, within an explicit context of unequal suspicion, since their very position as migrants from Muslim-majority countries marked them as likely sexists and homophobes.

The following year, the Dutch passed a law requiring a civic integration examination of all non-Western foreign nationals who wished to join their families in the Netherlands.[117] In this new format, applicants for citizenship had to take the test in their country of origin, with entry into the Netherlands based on their performance. To prepare for the exam, applicants were expected to purchase a study packet that contained a DVD of the film *Coming to the Netherlands*. This package, according to the Immigration and Naturalization Service's website, provided everything needed to prepare for the test, including demonstrations of Dutch lifestyles, customs, and communal modes of social interaction.[118] The website also offered a pointed warning about the film: "In the Netherlands, some things are allowed which may not be permitted in other countries. For example, women can walk around on the beach without very much clothing. People are allowed to express themselves freely: they may declare themselves to be homosexual, for example. The film includes scenes of these very typical aspects of Dutch life."[119] The images of bare-breasted young women on the beach and a gay couple kissing in a field of flowers sent an "unambiguous" message: namely, that "Dutchness" required "putting up with sexualized . . . images."[120] Official immigration protocols, in short, defined national belonging as requiring the acceptance of sexually modern values.

Such use of sexual democracy to construct a positive notion of national belonging was also at work in France during these years. In his campaign video for the 2007 French presidential election, candidate Nicholas Sarkozy declared: "I believe in *national* identity. France is not a *race*, nor an *ethnic* group; France is a *community of values*, an ideal, an idea. . . . In France, women are free, just as men are, free to circulate, free to marry, free to get a divorce."[121] The unspoken point here was to draw a distinction between *our* French women who are free and *their* Muslim women who are not. In this way, sexual democracy served not just as the litmus test for membership in a liberal democratic society (although it did that, too), but also as a precondition for entry into French, Dutch, and German national culture, more generally.

It's worth being explicit here about the reasoning at work in making sexual democracy the basis for membership in nations rooted in liberal values. As political theorist Anne Norton has observed, "sexual freedom becomes the form of freedom that comes to stand for all."[122] Or to put it another way, sexual democracy came to be understood as the epitome of democracy itself, as democracy writ large. In some instances, this particular model of democratic governance "replaces"—or even trumps—other freedoms and foundational principles.[123] The case of the late Dutch political leader Pim Fortuyn offers a particularly vivid example of how such prioritization worked. An open and unabashed homosexual, Fortuyn mounted a spectacular rise in Dutch politics based largely on his anti-immigration—and especially, anti-Muslim—stance. He was, according to Ian Buruma, "a populist who played on the fear of Muslims while boasting of having sex with Moroccan boys."[124] While this was not a typical formula for right-wing political success, it worked for Fortuyn, who, at the time of his 2002 murder by a Dutch animal rights activist, was expected to become the country's next prime minister in the approaching national elections. In an important respect, Fortuyn's in-your-face gay persona served to relieve constituents and members of his party, List Pim Fortuyn, of any doubts they might have had about holding openly xenophobic views of Muslim immigrants. "Fortuyn's flamboyant homosexuality," Norton has argued, "worked as a kind of secular exculpation. He enabled his supporters to affirm their tolerance even as they manifested their intolerance. Their acceptance of his homosexuality licensed their refusal of tolerance to Muslims."[125] Sexual democracy ultimately served both to disqualify Muslim immigrants from membership in liberal European societies and to excuse Europeans for their rejection of Muslim immigrants.

What, then, have been the broader effects of the consolidation of gender, Islam, and immigration in Europe? Most notable perhaps was the growing tendency in the wake of the Rushdie and headscarf affairs to treat religion not so much as a mutable form of culture, subject to change through social, economic, political, or other historical forces, but rather as something almost prior to culture—an entrenched body of beliefs, norms, and laws. Part of this stemmed from the growing tendency to equate "radical" Islam with Islam as a whole, even though the more fundamentalist strains of Islam that were emerging as a problem after 2000 were themselves relatively new. A good example of this process can be found in the Stasi Commission's 2004 recommendation for the headscarf ban, which justified its refusal to budge on the principle of *laïcité*. In its opening pages, the report declared no negotiation with religion—or at least no negotiation with "extremist groups." A few pages later, it clarified the specific target, asserting that Islam was less willing than other religions to "accommodate its dogmas to the requirements of a pluralist society."[126] While the report acknowledged that "there were some more 'rational' Muslims who understood the difference between political and spiritual power," it "nonetheless assumed that most followers of Islam would reject this distinction." "Extremist groups," in this way, came to stand in for the majority of French Muslims. And since "extremism," by definition, didn't recognize the values of liberty and *laïcité*, the report concluded that "there was no need to tolerate Islam."[127]

This pattern, it is important to note, was not confined to French officials. In her 2010 collection of essays *Die große Verschleierung*, for instance, Alice Schwarzer condemned what she called "Islamism" or radical Islam, rather than Islam the religion. But the publisher's description of her volume conceded that the line between the two was "appreciably more difficult to grasp."[128] This slippage between extremist versions of Islam and Islam as a whole pushed toward a much more rigid and blunt understanding of Islam per se in European public discourse. Conflated with radical extremism, Islam increasingly functioned more like older notions of race, more like the stuff of biology and embodied essences.

A second effect of the fusion of gender, Islam, and immigration was the narrowing gap between the political right and left. This convergence can be seen most clearly in the emergent discourse of "sexual democracy." On the one hand, right-wing politicians such as Sarkozy raised women's freedom to a principal feature of French national identity. He declared that French women are free to circulate, marry, and get a divorce. But he actually went even further: "The right to abortion . . . that too is part of our identity." This was a remarkable pair of claims. In making this leap, Sarkozy effectively incorporated key issues of second-wave feminism into his right-wing conception of national belonging. As Éric Fassin has noted, a sexual democracy that extends to abortion rights may "be the price that many conservatives are willing to pay to provide a modern justification to anti-immigration politics that could otherwise appear merely as reactionary xenophobia."[129] European conservatives, that is to say, were prepared to endorse specific women's rights that they had traditionally opposed in other contexts in order to make their stance on sexual freedom more consistent. In this way, it became possible to elevate sexual democracy into a defining "liberal value," a key litmus test of Western identity.

On the other hand, the new commitment to sexual democracy prompted at least some leftists to wonder about the limits of tolerance. In 2003, for instance, three self-identified German leftist feminists, including the respected documentary filmmaker Helke Sander, wrote an open letter to the Federal Integration Commissioner, Marieluise Beck. This letter described the situation of some women and girls in Germany who lived in what they termed "a rights-free space," a private realm of the family dominated by Muslim men. The authors, together with 125 other signatories, urged Commissioner

Beck to intervene on behalf of these women, declaring that as long as the government did nothing, it "tolerate[d]" crimes.[130] The state, they argued, was too lenient in permitting unregulated coexistence because it gave Muslim immigrants free reign in the private sphere, where men could commit all sorts of abuses and deprive women of the basic right to equality. These feminists worried that their own well-meaning support of cultural pluralism had inadvertently allowed an oppressive Islamic culture to run riot in the very heart of liberal-democratic Europe.

It is worth noting that secular Muslim women were instrumental in fostering these growing doubts about religious tolerance. Hirsi Ali, for example, famously chastised the mayor of Amsterdam, known as a champion of multiculturalism, for "adopt[ing] an unreflective, unexamined tolerance of Islamic communities and their activities."[131] More recently, Necla Kelek excoriated German leftist intellectuals for characterizing her open discussion of forced marriage, honor killing, and violence against women among Muslims as "Islamophobic" or "racist."[132] "There is a panicked fear," she observed, "of discriminating against Islamists because of their religion or background; one prefers to condone their infringement on fundamental rights instead."[133] In this view, Germans, especially those on the left, suffered from an "identity crisis" (and lingering weakness in their politics) because of the Holocaust: their "special feelings of guilt towards Jews, Sinti, Roma, homosexuals and others," Kelek argued, blocked a "clear view on today's realities of oppression and exclusion." In the face of an enshrined tolerance of difference, Kelek's statements seemed aimed at giving Germans permission to "discriminate" in order to address the ways Islamic culture compelled its adherents to violate liberal principles.

A final effect of the consolidation of gender, Islam, and immigration was a growing European sense that Muslim minorities posed a perilous threat to "freedom" itself. The first sign of this threat was the Rushdie affair, when Muslim Britons sought to curtail his personal rights—as author and critic—to free speech. This sense of danger resurfaced in the multiple headscarf affairs, which served as vivid examples of the way that Muslim culture seemed to regulate every aspect of that most personal of individual freedoms— sexuality. Muslims, according to this argument, repudiated homosexuals and denied women the right to make basic choices: what to wear, how to move through public spaces, whom to marry, whether and when to have children. The subsequent rise of sexual democracy movements was thus part of the broader effort to safeguard individual liberty.

For critics on the left, however, championing sexual democracy led in some strange and unexpected directions. Most notably, perhaps, it led growing numbers of self-identified left liberals to turn away from the older ideals of cultural relativism and pluralism. Long sacred to earlier generations of leftists, these ideals had been forcefully articulated in the early twentieth century by figures such as Randolph Bourne, Horace Kallen, and the anthropologist Franz Boas, who maintained that culture, rather than biology, was the crucial factor in human differentiation.[134] No culture, Boas argued, possessed a special purchase on civilizational advancement, and every group deserved to be understood within its own particular context. Thus, all of humanity—in its cultural diversity— was equally worthy of respect and tolerance. Cultural relativism, in fact, had long served as the guiding logic that allowed many on the left to reject older modes of racialist thinking, which defined particular social and behavioral characteristics as intrinsic, fixed, and universal across specific groups. Cultural pluralism, moreover, became an important basis— especially in the US and British contexts—for recognizing the contributions of multiple groups previously disenfranchised or undervalued: women, workers, and immigrants, as well as other ethnic and racial minorities. For much of the twentieth century, this ideal fueled demands for broader notions of democracy, for expanding the circle of social inclusion. In the wake of the Rushdie and headscarf affairs, however, many European leftists began to view Muslim immigrants as both an undifferentiated mass and a rising threat to personal freedom.

The broader implications here were profound, for they involved a redrawing of the political landscape. Where older forms of political allegiance had often divided along the lines of individualism versus pluralism (or inclusion versus exclusion), the European left's emphatic commitment to defending individual freedoms at the expense of immigrant tolerance threatened to scramble, or at least complicate, the older political calculus. Indeed, as the twentieth century came to a close, an increasing number of leftist commentators found themselves in the unexpected position of championing notions of freedom by ascribing illiberal behaviors to entire groups of people. Except that in this case, the characteristics now deemed illiberal seemed to derive from gender, sexuality, and religion, as opposed to the older biological essences that had previously served as the political weaponry of the right. And this reliance on cultural arguments to mark fundamental differences between Europeans and Muslim immigrants made leftists less self-conscious of how close to the right they had moved.

CHAPTER FIVE

The "Failure" of Multiculturalism

In October 2010, Chancellor Angela Merkel stood before the annual gathering of the joint youth organization for Germany's two center-right parties—the CDU and CSU—and declared, "the multicultural concept is a failure, an absolute failure."[1] This pointed statement elicited extended applause from the young conservatives, as well as considerable attention from the German press.[2] In retrospect, her pronouncement seems curious, since Germany had never embraced any vision of state-sponsored multiculturalism and had not even offered long-resident guest workers a formal path to citizenship before 2000. Still, her pronouncement resonated strongly—and not simply within German borders. Three months later, newly elected British Prime Minister David Cameron addressed the same theme, using his first official speech at a Munich security conference to condemn his country's decades-long policy of state multiculturalism. Within a few days, French President Nicolas Sarkozy joined the chorus. This, too, was somewhat surprising, given the fact that over many decades France had explicitly refused to consider multiculturalism as a guiding principle. Nevertheless, Sarkozy suggested during a television debate that "we've been too concerned about the identity of the new arrivals and not enough about the identity of the country receiving them."[3]

These pronouncements marked the culmination of a backlash against European multiculturalism that had been building for at least twenty-five years. By 2010, the idea that multiculturalism simply did not work in Europe was so self-evident— so obvious—that national heads of state felt comfortable declaring its failure without qualifications or caveats. Yet the sheer ease with which Merkel, Cameron, and Sarkozy issued their declarations also raised an important question: how, exactly, did this view become a kind of political common sense? It was one thing, after all, to be skeptical about Muslim immigrants' ability to integrate or to raise doubts about Islam's oppression of women. It was quite another to assert that the previously open question of European multiculturalism was now closed—a casualty of its tolerance of beliefs and practices incompatible with "Western" values.

To understand how this discourse of "failure" took hold— becoming a "recited truth" at the highest levels of public discourse—we must return to the late 1970s and 1980s.[4] The politics of this period were quite a bit more complicated than is often acknowledged. The dominant pattern, to be sure, was to consolidate a diverse immigrant population into a single group (Muslims) and to raise doubts about their "capacity" to integrate—a process that reached a kind of apotheosis around 1989. But it is also important to acknowledge what was happening apart from the conservative backlash, especially at the level of grassroots policy. While the first efforts at explicitly multicultural forms of policy making were pursued in a largely ad hoc manner by various local and nongovernmental institutions, they did seek to address the ongoing presence of immigrant communities (a presence that conservative scapegoating, after all, did not simply end). As such, these local efforts must be considered part of the larger history by which Western European nations came to view multiculturalism as a broader threat to their ways of life. To-day, we sometimes assume a quick and easy trajectory from the upheavals of 1989 through the politics of 9/11 and be-yond, but the ground-level process was quite a bit messier. As we shall see, the commonsense view of multiculturalism's "failure" built slowly over time and across multiple contexts. It was never a simple effect of acts of terrorism.

The other key wrinkle here involves another, very different set of critiques of multicultural policy making—in this case, issued by minority intellectuals who simultaneously rejected the conservative politics around immigration. Though not widely known, ethnic minority activists and intellectuals for-mulated some of the most sophisticated critical perspectives on the implementation of multicultural policies, having be-come disillusioned for reasons very different from those we have already considered. The fact that these arguments were most fully developed in Britain is no coincidence: it was there, after all, that the first and most elaborate efforts to put state multiculturalism into practice emerged during the 1980s. Brit-ish experiments with educational policies and local funding initiatives provided concrete touchstones for serious debate, with minority critics often describing such programs as "anti-democratic" due to failings that had nothing to do with car-icatures of Muslim culture. In most cases, they questioned the efficacy of multicultural policies to promote minority rep-resentation, rather than whether immigrants could ever truly adapt.

But how, then, did this volatile mix of grassroots experimen-tation and local critique coalesce into something closer to na-tional consensus? Certainly, 9/11 was a significant milestone in this process. The attack—and the localized cycles of terror that followed—powerfully accelerated earlier debates about the presence of Muslim immigrants. The expanding "war on terror," in turn, channeled these worries into a broader belief that the rise of Muslim parallel societies within Europe now posed a major security threat. In this respect, 9/11 catalyzed an expanding crisis around the idea of multiculturalism itself, unleashing unprecedented waves of criticism at every level.

And yet, the discourse of "failure" that took hold in the 2000s did more than just expand previous claims of Muslim incommensurability with European values. As we shall see, concerns across the political spectrum about the protection of individual freedoms became a major part of this process, too. One might argue, in fact, that the object of criticism slowly changed between 1990 and 2010: with initial concerns about the putatively illiberal and intractable nature of "Muslim culture" (as patriarchal, oppressive, intolerant, and so forth) now coalescing into a sweeping rejection of multiculturalism itself as a social blueprint for European society in the twenty-first century. This shift is easy to miss because the term "multiculturalism" has been invoked to mean so many things, whether demographic diversity on the ground or policies for managing that same diversity. By the time Merkel and her fellow leaders proclaimed multiculturalism a failed experiment, however, the political stakes had clearly risen. At issue in 2010 was not simply a brief wave of xenophobia or set of fears around localized acts of terrorism. Increasingly, the new object of public debate was the very nature of European society—or more specifically, what kind of society it wanted to be.

Multiculturalism on the Ground

Most histories of multiculturalism in Britain harken back to a 1966 speech by Home Secretary Roy Jenkins in which he rejected assimilation as a "flattening out process" in favor of a policy of "integration" that would promote "equal opportunity, accompanied by cultural diversity, in an atmosphere of mutual tolerance."[5] Jenkins's statement did not explicitly use the word "multiculturalism," but it did envision a more pluralistic model of British society, one based on the peaceful coexistence of different cultures. This speech marked the first time that a government minister had offered a public blueprint for (or, if you like, a broader philosophy of) Britain's increasingly multiethnic and multiracial society. Jenkins's speech was aimed at persuading members of Parliament to support a more robust Race Relations Act to replace the one passed in 1965.[6] That same year, a more practical effort to deal with ground-level diversity was also advanced: the new Local Government Act introduced the Section 11 provision, which offered grants to help defray the costs of providing resources for newcomers with different languages and customs to municipal authorities with high numbers of New Commonwealth immigrant residents.

By the mid-1960s, immigrant social and cultural differences were clearly emerging as a significant concern in the educational arena, sparked by the arrival of growing numbers of foreign-born children. Local educational authorities (LEAs), in fact, were among the first institutions to take advantage of Section 11, applying for funds to hire additional teachers and develop English as a second language courses. In addition to these measures, many LEAs initially dealt with new arrivals by working to "disperse" immigrant pupils in order to preserve academic standards by ensuring that no one school or district served too high a concentration of minorities. This strategy involved informal quotas for each area and bussing those in excess of the target number to other neighborhoods. As we have seen (in chapter 2), the plan by the London Haringey education authority to limit the number

of West Indians in its schools provoked an outcry from immigrant parents who not only mobilized to block the LEA initiative, but subsequently developed community-based forms
of supplementary education for their children.

For many teachers actually working in multiracial schools,
however, it quickly became clear that initial LEA efforts to
incorporate immigrants into the mainstream school system were not producing the desired results, with significant
numbers of ethnic minority children disadvantaged by poor
school results or being placed in remedial classes. In order
for a more effective process of integration to take place, these
teachers argued, schools needed to take into consideration
the cultural and religious differences of immigrants. Some
LEAs responded with initiatives to help teachers learn about
the backgrounds of pupils from outside of Britain, providing
information and in-service courses on the customs and practices of different cultural groups.

By the 1970s, the more cutting-edge LEAs developed what
they explicitly began to call "multicultural" educational policies. This marked the very first time the term was used in British efforts to manage the concerns and needs of immigrant
communities. The new approach sought to establish a distinctly different goal: instead of "remedying" the "perceived
problems of ethnic minority children," schools would address
their specific educational challenges and prepare all students
"for life in a multi-racial society."[7] Here, again, the changes
were at least partially the result of issues raised by immigrant
groups. In 1972, for example, a West Indian community organization presented evidence to the Select Committee on
Race Relations and Immigration, arguing for a fundamental
rethinking of the "books used, the type of teachers, and the
type of material read in the schools." "We believe," the organization asserted, that "school should reflect the contribution
by and participation of all ethnic groups. Through the teach-

ing of geography, history, drama, music, literature, West Indians could be seen as contributing to the school curriculum."[8]

Starting in the late 1970s, Asian immigrants also began to register concerns about the educational system their children encountered. Some issues overlapped with those raised by West Indians, such as curriculum reform, the need for teachers from minority backgrounds, and racism. But others were more specific to Asians, such as demands for mother-tongue language instruction, or provisions for meals and dress that met religious requirements. In the early 1980s, for instance, Asian parents in Bradford led a citywide campaign for halal meat in schools. In this way, the first attempts to develop an explicitly multicultural approach to education generally focused on responding to a broad range of parent demands, including employing more West Indian and Asian teachers, offering religious and mother-tongue language courses, and appointing special administrators to handle diversity issues.

It was only in the late 1970s that the federal government became more directly involved in the question of minority education, prompted by a 1977 study of the West Indian community that revealed the poor school performance among its children. An official inquiry in 1981 concluded that the main problems facing Afro-Caribbean students were low teacher expectations and racial prejudice. These findings, however, were dismissed by Conservative Secretary of Education Mark Carlisle, who subsequently appointed Lord Michael Swann to undertake an extensive investigation into the education of all ethnic minority groups. But the expansion of the inquiry produced some unexpected consequences—most notably, a shift from a specific critique of racism to a sweeping condemnation of the government's approach to education in a multiethnic society.

Released in 1985, the Swann report, titled "Education for All," offered a systematic assessment of British educational policies for ethnic minorities in the wake of postwar immigration. This landmark report rejected what it described as educational authorities' initial impulse to assimilate and integrate immigrant pupils, condemning the efforts to absorb these children into the school system with "as little disruption to the majority community as possible."[9] More specifically, Swann criticized the "problem-centered perception" of minority students, which produced policies such as teaching English to "compensate" for supposedly "deficient" language skills, channeling immigrants into "sub-normal" classes and schools, and, above all, seeking to prevent high concentrations of nonnatives that were assumed to lower the educational standard.[10]

But Swann also criticized the first "multicultural" policies developed by local authorities for recapitulating the earlier approach—that is, by tackling "perceived 'problems,'" rather than offering "a coherent and planned strategy."[11] He acknowledged the historical importance of these initiatives, many of which arose from the "effort and commitment of individuals or small groups of people around the country," but ultimately concluded that "multicultural education at the local level" had become "a range of ad hoc measures" that were "lumped together" under a "common heading" yet were "essentially unrelated."[12] In this way, the report explicitly rebuked the federal government for its "marked lack of clarity ..., guidance and leadership."[13] While Swann credited the government with recognizing the necessity of educating all children (not just those of immigrant backgrounds) about the "new reality" of Britain's diversity, he also made clear that "constant reiteration and exhortation to this effect" was not enough.[14] "Multicultural education," he concluded, should "involve far more wide ranging and fundamental changes in attitude and practice than had previously been envisaged."[15] Implicit in Swann's report was a very particular vision of multiculturalism, one that now imagined immigrants as positive contributors to a "new," "multicultural," and "multiracial" Britain.[16]

Swann's inquiry, it is important to remember, emerged in the context of Margaret Thatcher's simultaneous efforts to shore up the terms of national belonging and tighten the nation's borders. Thus, even before the report was released, conservative newspapers began to pillory the inquiry's efforts to promote multiculturalism in the schools. Anticipating recommendations for further educational reform, political commentator and informal adviser to Thatcher, Alfred Sherman, predicted that the report would endorse "a procrustean pidgin culture to be imposed on majority and minorities alike." These changes, he warned, would result in "cultural genocide" that would effectively "outlaw the concept of the English nation."[17] Simon Pearce, the deputy chairman of the Immigration and Race Relations Committee for the conservative pressure group the Monday Club, chimed in, condemning the report as "profoundly dangerous" and "contemptuous of the rights of the native inhabitants of the UK."[18]

These reactions were not especially surprising. Schools represented a key site of integration, a place where immigrant and ethnic minority children often had their only sustained contact with native Britons. After border control and immigration, education was typically the first place the state intervened in newcomers' lives. Above all, though, education immediately raised weighty questions of national self-conception and socialization. Seemingly small and specific decisions about curricula—the version of history taught, the languages offered, the religions recognized as part of the larger culture—as well as possible special provisions (i.e., of meals or uniforms) added up to a larger vision of British society and its normative way of life. Not surprisingly, then, efforts to develop multicultural education, whether as ad hoc policies or nationally agreed-upon objectives, faced resistance from the very start.

At precisely this moment, moreover, controversy exploded around the public denunciations of multiculturalism leveled by Ray Honeyford, headmaster of Drummond Middle School located in the immigrant-heavy Midlands city of Bradford. In a series of articles published between 1982 and 1984 for the *Times Educational Supplement* and the conservative *Salisbury Review*, Honeyford railed against the "current educational orthodoxies connected with race," highlighting what he considered the "dishonest" language used to promote multicultural education.[19] To Honeyford, the term "cultural enrichment," which he described as the "approved term for the West Indian's right to create an ear splitting cacophony for most of the night to the detriment of his neighbour's sanity," was one such example.[20] The euphemisms enforced by such "orthodoxies," he pointedly argued, meant that it was impossible to say what one really thought, thus making "freedom of speech difficult to maintain."[21]

As the director of a school where Asians composed 86 percent of the students, Honeyford authoritatively declared: "It is no more than common sense, that if a school contains a disproportionate number of children for whom English is a second language (true of all Asian children, even those born here), or children from homes where educational ambition and the values to support it are conspicuously absent (i.e. the vast majority of West Indian homes a disproportionate number of which are fatherless) then academic standards are bound to suffer."[22] Here he articulated exactly the assumptions the Swann commission condemned in its report the following year. Honeyford felt wholly justified in rejecting the idea that schools had a duty "to foster and maintain distinctive, foreign cultures in opposition to the majority culture."[23]

His negative opinion of many pupils'"cultures" only strengthened his resolve against any reforms. In relating his struggles
with Asian parents, he described Pakistan as "a country that
cannot cope with democracy," charged that it was wracked by
corruption as "the heroin capital of the world," and characterized "the political temperament of the Indian subcontinent"
as "hysterical."[24] His opinion of Afro-Caribbean students was
no better: he declared that "the roots of black educational
failure are, in reality, located in West Indian family structure
and values."[25] And perhaps worst of all, to Honeyford, was that
the predominance of these alien cultures in certain schools
resulted in the decline of the British educational system more
generally.

His inflammatory comments provoked a major protest by
school parents, who formed the Drummond Parents' Action
Committee and campaigned for Honeyford's dismissal. In
response, many national media outlets defended him as a
martyr to "vehement ideologues."[26] His "crime," according
to the *Times*, "was to tell the truth as he saw it," and "for this
truth he must be silenced" by "ruthless bigots."[27] The left-
leaning editorial board for the *Guardian* was more measured
in its assessment, observing that "Mr Honeyford would seem
to be the wrong person to hold the particular job which he
so masochistically seeks to retain," even as it cautioned that
"the mere accusation of racism" should not justify the "sack-
ing of a head teacher or of anyone else."[28]

Significantly, the Honeyford debate came to a head just as
the Swann report was submitted, and the two events seem to
have had reciprocal effects. In 1986, Honeyford was pushed to
accept early retirement and ushered off the national stage, but
the controversy also undermined Swann's call for a broad,
state-led vision of multicultural education that acknowledged the positive aspects of Britain's demographic diversity. Indeed, Thatcher's Conservative Party essentially ignored

Swann's injunctions and instead spearheaded its own version of national education reform, which culminated in the
passing of the Education Reform Act of 1988. The act allowed parents to designate a preferred choice school, enabled
schools to remove themselves from the jurisdiction of their
LEA, introduced a national curriculum with key metrics for
measuring achievement, and required "broadly Christian"
acts of worship in all schools.

Education, though, was not the only arena in which multicultural policy became an issue in 1980s Britain. Efforts to
reform local government constituted a second key site where
ground-level efforts to address the needs of ethnic minorities gained some traction. In many respects, the inclination
of many borough councils and municipal authorities to
shake up local administration is not especially surprising—
local politics attracted leftist activists disillusioned with the
crisis-ridden Labour Party of Harold Wilson and James Cal-
laghan and seeking "a new way of doing politics."[29] Many of
the "urban left," as they came to be known, cut their political
teeth on late 1960s protests for peace, antiracism, feminism,
and environmentalism, causes that "predisposed" them to
"respond sympathetically" to minority concerns about racism, discrimination, and representation.[30] Indeed, significant
numbers of young British leftists were inspired by and supported the civil rights movement in the United States. These
activists were also key participants in the antiracist campaigns
of the Anti-Nazi League, a broadly leftist coalition established
in 1977 to combat the far-right National Front and its violent
incursions into immigrant neighborhoods. It was precisely
this younger generation that began moving into local municipal politics in the late 1970s.

As we have seen, Ken Livingstone, leader of the Greater
London Council (GLC) from 1981 until its dissolution in

1986, was the most celebrated (and vilified) example of the urban left, but there were countless other Labour activists in metropolitan London, Manchester, and other cities who used their local government positions to advance a progressive political agenda. Leftist members of the Lambeth Council who were also active in the Anti-Nazi League, for instance, asserted that antiracism had to extend beyond simply confronting the overt bigotry of the far right. They criticized the fact that 30 percent of Lambeth's population was Afro-Caribbean, yet Lambeth had no black councilors or senior officers and the council employed only a handful of black staff. As a result, in 1978, the Lambeth Council created an "ethnic minorities working committee," which served as a template for similar units in the GLC and nine other radical London boroughs.[31] Such committees pushed for the presence of more people of color at all levels of local government, established equal opportunity procedures to ensure more transparent hiring processes, and introduced racial sensitivity training across many city departments.

Efforts proceeded on numerous fronts. Some councils revised the rules for allocating low-income housing to address the recurring pattern of minorities receiving the worst accommodations. Others raised the issue of racism within law enforcement that often manifested itself in racial profiling or refusing to treat "Paki-bashing" as a crime. And virtually every left-controlled urban council, imbued with an ethos of "do-it-yourself politics," emphasized the participation of ordinary citizens in government through self-organization. Municipal authorities worked hard to find minority leaders to serve as interlocutors and represent their communities. Officials also encouraged these leaders to identify community needs and develop their own plans to meet them. Local councils, in turn, offered grants and other forms of funding to support such efforts, enabling immigrant communities themselves to become "effective agencies of self-help and collective action."[32]

Beyond the more practical efforts to foster multicultural coexistence through local government, urban left members of the GLC also used their position to promote a new vision of London itself as a multicultural and cosmopolitan city. They cultivated this image by sponsoring free concerts and cultural festivals that showcased a wide variety of ethnic music and cuisine, events that made ground-level heterogeneity more visible and encouraged multicultural exchange as a form of ordinary practice (e.g., eating and cultural consumption). But they also planted the seeds of a new kind of marketing and branding for tourism: Britain's capital was a "world city" that celebrated its diversity as a source of creativity and dynamism.[33]

These attempts to recast multiculturalism in more positive ways—indeed, to make it a more concrete part of British life by offering greater access to local governance and channeling new resources to local communities—were quickly demonized by the conservative media. Livingstone became the object of recurring scorn after publicly stating that the 1981 Brixton riots had been caused by "years of neglect, high unemployment, resentment against racial discrimination and, in particular, insensitive, racist policing."[34] From the *Express* and *Star* to the *Mail*, as well as the *Mirror* and *Sun*, the tabloid press depicted the GLC administration as Marxist, authoritarian, undemocratic, and more concerned with the needs of ethnic minorities than with those of the white working class. "The real assault on the democracy of this country," declared the *Daily Mail*, "is by the Fascist left, which has gained a menacing hold on the power structures at union and local level within Mr Livingstone's Labour Party."[35] Of special concern were the various efforts to facilitate equal opportunity in employment, to require cultural sensitivity training, and to strengthen the Commission for Racial Equality's ability to prosecute racial discrimination. But rather than addressing actual policies, the gutter press favored a strategy of caricaturing the "loony left" for indulging in "multicultural" excesses. A rash of articles, for example, condemned Labour-led authorities for outlawing use of the word "black" as racist. One prominent set of stories claimed that the Haringey Council had banned black garbage can liners because they were "racially offensive." The *Mail on Sunday* reported that the council had "changed over to grey sacks—to avoid offending West Indian workers in the cleaning department."[36] But the most widely resonant controversy focused on the left-wing Hackney Council's supposed outlawing of the nursery song "Baa Baa Black Sheep."[37] These "loony left" caricatures reinforced the sense that Labour-led municipal authorities were "irrationally obsessed" with "fringe issues," which in turn allowed their antiracist and equal opportunity policies to be dismissed both as crazy and as draconian forms of political correctness.[38]

Against this backdrop, Margaret Thatcher began a concerted attack on Labour-controlled local government. In 1981, she was already accusing Labour councils of being "big spenders of other people's money."[39] By 1983, Thatcher charged that the GLC was "a wasteful and unnecessary tier of government," and the Tories campaigned on a promise to abolish the GLC and other metropolitan authorities. But at least one major newspaper, the *Irish Times*, reported in 1985 that the claim that this would lead to financial savings had "not stood up." The move was thus recognized—at least by those on the left— "as having a large element of political malice."[40] It was seen as an effort to bring to heel activist, Labour-led local councils seeking to implement ground-level policies that promoted ethnic pluralism and fought discrimination.

For sociologist Paul Gilroy, the 1986 shuttering of the GLC (as well as the contemporaneous closing of the Inner London Education Authority) marked the end of any serious British effort to pursue multiculturalism as an "active ideology."[41] And in certain respects, this is true: the demise of the GLC initiatives certainly ended the most highly visible programs. The shuttering, however, was never absolute. The Midlands city of Leicester, for instance, invested in ethnic minority inclusion measures that championed diversity, including displaying multilingual school signs, welcoming the first consecrated Jain temple in the Western world, and celebrating the Hindu festival of Diwali as a municipal event that drew thousands of people each year. Meanwhile, many London boroughs continued to print their informational leaflets in multiple languages and provide "race awareness" training for workers in health and social services. Local councils in London, Birmingham, and Leeds even developed campaigns to encourage ethnic minorities to vote in larger numbers.[42]

At the national level, too, hard questions about continuing patterns of British racism did not simply disappear in the 1990s. In April 1993, for instance, a black teenaged architecture student, Stephen Lawrence, was murdered in a racially motivated attack while waiting for a London bus. After delayed arrests and a botched investigation, the five suspects were acquitted. This outcome prompted a major public outcry, but it was not until the Labour Party returned to power in 1997 that Home Secretary Jack Straw appointed Sir William Macpherson to head a formal inquiry. The subsequent Macpherson report openly condemned the Metropolitan Police Service for incompetence and systemic errors, including failing to follow obvious leads and arrest suspects. The document suggested that senior law enforcement in London had ignored the recommendations of a previous inquiry (the Scarman report, issued after the Brixton riots) to address misconduct; it ultimately concluded that the Metropolitan Police—as well as the broader criminal justice system—was institutionally racist. In this way, the Lawrence murder, which focused public attention on a highly sympathetic victim, reignited debate about racism in British society and prompted calls for major reforms in policing around ethnic minorities, especially providing a clear definition of racist crimes.

Nongovernmental organizations also served to facilitate this kind of institutionally transformative work. In 1998, for example, the Runnymede Trust, an independent think tank dedicated to promoting racial justice, established the Commission on the Future of Multi-Ethnic Britain. It appointed political theorist Bhikhu Parekh as chair and enjoined the committee "to analyse the current state of multiethnic Britain and propose ways of countering racial discrimination and disadvantage and making Britain a confident and vibrant multicultural society at ease with its rich diversity."[43] The Commission released its findings in 2000, offering a strong statement about how to think about diversity in explicitly multicultural terms. The so-called Parekh report declared that Britain was "both a community of citizens and a community of communities, both a liberal and a multicultural society."[44] In particular, it argued for a synthesis of a common liberal political culture and respect for a plurality of communities within the nation.[45] "Cohesion in such a community," the report explained, would derive from "widespread commitment to certain core values, both between communities and within them: equality and fairness; dialogue and consultation; toleration, compromise, and accommodation; recognition of and respect for diversity; and . . . determination to confront and eliminate racism and xenophobia."[46] This is the language that led prominent critics such as Indian-born British journalist and author Kenan Malik to describe the Parekh report as a key moment, the crystallization of state-sponsored multiculturalism. More importantly, perhaps, the report represented a crucial intervention in terms of naming and claiming multiculturalism as a bedrock British value. The very fact that the report was commissioned and issued in a climate of growing wariness toward Muslim immigrants and lack of federal policy leadership only reinforces its importance as evidence of one influential institution's effort to keep these ideals alive.

In West Germany, meanwhile, efforts to promote something explicitly described as "multiculturalism" were also emerging at the grassroots level—and this despite national leaders' insistence (by the CDU) that Turks could never be a part of German society. As early as 1980, for example, the Catholic and Protestant churches sponsored the *Tag des ausländischen Mitbürgers* (Day of the Foreign Co-Citizen), an event to celebrate "Germany as a multicultural society." The planners consciously chose the expression "multicultural society," according to one organizer, in order to broaden the public's awareness of long-term foreign residents (and their contributions to German society). The term, he noted, encouraged native Germans to see their "foreign fellow citizens" as bearers of rich customs and traditions that might enhance German culture in the very process of integration. The use of "multicultural" here suggested not only that it was possible for different cultures to coexist in a single society, but also that German society would be expanded and improved by the contributions of its "foreign fellow citizens."[47]

Conservatives, however, remained skeptical. A couple of years later, journalist and features editor of the *Frankfurter Allgemeine Zeitung* Konrad Adam published an article titled "The Price of Multiculture." Adam was prompted to write his piece by the Protestant Academy of Arnoldshain's declaration that multiculturalism was a "foregone conclusion" in Germany. He dismissed such "utopian calls" to "broaden one's horizons" or embrace "the possibilities of other cultures," insisting that social progressives needed to answer a more basic set of questions: How is "mutual integration" to be "concretely represented"? "What is given and what is taken?" "Under which conditions and at what price must Germans adapt to 'the new relationships of multicultural coexistence'?" And "where does this task conversely fall on foreigners?"[48] Adam worried about the lack of a specific framework for valuing one set of principles over another—an absence, he feared, that might allow retrograde customs and undemocratic absolutisms (such as "renunciation of women's equality" or "revival of corporeal punishment in schools") to be celebrated under the guise of cross-cultural enrichment. Deeply suspicious of blanket tolerance, he sought a clear standard for which values and customs would be sanctioned in a multicultural Germany.[49]

In the meantime, though, the federal government's return to the mantra of Germany as a "non-immigration country" meant that metropolitan areas with large guest worker populations were forced to develop ad hoc strategies to respond to foreigners' needs. In 1981, West Berlin mayor Richard von Weizsäcker created the post of "commissioner for foreigner affairs" to spearhead a city-based effort to incorporate guest workers and their families into German society. This office was the first of its kind at the local level and became a model for similar positions in other West German cities.[50] The moderate CDU politician Barbara John became Berlin's inaugural commissioner, functioning as the city's principal representative on all matters related to "foreigners" during her more than twenty-year tenure (1981–2003). John herself often appeared at religious celebrations, community meetings, neighborhood roundtables, academic conferences, and other public events that highlighted the presence of Turks. She was such a familiar figure at these gatherings that Turkish Berliners often referred to her as "John Abla," or older sister John.[51] Her office was responsible for providing financial support to groups of native Germans that wanted to work with the Turkish community, as well as to a handful of organizations run by de facto immigrants themselves. John and her staff established an institutional framework for tackling issues important to guest workers and their families (including housing, social services, education, religious observation, and community life), essentially facilitating the integration of new immigrants—even if the CDU refused to acknowledge them as such.

By 1989, the refusal of national leaders to admit the enduring presence of Turks and other guest workers in Germany was giving way to an explicit public debate about multiculturalism as a social blueprint. During a community meeting in Berlin's predominantly Turkish Kreuzberg neighborhood, Commissioner John called for the liberalization of the German citizenship law. The nation's resident migrants needed access to citizenship, she argued, so they would be "politically equal" even as they were able to "go their own cultural way." "National citizenship," she concluded, needed to "finally be detached from cultural identity."[52] The view advanced by John was one in which cultural identities would remain untouched, while national citizenship would be expanded, open to long-term residents who were willing to pledge their allegiance to the German liberal democratic state. This approach targeted Germany's old, largely outmoded citizenship law, which defined ancestry as the sole basis for accessing the status of German citizen. Because traditional German citizenship collapsed ancestry and national culture, any new law would necessarily have to decouple national citizenship from cultural identity. The goal was to establish a more open conception of national belonging, one that no longer relied on a blood-based standard.

This meeting in Kreuzberg took place just as the Rushdie affair was exploding in Britain. In practice, this meant that even as John and like-minded activists were pushing for a new citizenship law, opponents were pointing to the Rushdie affair as a cautionary indicator of multiculturalism's dangers. The conservative commentator Dankwart Guratzsch, for instance, characterized Khomeini's fatwa as a blatant example of intolerance. He argued that it represented a "foreignness between cultures" that rendered any multicultural vision of society unworkable.[53] The progressive critic Claus Leggewie, in contrast, discerned two major issues in the controversy. First, he argued that those who championed the coexistence of many cultural "communities and colonies" as an alternative to "national homogenization" were in fact promoting a "childish" celebration of differences that often fed the desire for exoticism. Second, he worried that such undertheorized multiculturalism failed to offer disparate ethnic communities any shared institutions that would bind them together. A society that viewed everyone's cultural particularities as worthy of protection but shared no basic values or institutions, Leggewie claimed, would invariably succumb to illiberal acts. The key, he insisted, was access to German citizenship. Leggewie therefore pressed for an easing of naturalization procedures for guest workers and their families: migrants with a stake in civil society would be less likely to turn to extremism.[54]

As these debates around what German multiculturalism might look like unfolded, more immediate and practical efforts at integration continued apace. In Frankfurt, the local Green Party had been pushing hard for the creation of an Office of Multicultural Affairs (Amt für multikulturelle Angelegenheiten, AmkA) to counter rising xenophobia. This initiative seemed especially urgent because Frankfurt had neither a local commissioner for foreigner affairs nor a citywide foreigners' council (institutions that had begun to spring up across the country to address "foreigner issues" during the 1980s). Finally established by mayoral decree in July 1989,

the office was overseen by the former student leader of the
Paris 1968 revolts, Daniel Cohn-Bendit, who became deputy mayor in charge of "multicultural affairs." The title itself
was a political statement, deliberately avoiding older tem-
plates that stressed outreach to "foreigners." Indeed, it had
been intentionally chosen to emphasize the unit's mandate
to promote a new vision of integration. "Integration," office
director Rosi Wolf-Almanasreh explained, was becoming "a
two-way process for all those involved," including the German residents of Frankfurt.[55]

The AmkA positioned itself as a resource for the city's socially disadvantaged groups, including the homeless, homosexuals, national minorities (e.g., the Roma), and foreigners.
It concentrated on two principal tasks. First, armed with an
open-ended mandate to "handle general integration questions," the office coordinated these efforts across the city's
complex bureaucracies. AmkA staff, for instance, often mediated between the schools and the city's social welfare office, facilitating mutual cooperation. Second, the AmkA focused on the work of antidiscrimination, a task that became
increasingly urgent in the face of rising complaints about
prejudice and xenophobia. Despite the absence of federal
laws against discrimination, the AmkA director maintained
that "one of the most important tasks of human municipal
politics" was to "fight xenophobia" and "cultural racism."[56]
In its work with Frankfurt law enforcement, for example,
the AmkA provided the police with positive images of foreigners and helped to deconstruct stereotypes about foreigners and criminality.[57]

These local integration efforts, along with a building momentum to reform the citizenship law, seemed to point to
the possibility of a radical revision of German self-definition
along multicultural lines. But this possibility ground to a halt

amid the fall of the Berlin Wall in November 1989 and the rapid drive toward reunification in October 1990, milestones that touched off inward-looking debates about a more narrowly construed national identity.[58] Even though the consolidation of the two German states diverted public attention away from the status of guest workers, reunification actually removed a key justification for maintaining the 1913 citizenship law, which defined German belonging according to the principle of descent. During the Cold War years, this definition had facilitated extending citizen status to East German refugees, but it also prevented Turks and other long-resident guest workers from naturalizing.

The push for nationality reform reemerged only after a series of shocking arson attacks against foreign workers, refugees, and Turks in Hoyerswerda (1991), Rostock (1992), Mölln (1992), and Solingen (1993). These tragedies convinced many constituencies—including the Green Party, the SPD, the FDP, and even some members of the CDU, along with many churches, trade unions, and intellectuals—that a citizenship law based on descent was incompatible with a democratic society transformed by immigration.[59]

It was the SPD victory in the 1998 federal election that ultimately opened up the opportunity for major change. The new Socialist-Green government affirmed that Germany had experienced an "irreversible process" in recent decades that required the "integration of those immigrants who live in Germany on a permanent basis and who accept Germany's constitutional values."[60] First among its policy goals was citizenship reform. The original proposal advocated dual citizenship and the principle of granting automatic citizen status to those born on German soil. But the political process was contentious, with the CDU mounting a signature campaign against "double passports" that forced an awkward

compromise. The final law embraced jus soli (birthright citizenship), but opposed dual citizenship: children granted
German citizenship by virtue of being born in Germany
would maintain their parents' nationality until they reached
the age of majority (eighteen), at which point they would
have until their twenty-third birthday to decide between
the two.[61] Despite these limitations, the revised law, which
was passed in 1999 and went into effect in 2000, marked a
crucial milestone in German efforts to come to terms with
its postwar heterogeneity. Only by offering Turks and other
guest workers a legal path to national belonging did Germans finally create the conditions that would allow for a
serious conversation about multiculturalism as a model for
social organization.

In France, early "insertion" initiatives that had acknowledged cultural differences as part of a pragmatic strategy to
support labor migrants (largely from Algeria) ultimately gave
way to an explicit rejection of multiculturalism that began in
the 1980s. This shift, which took place in the context of the
so-called nationality debates, was marked by a new focus on
urban renewal. To a certain extent, the emphasis on neighborhoods, suburbs, and "space" as a framework for dealing
with diversity issues should come as no surprise. In 1958, the
introduction of the category of priority urban development
areas (ZUPs, zones à urbaniser en priorité) had specifically
targeted areas with high concentrations of Algerian workers
and their families. The immediate goal had been to disrupt
FLN networks in the *bidonvilles* during the Algerian War,
and the means involved relocating Algerians from shantytowns, first to temporary lodgings (*cités de transit*) with centralized running water, public bathrooms, and shared cook-
ing facilities, then to large-scale public housing complexes
(*grands ensembles*) that included large apartment blocks,
schools, recreational facilities, and shops.[62] In practice, these

massive housing projects in the suburbs of Paris, Lyon, and Marseille were never ethnically homogeneous. Their inhabitants consisted of French working-class people, as well as laborers from Algeria (many with French citizenship), Turkey, Africa, and Asia.[63] This heterogeneity made space a useful rubric to address the needs of multiple groups, especially after the mid-1980s, when French leaders across the political spectrum emphatically reaffirmed the core principles of republicanism and national integration. By targeting the *grands ensembles* and *banlieues*—or so the theory went—the French state could tackle "distress" and "disadvantage" without referring to the specific needs or problems faced by specific minority communities and thus compromising its color-blind policies.[64]

Once economic stagnation set in after 1973, those living in the suburbs suffered disproportionately from deindustrialization (especially the contraction of the French auto industry). Downsizing produced high unemployment and growing inequality, and the inhabitants of the *grands ensembles* faced particular difficulty in finding new work because they lived far from city centers and lacked public transportation. Substandard schools in project neighborhoods, moreover, exacerbated the gap between the needs of a tighter labor market and the rising number of unskilled working-class youth in the suburbs. Tensions in the *banlieues* came to a head in 1981, when riots broke out in the Minguettes projects in the suburbs of Lyon. These clashes prompted the central government to devise new policies to "tackle the causes of neighborhood decline," including poor schools and insufficient vocational training.[65] Over the course of 1981–82, the state established a new agency, the Commission nationale pour le développement des quartiers, and began to identify Education Priority Zones (which often overlapped with Urban Priority Zones) for extra funding and resources.

Notably, the government explicitly involved local authorities in the policies' implementation, an approach that grew
directly out of Prime Minister Mitterrand's efforts to promote regionalism and move away from the usual patterns of
centralized, top-down policy making.[66] These urban development initiatives tended to be carried out by "activists and
organizers who denounced the centralized, state-run and, in
their view, undemocratic housing policies implemented in
the 1950s and 1960s."[67] In this respect, the teachers, social
workers, and local government officials on the front lines in
France came from similar milieus as those engaged in grassroots integration efforts in Britain and Germany. Here, too,
French activists trying to spearhead integration emphasized
neighborhoods as the "locus of urgent social problems."[68]
More specifically, they worked to create neighborhood committees, facilitate dialogue between public housing corporations and residents, and fund youth associations.[69] These activists, one suspects, may have struggled to develop programs
that squared their more fine-grained knowledge of the specific difficulties facing disadvantaged suburban populations
(including the effects of discrimination and racism) with the
state's insistence that the problems confronting the inhabitants of the *grands ensembles* were simply structural problems
of the *banlieues* themselves. For the state, as one official suc-
cinctly put it, it mattered "little whether inhabitants of distressed areas" were "foreign or French of foreign extraction.
They experience[d] the same difficulties, namely unemployment and lack of skills."[70] At the same time, the relentless
focus by government officials and the media on the suburbs,
their description as "distressed areas" (*quartiers sensibles*), and
their association with delinquency and criminality resulted
in the pervasive stigmatization of the neighborhoods and
their residents.[71] *Banlieues*, that is, quickly came to serve as a

euphemism for people defined by their ethnic background, even as this spatial rhetoric deliberately obscured questions of multiethnic diversity.[72]

Despite major state efforts to address social and economic issues in the *banlieues*, the problems associated with these areas did not go away. Another highly publicized riot on the outskirts of Lyon in 1990—this time involving three nights of confrontation between the police and local youths at the Mas du Taureau projects—ushered in a pattern of urban disorder that continued through much of the decade.[73] These clashes suggested that the policy of urban renewal was not working: during the 1980s, in fact, Mas du Taureau had been a beneficiary of substantial urban development resources, and its Communist mayor had been actively involved in implementing these programs.

The state's response was to embrace a law-and-order approach. Seeds of this new policy emphasis were planted when conservative President Giscard d'Estaing passed the controversial 1981 Security and Liberty Law (just before Mitterrand's election) to shore up the French criminal justice system's ability to "deal effectively with crimes of violence."[74] And when the conservatives returned to power under Chirac in 1993, they immediately cracked down on juvenile delinquency, violent crime, and riots with a heightened police presence in the *banlieues*, a strategy that exacerbated the confrontations between young male residents and law enforcement.[75] The combination of addressing social and economic disadvantage through a spatial lens and focusing on law-and-order issues effectively cast immigrants as "people who create[d] problems rather than people who face[d] problems; the consequences of discrimination became irrelevant, even invisible in this frame."[76]

Indeed, what the state steadfastly refused to countenance was the possibility that racism and discrimination played a role in shaping the social and economic conditions of immigrants and ethnic minorities living in the *banlieues*.[77] The antiracist organization SOS Racisme sought to challenge this blind spot by conducting an investigation to expose the racist hiring practices of French companies. The group sent two identical résumés listing the same qualifications, professional experience, and knowledge to a range of businesses under two different names, one French and the other foreign.[78] It found that many potential employers simply discarded the applications with foreign names.[79] At the same time, the refusal to acknowledge the deleterious impact of race and ethnicity did not prevent the highest government officials from using racialized language to describe suburban youth. In highly publicized episodes during the 2005 riots, which began in Paris and raged across the country during the late fall, Interior Minister Sarkozy promised to "clean out the projects with a power washer" (*Kärcher*) and referred to rioters as "scum" (*racaille*). Even as the state disavowed discrimination and racism as factors that affected Algerians and other ethnic groups, it was clear that racialized assumptions shaped the very conditions of their belonging in France.

The French efforts to deal with ethnic and cultural diversity, then, operated within national integration policies that required the systematic effacement of differences. Yet the recurrent flare-ups of violence in the *banlieues* underscored their failure: integration had not taken place. Lacking a political and ideological framework for admitting that cultural differences existed and that racism affected certain segments of the population within the larger category of "disadvantaged," however, the French state was only able to throw money and resources at problems they called by other names.

Minority Critics of Multiculturalism

The rising tide of conservative backlash against multiculturalism is well known; far less familiar are the critiques that emerged from leftist intellectuals with roots in immigrant and ethnic communities. As the effects of multicultural policies started to become clear, minority activists began weighing in on some of their unanticipated consequences. This was especially true in Britain, where the basic premise of cultural pluralism was largely accepted (unlike France) and ethnic minorities enjoyed a relatively secure legal status (unlike Germany).

Perhaps the earliest minority critic of multiculturalism was Ambalavaner Sivanandan, the Sri Lankan–born British director of the Institute of Race Relations (IRR) in London. Sivanandan had been the IRR's librarian during the 1960s, when the institute served as a think tank to help strategize national concerns relating to the future of Britain's ex-colonies. During the early 1970s, a number of institute staff began to question the IRR's connection to the government and how this coziness might be influencing the kinds of research it supported. In a showdown with the IRR staff, the governing council—made up of executives from leading multinational corporations, politicians from the Houses of Commons and Lords, and newspaper editors—found itself outvoted and resigned en masse. Despite withdrawal of financial support from the corporate sector and large foundations, the IRR managed to regroup, appointing Sivanandan as its new director and reorienting its mission toward supporting community organizations and fighting racism.

As a socialist and antiracist, Sivanandan took aim at the way that state-sponsored forms of multiculturalism were playing out at the local level. In a series of essays from the late 1980s, he elaborated the emergent problems. He started by describing the multiethnic coalition of Asians, Afro-Caribbeans, and white Britons that had fought racism and discrimination in employment, housing, and social services during the 1960s and 1970s. This joint fight, he claimed, led to the government's antidiscrimination legislation and enabled cultural diversity to flourish. But as multiculturalism became institutionalized, it was "stripped of its anti-racist roots and remit. It ceased to be an outcome of the struggle from below, and became government policy imposed from above. And as the anti-racist component of the struggle ebbed, multiculturalism as policy began to degenerate into . . . culturalism or ethnicism."[80] By using the term "culturalism," Sivanandan highlighted the fact that racism was no longer understood as a "matter of racial oppression and exploitation, of race and class, but of cultural differences and their acceptability."[81] Prioritizing cultural differences, in other words, took attention away from the racism embedded in the deeper structures of social life: disparity of resources, differential access to government services, unequal treatment by the police, and so forth.

The emphasis on culture, Sivanandan charged, led to a facile understanding of structural racism, suggesting instead that bigotry was simply caused by a lack of familiarity or cross-cultural understanding. One consequence of this view was that proponents of multiculturalism—especially in the educational arena—often assumed that discrimination could easily be remedied by teaching about "other" cultures, primarily through superficial characteristics like cuisine, dress, and festivals. This strategy promoted what came to be caricatured as the "saris, samosas, and steel drums" version of multiculturalism—a trite and shallow celebration of cultural diversity.[82] Another effect was that racism became an issue of "ethnic disadvantage" that could be solved by targeting problem groups rather than addressing the racial hierarchies structuring British society and institutions. In assessing the government response to the early 1980s urban uprisings in Brixton, for example, Sivanandan pointed out that political leaders "identified the underlying problem as individual prejudice and 'ethnic disadvantage,'" rather than institutionalized police racism. This approach gave rise to the belief that "meeting the cultural needs" of Britain's black population "would somehow stave off protests about inequality and injustice."

Sivanandan also saw multiculturalism as divisive. While antiracist struggles had brought different groups of Asians, Afro-Caribbeans, and other immigrants together with white activists, multicultural state policies encouraged competition among various communities and thereby entrenched a "dangerous ethnicized patronage in local politics." When local authorities distributed state funds for urban renewal, grants, and favors based on specific ethnic needs and problems, it deepened ethnic differences and fostered rivalries among minority communities, while simultaneously encouraging groups to organize themselves around single categories of ethnicity and culture to access earmarked funds. When "cultures exclude each other through a hierarchy of racial discrimination," warned Sivanandan, multiculturalism becomes "regressive."[83]

Other minority activists extended these critiques in new directions. For example, Southall Black Sisters (SBS) was established in 1979 by Asian and Afro-Caribbean feminists to add women's voices to the black (that is, Afro-Asian) antiracist struggle and challenge "the right of male community leaders to speak for" women of color.[84] Although most SBS feminists had begun their activist careers in the antiracist movement, their commitment to addressing women's concerns led them to criticize both multiculturalists and antiracists.

The ideal of respecting differences, the group charged, encouraged multiculturalists to take "a non-interventionist line
with regard to Asian families," rather than fighting for "equal
opportunities for girls."[85] At the same time, SBS condemned
antiracists for celebrating black women "when they came
out in the thousands to oppose the presence of fascists in
the streets," but not when they raised other difficult issues
such as domestic violence (which challenged the notion of
a unified black community).[86] SBS attacked the "anti-racist
consensus" for refusing to acknowledge "the patriarchal control within black communities" out of fear that such an admission would provide "further fodder" to "reinforce ideas
of Asian men being more sexist than white men and Asian
families being particularly barbaric and tyrannical."[87]

These perspectives, moreover, shaped the SBS view of British state multiculturalism. According to SBS, the practice of
relying on unelected ethnic representatives to help local governments identify projects for funding tended to empower
the most conservative (and male) community leaders, who
often exploited the isolated nature of ethnic communities
to preserve their own patriarchal privilege. One result was
that state representatives tended to treat minority communities as monolithic and homogeneous, with little sense of
their variegated and conflicting needs. This strategy, SBS
feminists argued, ultimately "ignored social divisions and hierarchies within communities" and "circumvented the very
political processes designed to ensure accountability and address disadvantage."[88] For SBS, then, the institutional practices of state-sponsored multiculturalism actually undermined the efforts to fight for women's rights within minority
communities.

With the benefit of hindsight, former member of the far-
left Socialist Worker Party member Kenan Malik has elabo-

rated on these criticisms. Describing the Birmingham council's response to the riots in the Handsworth neighborhood
in 1985, he explained that the city "borrowed the GLC blueprint to create a new political framework through which to
reach out to minority communities."[89] Birmingham established nine "umbrella groups" based on ethnicity and faith—
such as the African and Caribbean People's Movement, the
Bangladeshi Islamic Projects Consultative Committee, the
Birmingham Chinese Society, and the Hindu Council—to
represent their communities, help local authorities develop
policies, and make recommendations for the allocation of
funds. The goal was to draw minority communities into the
democratic process while simultaneously preventing ethnic
frustrations from spilling onto the street. The problem, according to Malik, was that "there was precious little democracy in the process. The groups themselves had no democratic
mandate . . . , no mandate at all."[90]

In this view, the strategy for giving immigrants and minorities a stake in British society did little to empower individuals within their larger communities, but rather raised
the stature of so-called community leaders, "who owed their
position and influence largely to the relationship they possessed with the state."[91] "Birmingham's policies," Malik concluded, "did not respond to the needs of communities, but to
a large degree created those communities by imposing identities" on diverse urban populations (e.g., Afro-Caribbeans,
Bangladeshis, Chinese, Hindus) and "by ignoring internal conflicts which arose out of class, gender and intra-religious differences."[92] Thus, according to Malik, the earliest local attempts
at implementing multiculturalism as a social blueprint had
the unintended effect of producing a more fragmented British society, exacerbating (if not actually engendering) the very
problems they were supposed to resolve.[93]

Beyond condemning the effects of this approach in practice, Malik also issued a more fundamental critique of multiculturalism in its pluralist guise, namely, that it treated cultures as under threat and in need of preservation.[94] This view
translated into the assumption that minority groups were
"uniform, single-minded, conflict-free and defined by ethnicity, faith and culture." "For all the talk of culture as fluid and
changing," he observed, the official forms of "multiculturalism invariably lead people to think of human cultures in
fixed terms."[95] For Malik, then, the greatest problem with this
model of managing diversity was that it shared a crucial assumption with its ostensible opposite: the racialist ideologies
of the right. In both cases, differences among groups of people
(whether framed as biological or cultural) were understood as
predetermined, natural, and unchanging.[96]

Between the 1980s and early 2000s, then, a more nuanced
set of minority critiques began to emerge in Britain, aimed
at the ways in which state policies of multiculturalism were
playing out in actual practice. This was a very different set of
critiques from the conservative attacks raising the alarm that
Britain was being overwhelmed by alien traditions. None of
these minority critics took aim at immigration or the ground-
level diversity that such influxes produced. Rather, they pointed
to emerging blind spots in state policies that gave rise to some
surprisingly undemocratic effects. For Malik, in particular,
the problem with multiculturalism was not multiracial society or the celebration of diversity per se, but the essentialized
assumptions about race and ethnicity that shaped the specific
mechanisms of resource allocation and policy making at the
local levels. Ultimately, these critiques did not seek to end efforts to expand notions of British belonging or incorporate
ethnic minorities. Instead, they sought to make this expansion more inclusive and democratic.

How Multiculturalism's Failure
Became Common Sense

How, then, did these broad, but largely diffuse criticisms of multiculturalism coalesce into a more generally accepted discourse of failure? In what ways did such divergent forms of critique—left and right, white and nonwhite—ultimately come together? Here, it is useful to return (one last time) to the broader effects of the Rushdie affair. As we have seen, this episode began to transform critiques of specific policies and programs into a more generalized attack on multiculturalism, while simultaneously connecting it to a particular group of problematic immigrants—Muslims. Rather than responding to the initial conflict by addressing the actual organizers of the protests against *The Satanic Verses*, Home Secretary Douglas Hurd went to the Central Mosque in Birmingham to deliver a speech to the British Muslim community as a whole. Rather than treating each issue that emerged during the controversy (the demand that Penguin halt publication, the symbolic book burning, the request for equal treatment under the blasphemy law) on a case-by-case basis and identifying certain behaviors as violating specific British norms and laws, Home Office Minister of State John Patten chastised the country's entire Muslim community for being "un-British." Rather than condemning the Ayatollah Khomeini for issuing his fatwa, editorials in newspapers such as the *Independent* dismissed Islam in total, arguing categorically that "Islam is not a tolerant religion and makes no pretence of being so."[97]

To be sure, the mass cultural optics of the conflict encouraged commentators to make such leaps of association. As depicted by the British media, the controversy revolved around the Muslim community's efforts to intimidate and suppress an individual from its own ranks; an individual who was erudite, was articulate, and displayed the trappings of bourgeois success, precisely the kind of ethnic representative prized and celebrated as a model of assimilation. Because opponents of the novel had initially struggled to receive a hearing in the public sphere, they organized large-scale demonstrations in London and Bradford that suggested a much larger and more united community. The book burning, in particular, crystallized a vision of this community's ire and fanaticism bubbling to the surface in a distinctly illiberal way. Khomeini's fatwa, moreover, made it easy to assume that Islam as a religion brooked no insult and sanctioned violence as retribution. This action seemed to implicate not just a single theocratic leader, but all Muslims in what observers increasingly described as a "clash of civilizations." Following this associational logic, Western critics began to make a powerful argument: under the guise of safeguarding differences, multiculturalism had allowed an intolerant Islam to flourish and take root in the heart of liberal democratic societies.

This pattern quickly extended to the first French headscarf controversy just a few months later. What began as a local school conflict over the enforcement of stricter rules about headscarves soon escalated into a national discussion of Muslim immigrants' threat to secular values. At the same time, though, the French headscarf affairs added new and crucial layers to the view of Islam and Muslim immigrants forming in Europe. Where the Rushdie affair fueled public perceptions of Islam as vengeful and intolerant, the headscarf affairs conjured an inherently patriarchal tradition that was particularly "bad for women."[98] In this view, the fact that Muslim girls insisted on wearing the headscarf to school— even after multiple rounds of reasoned negotiation—only confirmed their subjugation and proved that Islam stripped women of individual liberty and self-determination in even the most basic aspects of their lives.

Once communism began its rapid collapse and the push for European unification intensified after 1989, moreover, commentators started to articulate doubts about multiculturalism in distinctly new registers. This trend first emerged in the Netherlands, the only other country besides Britain to adopt a state policy of multiculturalism, within its traditional framework of "pillarization." In a 1991 speech titled "On the Collapse of the Soviet Union," Frits Bolkestein, the leader of the Dutch conservative-liberal People's Party for Freedom and Democracy (VVD), called for a wholesale rethinking of immigrant policy. "Our official policy used to be, 'Integration without prejudice to everyone's own identity,'" he explained. "It is now recognized that this slogan was a bit too easy."[99] Indeed, by the late 1980s, other Dutch authorities had begun to question the efficacy of institutional pillarization, arguing that the protection of collective rights had encouraged minorities' social isolation.[100] Quickly, however, Bolkestein pushed his critique further. Warning that "very important aspects of our Western culture such as individual freedom and equality are under attack," he vigorously defended the achievements of European civilization (separation of church and state, freedom of expression, tolerance, nondiscrimination) against the "world of Islam"—a world, he argued, in which "religion" was a "way of life."[101] Here, Bolkestein echoed British historian Bernard Lewis, who had published an essay in the *Atlantic Monthly* the previous year describing a perpetual struggle between Islam and Christendom going back to the seventh century.[102] For Bolkestein, this age-old "clash of civilizations" had major implications for Dutch multiculturalism. "We must go back to our [European] roots," he declared. "Liberalism has produced . . . fundamental political principles. . . . Here there can be no compromise and no truck."[103] In arguing for "integration with more guts," Bolkestein insisted that the Dutch should not accommodate the cultural differences of Muslim immigrants. But his target was much broader than a handful of putatively illiberal practices. Islam as a "way of life," he argued, was simply irreconcilable with core European liberal values.

Scholars have come to describe what was emerging in Bolkestein's tough talk as "new realism."[104] The three crucial hallmarks of this novel approach were a perceived honesty—no longer bound by so-called political correctness—about the problems brought by immigration; validation of the perspective of a putatively typical native Dutch citizen; and critique of excessive tolerance.[105] New realists positioned themselves as public figures that dared to be frank, straightforward, and realistic about the more difficult, less celebratory aspects of multiethnic coexistence. They also set themselves up as spokespersons for regular folk, who "knew from day-to-day experience" what was "really going on."[106] They further criticized the pervasive fear of appearing racist in the Netherlands, which, they believed, led to excessive tolerance of Muslims' illiberal behavior and actions.

Within a decade, significant aspects of Bolkestein's critique had become standard talking points among the political opposition. In 2000, Dutch urban studies scholar and prominent Labor Party member Paul Scheffer published an article, "The Multicultural Tragedy," in the leading national newspaper NRC Handelsblad, in which he warned of a rising ethnic underclass in major Dutch cities, characterized by high rates of unemployment, criminality, and high school dropouts.[107] Scheffer blamed the "good old strategies of peaceful coexistence through deliberation and compromise"[108] as fostering a situation in which ethnic minorities—and especially Muslims—"did not feel attached to Dutch culture and society, and . . . were unwilling and unable to integrate."[109] Previous efforts to "emancipate" minorities within their own pillarized institutions had, Scheffer said, fueled segregation and separation from mainstream society. Above all, he insisted that state-sponsored multiculturalism "was incapable of remedying the most pressing problem among immigrants and their offspring, unemployment and economic marginalization."[110] Because of the refusal to confront the serious problems of a diverse society, he claimed, the Dutch had actually created and institutionalized social inequality.

Scheffer's proposed solution—what he called a "civilization offensive"—picked up on Bolkestein's rhetoric.[111] On the one hand, Scheffer argued that the state needed to become more active in the previously neglected socioeconomic arena of integration, developing strategies to help immigrants overcome poverty and economic disadvantage. Rather than treating ethnic minorities as groups with separate institutions, the new approach should emphasize the integration of immigrants as individuals. On the other hand, he pushed for a more rigorous set of requirements—namely, that immigrants adapt to the principles of liberal democracy and acquire a much better knowledge of Dutch culture and history. He recommended, in short, that strong affirmations of Dutch identity serve as an antidote to the problems created by state multiculturalism.[112] While Scheffer remained silent on whether such affirmations would also require Muslims to relinquish their religion in a kind of zero-sum choice, he was clearly moving away from pluralist impulses as a means of managing diversity.

Here we can see the first outlines of a new bipolar worldview, one in which Muslim culture—increasingly defined by intolerance, religious fanaticism, and patriarchal oppression—stood in opposition to a collective "European" culture, representing tolerance, secularism, and freedom of the individual. This worldview had begun to coalesce well before 2001, but the events of 9/11 went a long way to making them seem more obvious and natural—a new commonsense consensus on questions of European diversity. What the attacks in New York City and Washington, DC seemed to provide was incontrovertible evidence of all the suspicions that had been expressed in the wake of the Rushdie and headscarf affairs. Muslims had failed to integrate in Western democracies and were actively hostile toward their host societies. The 9/11 attacks were especially effective at consolidating this reasoning because they tied the threat of Islam not just to images of localized protests or book burnings, but to an actual, large-scale terrorist assault conducted on a liberal democracy. As the United States mobilized NATO allies against a newly declared "war on terror," European leaders began to worry that isolated Muslim immigrant communities might become breeding grounds for future recruits. In this climate, the decades-long failure (or even refusal) to develop national integration policies in Britain, France, and Germany was replaced by a rush to condemn the earliest efforts at state multiculturalism—now seen as having strengthened ethnic identities and allowed parallel societies to flourish on Western soil. The events of 9/11, in other words, hardened the emerging bipolar worldview because it raised the stakes: it was not just that Muslim immigrants seemed potentially incompatible with Western society; now they posed a security threat to the very existence of Europe itself.

Very quickly, arguments against multiculturalism became more strident and stark. Ayaan Hirsi Ali, for instance, published *The Caged Virgin* just a few years later. While her immediate target was what she characterized as the oppressive nature of Islamic sexual morality, she ultimately issued a sweeping condemnation of Islam as a totalizing worldview.

"The basic principles of traditional Islam," wrote Hirsi Ali, "clash with the elementary values and standards of Western society. . . . I argue that the Islamic faith lends itself more than any other to the preservation of premodern customs and traditions."[113] These "fossilized religious concepts," she asserted, prevented Muslim immigrants from integrating successfully in the Netherlands.[114] Hirsi Ali rejected Dutch policies that she said granted Muslims special privileges and allowed them to preserve their orthodox mentality. Drawing sharp lines between a premodern Islamic tradition and Western emancipation, she popularized and legitimized an emerging view of Muslim culture as antithetical to the fundamental tenets of liberalism—especially its valorization of individual freedom.

At the same time, Hirsi Ali explicitly tied Muslim women's oppression to this "clash of civilizations." Because of Islam's "patriarchal mentality and culture of shame," she maintained, Muslim men insisted on controlling every aspect of women's sexuality, stripping Muslim women of their basic right to self-determination. This emphasis on the status of women, as we have seen, provided those on the left (especially feminists) and on the right with something on which these traditional foes could agree. In the context of a struggle between civilizations, sexual democracy now served as the crucial line in the sand. For feminists and other leftists, safeguarding women's rights increasingly became a zero-sum choice, with personal freedoms now counterpoised against tolerance for cultural difference. Sexual liberty represented the outer limit for how much diversity Western feminists were willing to accept. For conservatives (at least in Europe), by contrast, the categorical demand that ethnic minority groups respect individual freedom ultimately required them to extend that same notion of liberty to women and questions of sexuality. Sexual freedom, both sides thus affirmed, had to be preserved as a core value of liberalism. It was precisely this calculus between embracing homosexuality—one form of sexual freedom—and rejecting intolerant Islamic culture that fueled the remarkable rise of Dutch politician Pim Fortuyn in 2002. A similar set of concerns informed the blunt presentation of Dutch culture laid out in the Netherlands' naturalization procedure, as well as the citizenship test questions proposed in 2005 by the German states of Hesse and Baden-Württemberg.

Increasingly, rejections of state multiculturalism began to extend beyond conservative quarters. David Goodhart, the left-liberal British journalist and director of the think tank Demos, raised this fundamental question in his hotly debated 2004 *Prospect* magazine essay "Too Diverse?" Goodhart started from the premise of the liberal left's commitment to the comprehensive welfare state, which provided generous social support paid out of a progressive tax system. Quoting the British Conservative politician David Willetts, he observed: "The basis on which you can extract large sums of money in tax and pay it out in benefits is that most people think the recipients are people like themselves. . . . If values become more diverse, if lifestyles become more differentiated, then it becomes more difficult to sustain the legitimacy of a universal risk-pooling welfare state."[115] The "progressive dilemma," argued Goodhart, was that "sharing and solidarity" can conflict with "diversity."[116] For too long, he claimed, the liberal left had supported diversity, while ignoring the "self-evident truth" that large-scale immigration eroded the bonds of mutual obligation. Specifically, he proposed that "the laissez-faire approach of the postwar period in which ethnic minority citizens were not encouraged to join the common culture should be buried. Citizenship ceremonies, language lessons and the mentoring of new citizens should help create a British version of the old US melting pot. This third way on identity can be distinguished from the coercive assimilationism of the nationalist right, which rejects any element of foreign culture, and from multiculturalism, which rejects common culture."[117] Here, Goodhart blamed the government's poor management of immigration, suggesting that its hands-off approach to tolerance had failed to push newcomers to "join the common culture."

In the heated debated that followed, the black British journalist, Labour politician, and chairman of the Commission for Racial Equality Trevor Phillips scathingly rebuked Goodhart. Phillips accused his fellow left liberal of peddling what appeared to be a progressive argument against immigration, but was actually "genteel xenophobia."[118] "If today's immigrants were white people from the old Commonwealth," he charged, "Goodhart and his friends would say they pose no threat because they share Anglo-Saxon values. They may not even object to Anglophile Indians—as long as they aren't Muslims."[119] The defense of welfare state provisions thus masked a troubling liberal racism. But Phillips took his criticism even further. He put his finger on an undeveloped yet crucial implication in Goodhart's assertion that "as Britain becomes more diverse common culture is being eroded."[120] Phillips ultimately suggested that Goodhart's critique betrayed a "wilting commitment to multiethnic Britain"—in other words, serious doubts about multiculturalism as on-the-ground diversity.

Just three months later, however, Phillips issued his own condemnation of multiculturalism that echoed many of the earlier minority critiques such those leveled by Sivanandan. The real question, he insisted, was how to "manage the process of integrating migrants."[121] Phillips characterized multiculturalism as "celebrating diversity," but accused the approach of "ignoring inequality" and suggested that this strategy "inevitably leads to the nightmare of entrenched segregation."[122] For Phillips, state-sponsored multiculturalism recognized—and even celebrated—differences, but failed to provide meaningful redistribution of economic resources and opportunities. Indeed, it effectively reinforced institutional racism.

In the aftermath of the 2005 London bombings, however, Phillips moved in a different direction. Multiculturalism, he now maintained, had allowed Islamist extremism to grow unchecked in British society. In this context, multiculturalism was not simply facile and superficial. More problematically, it was an engine of immigrant isolation. The fact that the London bombers were born and raised in Britain only proved that multiculturalism had gone awry. Britain, Phillips ominously warned, is "sleepwalking to segregation."[123] To combat this dangerous drift, he called for "a new emphasis on integrating minorities to 'British values.' "[124] These included "some simple truths that should bind us together": "an attachment to democracy, freedom of speech, and equality."[125]

This emphasis on shared values, in fact, became a central component of the revised approach to immigrants that liberal Labour Prime Minister Tony Blair adopted after 7/7. In a major policy speech titled "The Duty to Integrate," Blair continued to endorse the basic idea of social heterogeneity. "We like our diversity," he stated. But Blair also insisted that "when it comes to our essential values—belief in democracy, the rule of law, tolerance, equal treatment for all, respect for this country and its shared heritage— . . . that is where we come together, it is what we hold in common. It is what gives us the right to call ourselves British. At that point no distinctive culture or religion supersedes our duty to be part of an integrated United Kingdom."[126] While Blair was not prepared to repudiate "multicultural Britain," he made clear that no social blueprint for multiculturalism—be it recognition of cultural differences, granting of minority rights, or laissez-faire coexistence—should take precedence over the full acceptance of British common values.

Death Knell for Multiculturalism

By the time Merkel, Cameron, and Sarkozy delivered their sweeping pronouncements, the putative failure of multiculturalism in Europe had been well established. These declarations, however, raised the discourse to a new level: the three were speaking, after all, as the leaders of the most powerful nations in Europe. Their statements lent authority (and visibility) to the growing conviction that multiculturalism was simply unworkable for European society in the twenty-first century. But what exactly did this mean? Unworkable, how? Significantly, when Merkel spoke of multiculturalism as an "absolute failure," she also acknowledged that the number of young people with a "migration background" was increasing, not decreasing. She reminded her audience that "we as a country brought guest workers to Germany at the beginning of the 1960s."[127] "For a while," she admitted, "we kidded ourselves. We said they won't stay, at some point they will go. This is not the reality. And of course the tendency was: let's be 'multikulti' and live next to each other and enjoy being together, but this concept has failed, utterly failed." Especially striking here was Merkel's acknowledgment of Germany's own role in creating the conditions for postwar diversity and in perpetuating the myth that the new diversity was merely "temporary." The German chancellor was admitting some responsibility for the lack of a more coordinated and energetic *national* response to the demographic realities on the ground.

And yet Merkel's retrospective portrayal of "multiculturalism" as the very essence of that nonengagement—an ad hoc response based on tolerance rather than concrete policy making—was in many respects a caricature. She offered glib descriptions of a "multikulti" coexistence that neglected the more serious work of socialization and cultivation of liberal values that multiculturalism, at its best, had involved. Particularly troublesome, she seemed to suggest, was the naïve celebration of cultural differences and the way it had fostered an unmanaged approach to life in a diverse nation. Implicit throughout her speech was a new and tougher approach to dealing with immigrants. "Those who want to have a part in our society," she explained, "must not only obey our laws and know the constitution, they must above all learn our language." And from there, she turned to the familiar tropes of language, schools, and girls: "It is right that a language test be taken in union-governed states. It is important that students who go to school understand their teachers. . . . And it is, without question, important and right to say that young girls must attend school field trips and participate in gym classes, and that we do not believe in forced marriages—they are not compatible with our laws." In this formulation, successful management of social diversity required immigrants to meet a concrete set of demands: facility in German, full participation of girls in civic life, and equality within marriages—issues linked in the popular imagination almost exclusively with Muslim Turks. Muslim Turks' shortcomings in these areas, Merkel implied, reinforced their isolation from mainstream German society and left them outside German law. Merkel now proposed a more one-way model of integration, demanding that guest workers and their descendants adjust to norms and values explicitly marked as German (or European). Ethnic distinctiveness, in this view, had to yield to a single *Leitkultur* (dominant culture). For the chancellor, any hint of integration based on the mutual recognition of cultural differences (or the reciprocal transformation thereof) was over. The larger approach here was not an argument against diversity so much as a set of ultimatums that represented a new vision for preventing illiberal values and practices from gaining ground in the Federal Republic.

British Prime Minister David Cameron picked up on some of these themes, but now framed his pronouncements (which came a few months later) more explicitly in terms of Islamist extremism and the threat of homegrown terrorism. Delivering his first major policy speech as prime minister at an international security conference in Munich, Cameron assailed the very notion of state multiculturalism as encouragement for "different cultures to live separate lives, apart from each other and apart from the mainstream."[128] Because of this, he argued, "we've even tolerated . . . segregated communities behaving in ways that run completely counter to our values." "When a white person holds objectionable views, racist views," Cameron explained, "we rightly condemn them. But when equally unacceptable views or practices come from someone who isn't white, we've been too cautious frankly— frankly, even fearful—to stand up to them." Like Merkel, Cameron pointed to "forced marriage" as an example of just such a practice. But instead of simply pronouncing this custom illegal (as the German chancellor did), the British prime minister was more aggressive.

"This hands-off tolerance," he claimed, "has only served to reinforce the sense that not enough is shared. And all this leaves some young Muslims feeling rootless. And the search for something to belong to and something to believe in can lead them to this extremist ideology." "For sure," Cameron continued, "they don't turn into terrorists overnight. What we see is a process of radicalization." In this view,

multiculturalism did not simply foster atomization or isolation among second- and third-generation British Muslims. It also promoted a "hands-off tolerance" that weakened
any notion of a common British culture. For young people who lacked any sense of broader "connection," Cameron
concluded, this process opened the door to new forms of
extremism that, whether through Internet chatrooms or radical mosques, offered alternative forms of belonging. Or
to put it another way, the putative failure of multiculturalism had sowed the seeds for homegrown terrorists.

In response, Cameron proposed a new model of "muscular liberalism," one that would "enforce the values of equality,
law and freedom of speech across all parts of society."[129] He
warned that European governments should be "shrewder in
dealing with those that, while not violent, are in some cases
part of the problem."[130] In this vein, Cameron pledged to
withhold state funding from all Muslim groups that encouraged community isolation or refused to endorse women's
rights. He further argued that Britain and other European
countries must forswear "passive tolerance" in favor of an
"unambiguous" and "hard-nosed defence" of our fundamental "liberties," including freedom of speech, freedom of worship, democracy, the rule of law, and equal rights regardless
of race, sex, or sexuality.[131]

For French President Nicolas Sarkozy, the occasion to
weigh in on these issues came when he appeared on the television channel TF1's political issues show *Paroles des Français*
less than a week after Cameron's speech. In the course of the
program, the moderator posed a question that had been submitted to the station by a viewer online: "Do you not find
multiculturalism a failure and the origin of many problems
of our society?"[132] One plausible response here, of course,
would have been for Sarkozy to point out that state multiculturalism was not applicable in France. According to its

own laws and governing principles, French policy toward its population with immigrant backgrounds was based on republican values, an approach that demanded assimilation to a singular culture through a shared language, history, and political ideology. Sarkozy might have insisted, as well, that multiculturalism was a uniquely Anglo-American concept, one deeply flawed because it creates a society riven by ethnic conflicts. The French state, he might have concluded, had, since at least the early 1980s, consistently rejected this approach.

Instead, and instructively, Sarkozy chose to respond to this question as if multiculturalism *did*, in fact, exist in France. Indeed, both the question itself and Sarkozy's energetic engagement with it suggested that everyone at TF1 perceived multiculturalism as a reality of French society, one that was already producing clear effects. For the president, as for the questioner, these effects were clearly negative. "Yes, it is a failure," he answered.[133] "In all our democracies," he claimed, speaking expansively for Europe, "we are too concerned about the identity of those who arrived and not enough about the identity of the country that welcomed them."[134] Addressing the French situation in particular, Sarkozy insisted, "We do not want a society" where communities simply "coexist next to each other. If you come to France, you agree to melt into a single community, the national community. If you do not accept this, don't come to France."[135] For Sarkozy, the lesson was clear: assimilation to French life required immigrants to surrender their distinct cultures and practices in the name of a greater national community.

Here, then, were three versions of an obituary for European multiculturalism, at once distinctive in their points of emphasis, but also convergent in their broader logics. For Merkel, multiculturalism's social blueprint had failed to establish clear guidelines for dealing with immigrants whose practices were at odds with German liberal values. For Cameron, it promoted a "hands-off" tolerance that produced isolated minority communities, allowed core British principles to languish, and encouraged homegrown extremists. For Sarkozy, it undermined French republican identity, a vision of national cohesion that relied on indistinguishable individual citizens.

Yet, arguably, these were three versions of the same basic position. In each case, they demanded integration and offered strict stipulations about what that looked like. Each called for assimilation without compromise. Above all, they insisted on a new and more aggressive (or in Cameron's terms "muscular") brand of "liberalism" to defend European ways of life. The three leaders, that is, asserted a recommitment to liberal values, underscoring the primacy of individual freedom, especially in relation to gender and sexual relations. These statements effectively drew a line in the sand. Liberalism, each leader suggested, had to be defended at all costs. The very survival of European society was at stake.

The Future of Multicultural Europe?

Given the longer history we have just considered, it may be that multiculturalism has outlasted its usefulness as a viable blueprint for Western European societies. The term has been saddled with criticism—both thoughtful and spurious—from every imaginable political quarter. The sheer weight of these condemnations may simply be too difficult to lay aside or overcome. Even commentators who are committed to "lived multiculture" in Europe have urged its abandonment, and some have offered alternative concepts such as conviviality.[1] At the end of the day, however, such calls for abandonment raise a number of urgent questions: What exactly do Europeans imagine as a replacement for multiculturalism? How will they come to terms with multiethnic diversity moving forward? What will be the grounds on which such a negotiation can take place? Do Europeans possess the determination to build strong and peaceful societies together with their long-resident immigrant populations?

Certainly, the death knell pronouncements by Angela Merkel, David Cameron, and Nicolas Sarkozy offered one

vision of multiculturalism's successor—what Cameron so
vividly described as a "muscular liberalism," a commitment
to protect the shared liberal values that ostensibly define
the European way of life. Such a vision, as we have seen, had
been crystallizing over the course of a decade. Raised to a
national priority under three conservative leaders, this alternative was not the exclusive preserve of the right. In fact, it
was championed across the political spectrum, including by
liberals, feminists, and others on the left.

Significantly, there was widespread agreement on what
constituted the core common values—namely, individual
freedom and sexual democracy. Yet this is a highly specific
conception of liberalism, one that subsumes other liberal
values such as democracy, equality, and pluralism under the
first principle of personal liberty and its extension into the
domains of gender and sexuality. This vision of liberalism
has played a dual role in the crisis of European multiculturalism. It served as the ground on which the critique of pluralism played out, becoming the lingua franca of multiculturalism's myriad critics. And it simultaneously provided
the model to replace the now discredited social blueprint.

These specific liberal values, then, have become the crucial criteria for deciding who is included in what historian
David Hollinger has called the "circle of we."[2] "How wide
the circle of 'we'?" is *the* great question in an age of ethnos-
centered discourse," according to Hollinger's account of
multiculturalism in the United States.[3] But in an ironic
twist, this circle, once defined by the narrower criteria of
ethnicity and culture, is now determined by adherence to
supposedly universalist liberal principles. What do "we" Europeans owe immigrants who don't follow "our" liberal values? Should "they" have access to "our" welfare provisions?
Should "they" be allowed to remain in "our" democratic
societies? By writing off multiculturalism, Europeans have

reduced a complicated discussion about how to deal with ethnic and cultural diversity to a simplistic demand that Muslim immigrants adopt liberal values as the crucial precondition for inclusion in European society. In this way, the convergence that I've been tracing is much more than just a common critique; it is also an attempt to define something new—a shared fault line (that is, sanctioned by the right and the left), which is ultimately reinforced at the levels of both policy and ideology by pronouncements that multiculturalism has failed.

Here we must acknowledge the slippage between different efforts to uphold and promote liberal values. Conservatives tend to see these values as belonging exclusively to European civilization, an expression of European culture in its highest form; whereas liberals emphasize the universalistic aspects of these values, which—they maintain—have proven to be the most egalitarian and progressive basis for organizing society and which are theoretically available to all. But precisely because the European rejection of multiculturalism has been articulated through a common reassertion of liberal values, these important differences between a more exclusionary position and the more inclusive, classically liberal one have been blurred.

There is a further paradox in the collective push to defend liberal values as Europe's common core. The whole ethos of liberalism rests on the principle of individual freedom: the individual needs to be free to decide how best to live and realize his or her full potential.[4] This disposition privileges single citizens over communal groups (according to the traditional liberal critique of communitarian multiculturalism), but it also stresses a hands-off approach to governing the individual and society. Liberalism, in the classic version, typically meant that the state's authority was limited: individuals had to be free to exercise their moral autonomy, just as the market had to be free to regulate itself. But with the shared European conviction that liberal values require safeguarding, multiculturalism has been held up as an example of laissez-faire policy gone awry. In accepting a multicultural approach to dealing with immigrants, that is, European states failed to insist on shared principles and a common culture—or at the very least, to set basic limits on cultural tolerance. Misled by the liberal respect for individual freedoms, these countries allowed immigrants to settle without any real regulation and standards, enabling retrograde ethnic cultures to run amok and flourish. The lack of strong state intervention inadvertently facilitated a weakening and deterioration of the shared liberal core.

Perhaps the groundswell of criticism directed at the possibility of state-sponsored multiculturalism since the Rushdie affair has made it impossible to return to older notions of pluralism, at least within their conventional parameters. But giving up on pluralism itself in the name of holding the line on individual freedom has come with some serious costs. This is particularly true for the left, since it is among left liberals that the shift has been most dramatic. While those on the right have been consistent in their opposition to immigration, diversity, and multiculturalism, those on the left have a long history of tolerance vis-à-vis immigrants and have often championed pluralism as a way to fight racism and cultural prejudice. For leftists, then, the conclusion that multiculturalism is now antithetical to personal freedom has resulted in a major renunciation of some of their core commitments and political foundations.

Of course, most self-identified European leftists would never describe this transition in such starkly ideological terms. Instead, as we have seen, they might argue that the encroaching threats posed by Muslim culture to individual liberty forced a new kind of "tough-mindedness" on questions of coexistence and tolerance across multiple forms of differ-ence. Less often acknowledged, however, is that these recent threshold tests around the protection of individual freedoms have involved a major reordering of left-liberal values. In the wake of the Second World War, culture assumed a special importance for leftists and liberals, particularly once the magnitude of Nazi racial crimes became clear with the Holo-caust. Conceptualizing cultures as both mutable and relativis-tic presented a useful way to challenge the category of race— and especially the legitimacy of scientific racism—because doing so offered a more fluid understanding of human dif-ference. Whereas race had denoted "biological differences" understood as permanent (and thereby bolstered theories of inferiority and superiority), culture pointed to "historically or socially constructed differences," which contained fewer connotations of permanent hierarchical distinctions."[5] The mid-twentieth-century convention that every culture oper-ates according to its own specific logics—and, by extension, that no culture is simply superior or inferior to any other— was an insight crucial for dismantling older ideologies of ra-cial inequality, colonialism, and Social Darwinism. The values of cultural pluralism and relativism thus played vital roles in combating efforts to denigrate social groups deemed cul-turally different, strange, or foreign.

In the wake of postwar migrations, however, the pitfalls of deploying culture in these ways became clearer. First and foremost, replacing biological explanations of difference with cultural ones did not necessarily disable the basic assump-tions of racialist thinking. The new emphasis on culture as opposed to biology may have softened some of the hierar-chical aspects of previous forms of racialist thinking, but it did little to block the impulse to divide according to indel-ible differences. Culture, in other words, was also suscepti-ble to particularist interpretations and exclusivist agendas.

In Enoch Powell's vision, for instance, English culture de-noted a common past and set of traditions to which West Indians and Asians could never lay claim, even if they were British citizens. Similarly, Jean-Marie LePen was able to turn Algerians' demands that the French state acknowledge their "right to difference" into an exclusionary right of the French to be French. But even well-meaning advocates of multicul-turalism—including municipal governments and school dis-tricts in Britain—often treated cultures as unique and self-contained, as isolated traditions, practices, or beliefs that were passed down from one generation to the next.[6]

The growing emphasis on culture, moreover, tended to push the semantics of political struggle toward the recogni-tion and preservation of difference. Since each culture was understood to operate according to its own specific princi-ples, the logical focus of politics became the championing of differential rights for different groups. Indeed, some of the first multicultural campaigns in Britain revolved around granting special provisions for the unique religious and cultural customs of ethnic minorities. As early as 1969, for example, Sikh bus drivers won the right to wear turbans while on duty in the British city of Wolverhampton. But for some minority activists, this culturalist bent proved in-creasingly problematic because it drew attention and en-ergy away from broader social and economic inequalities. In Britain, for example, the antiracism activist Sivanandan provocatively declared himself a "heretic," "a disbeliever in the efficacy of ethnic policies and programmes to alter, by one iota, the monumental and endemic racism of [British] society" that often structured material conditions and re-sulted in unequal social services.[7]

For other critics, the emphasis on differential rights en-couraged immigrants to highlight the inequalities between ethnic minority groups, rather than focus on common concerns or struggles. This was especially true in Britain once the first forms of multicultural policy making began to tie financial resources and political power to ethnic identities.[8] In contrast to the mid-1970s British antiracist movement, which fostered cooperation among Asians, West Indians, and white leftists, these efforts at multiculturalism through local governments offered powerful incentives to organize around ethnicity and culture—and, in the process, helped freeze those very identities and communities in place.[9] A focus on culture, in short, could and did prove both isolating and divisive in actual practice.

The other crucial lesson here was culture's potential to inadvertently serve as an engine of homogeneity, emphasizing cohesion and sameness within ethnic groups. Reflexive celebrations of cultural tolerance (or cultural differences) sometimes had the practical effect of obscuring the specific needs of individuals (or subgroups like women) within ethnic minority communities. The Birmingham City Council, for instance, developed policies that "treated minority communities as homogeneous wholes, ignoring conflicts within those communities."[10] An internal report admitted as much, stating "the perceived notion of the homogeneity of minority ethnic communities" created "an over-reliance on individuals who are seen to represent the needs and views of the whole community and thus resulted in simplistic approaches to tackling community needs."[11]

Given these lessons of the 1980s, then, it is not especially surprising that many self-described leftists began to rethink the reflexive celebration of cultural differences and turned instead to the protection of personal freedoms within liberal democratic society. And yet, just as with the turn to culture, the unqualified promotion of freedom has come with its own unintended consequences. If the Enlightenment emphasis on human reason and dignity gave rise to the call for individual self-determination and rights as a potentially universal project, the recent efforts to champion personal liberty have been less broadly applicable. For one thing, many critics of multiculturalism who defended individual freedom did not just hold up this value as a principle worthy of general embrace, but claimed it as the unique inheritance of European civilization. Implicit here was the belief that Enlightenment values defined a specific group of people—Europeans—and were thus less immediately accessible or desirable to others, especially Muslims. This was precisely the sort of argument made by various groups of European conservatives from the late 1980s on; more surprising was the ease with which many self-described European liberals also jumped on the bandwagon.[12] In the Netherlands, for example, Ian Buruma has pointed to a pattern of Dutch "leftists," "embittered by what they saw as the failure of multiculturalism, or fired up by the anticlericalism of their revolutionary past," who subsequently "joined conservatives in the battle for the Enlightenment."[13] In this way, some on the left have turned what historically were emancipatory, democratic values to a more particularist—and even exclusionary—purpose. With the willingness of such critics to make "personal freedom" a badge of tribal attachment, the liberal left effectively ceded the ground from which to challenge the growing sense of civilizational struggle between an enlightened West and retrograde Muslim populations within its borders.

In so doing, however, these left constituencies have largely given up their role as a progressive vanguard in relation to immigration and social tolerance—one that long pushed Western European societies to live up to their own stated ideals. If the whole point of insisting on the primacy of the individual was to assert that all humans are free and equal and ought to be judged on their own merits, Muslims have certainly not enjoyed the benefits of such consideration in recent debates. As we have seen, a crucial strategy in arguing for the failure of multiculturalism has been to treat Muslims as a monolithic group. European feminists, for example, have often been quick to assume that the plight of the specific Muslim women they encountered represented the predicament of all Muslim women. And if all Muslim women suffered from patriarchal oppression, then it followed that Muslim culture, as a whole, sanctioned the circumscription of women's freedoms and rights, more generally.

Much of the broader discourse of multiculturalism's putative failure, in other words, has framed the choice between individual freedom and cultural pluralism in zero-sum terms: either one tolerates cultural differences and succors illiberal values, or one defends freedom and dispenses with cultural tolerance. But what is perhaps most problematic about this framework was that it treated the meaning of freedom as self-evident and fixed (as freedom writ large), even though it actually relied on a very particular definition of the concept. The vision of Western European freedom that began to emerge during the 1980s put the individual first, and had as its goal maximum self-determination for each citizen. It prized, above all, freedom of expression and freedom of choice. Indeed, these were precisely the values that both European leftists and conservatives identified as inviolable in the Rushdie and headscarf affairs.

Historically, however, other notions of freedom have often been in play. As recently as the immediate postwar period, European leaders across the political spectrum agreed that freedom from want was a top priority for rebuilding their states and societies. In the wake of catastrophic war, many shared the idea that ordinary people—not just the privileged few—should be free from worry about how to keep a roof over their heads, put food on the table, provide for their families, and educate their children. This notion of freedom prioritized the many—the social collective—and was willing to set aside the absolute rights of individuals in order to achieve freedom for the whole. These ideas relate to the criticism made by the economist Karl Polanyi of the liberal tendency to reduce the concept of freedom to a free market. For Polanyi, the basic problem with this definition is that it offers freedom only to the "comfortable classes," failing to acknowledge the predatory effects of a market economy on the rest of society.[14] As an alternative, Polanyi proposed a broader-based definition of freedom, one that relied on a rather different set of tools for its achievement: "The passing of market-economy can become the beginning of an era of unprecedented freedom. Juridical and actual freedom can be made wider and more general than ever before: regulation and control can achieve freedom not only for the few, but for all. Freedom not as an appurtenance of privilege . . . , but as a prescriptive right extending far beyond the narrow confines of the political sphere into the intimate organization of society itself. . . . Such a society can afford to be both just and free."[15] The point here is not to question the importance of individual freedom as a cornerstone of liberal democracy, but rather to suggest that other notions of freedom have largely been erased in the recent rush to hold the line against the putative illiberalism of certain groups of postwar immigrants. Ultimately, the zero-sum logic of such arguments against multiculturalism pushed the liberal left to accept an individually centered conception of freedom. This logic obscured the fact that freedom and social solidarity have been able to coexist—albeit in a relational tension—at other moments in Western history. In this way, many European leftists unwittingly abandoned their previous commitments to the more collective and pluralist notions of freedom that had guided their politics across the twentieth century.

———

At the end of the day, we turn to history to provide us with critical lessons and tools for self-reflection. In that spirit, I close with some conclusions about what the history of European multiculturalism might teach us as we ponder an uncertain future. In so doing, I also offer some parameters for a more robust political engagement with diversity, one consistent with Europe's professed commitment to democratic inclusion and equality.

It should be clear by now that simply declaring multiculturalism a failure is supremely unhelpful. While various commentators have made acute and thought-provoking criticisms of multiculturalism over several decades, blanket declarations of its demise have too often served to elide the demographic realities that have transformed Europe over the past seventy years. In this respect, the statements made by Merkel, Cameron, and Sarkozy in 2010 and 2011 were profoundly blind—perhaps willfully so—to the social realities of their countries. A major implication of their claims that multiculturalism had failed—and the one that has received the most traction in the international press—is that cultural diversity is simply unworkable in Europe. But the basic fact is this: the multicultural populations that exist in Europe are not going away. In Britain, France, and Germany, people with non-European backgrounds have put down deep roots. This diversity is readily apparent in cities, big and small. It is there on the streets and in the subways, visible in countless restaurants and public markets. It is also increasingly manifest in commercial media and mass entertainment. Every Western European national football team now boasts key

players of immigrant heritage, just as news presenters are
no longer uniformly white. One can see the shifts, as well,
in television programming such as the highly popular German show *Turkish for Beginners*; or in prominent theatrical
productions such as *The Big Life* (about the *Empire Windrush*) in London's West End; or in critically acclaimed cultural performance venues such as Ballhaus Naunynstraße in
Berlin's Kreuzberg. There is now a museum devoted to the
history of immigration in Paris, as well as a documentation
center and museum of migration in Cologne. In politics,
too, immigrants are members of the Houses of Lords and
Commons; represent constituencies in the Bundestag, the
French National Assembly, and European Parliament; and
have led major parties like the German Greens. Former colonials, guest workers, refugees, and their descendants, in
short, are now woven into virtually every aspect of European public life.[16]

The motors driving this heterogeneity, of course, are not
simply a thing of the past. Although European governments
closed their borders to unskilled labor migrants decades ago,
non-Europeans continue to arrive. Over the course of 2015–
16, thousands upon thousands of Syrian refugees landed in
Southeastern Europe and made their way northwest. This
most recent refugee crisis—with masses of people trying to
reach the European Union by boat, truck, train, and foot—
has forced its member states to allow more than a million
migrants to enter their countries and apply for asylum. Western European leaders have grudgingly done so, with only
Merkel affirming the EU's obligation to accept refugees and
establishing an open-door policy to Germany. But this hes-
itant welcome has come under the guise of responding to a
"humanitarian" crisis. Such a framework emphasizes the al-
truism of Western values, even as it dodges crucial questions.
The status of the diverse populations already resident in

those countries, the effective integration of refugees, and the broader impacts of these new arrivals remain issues of life-and-death significance, which are only partially addressed within the more comfortable rubric of "humanitarian" considerations. Even with the benefit of historical hindsight, avoiding serious and hard public discussion of the long-term social consequences of the European migration crisis has thus far remained the political strategy of choice.

What history has taught us, however, is that collective disavowal of demographic facts and political silence on matters of policy actually create the conditions for a far more destructive set of outcomes. Just as the postwar German taboo against race did not eliminate racialized thinking and the French state's refusal to acknowledge color did not prevent the development of significant social inequality along racial lines,[17] so simply pronouncing multiculturalism over has not erased the social pressures of lived diversity. Nor has disavowal provided practical strategies for a more democratic and equitable model of coexistence. Indeed, one might argue that this lack of leadership from European heads of state has in fact made the necessary work of debating questions of ethnic and cultural diversity all the more difficult. In renouncing multiculturalism, political authorities essentially discredited the lone concept that had been used to "publicly manifest the significance of" cultural diversity.[18]

In this respect, the broader dismissal of multiculturalism has been profoundly undemocratic. On the one hand, it has silenced those people and groups who were figured as part of the multicultural fabric itself. Declaring multiculturalism "dead" is a way of white Britons, Germans, and French telling immigrants, "We don't recognize you; you aren't a part of our society." Such blanket dismissals deny immigrants a legitimate place in European society and effectively refuse them any status as social and political actors. It writes them out of the debate by ignoring their presence. In this sense, such patterns of disavowal are not a naïve oversight. Rather, for immigrants who have lived in Europe for many generations now, they constitute something closer to ideological violence and raise the specter of social apartheid.

In practical terms, the shared presumption that multiculturalism is a failure has also largely terminated meaningful debate about how to manage diversity through concrete forms of policy making. Regardless of how one assesses previous iterations of multiculturalism and its policy forms, the concept itself opened up a space in which to grapple with the place of immigrants and their cultural differences. What had been more of a discussion—albeit, one often fraught with political hyperbole and by no means fully representative—has now become, in a best-case scenario, a series of "hard-nosed" and "muscular" demands for integration issued by European leaders to their Muslim immigrant populations. By declaring multiculturalism moribund, the possibility for contemplating and wrestling with more inclusive or open-ended conceptions of European society has largely been taken off the table. Indeed, this is precisely what makes the present moment so disturbing: there is no argument, no debate, no discussion about how best to move forward. In part, this is because the left has relinquished much of the ground of previous debates. But the elimination of this contested political space also sends a deeply troubling message. It suggests to immigrants that Europeans are highly selective in their application of "liberal" values. They profess democracy, but deny open (or even any) debate when it comes to problematic issues like how to coexist with their ethnic minorities.

How, then, might we begin to envision a more effective politics around European diversity? What are some of the necessary conditions for a more productive engagement to take place? The first condition, it seems to me, involves recognizing that—whatever we choose to call it—the political, cultural, and discursive space opened up by the "multicultural question" must resonate within the public sphere for European democracy to function properly. In this respect, it is actually important that multiculturalism existed as a *contested* political idea. This contest created the possibility of those perspectives most easily ignored or elided becoming visible to society at large. It made the boundaries of national belonging an open question that could be sorted through and argued over. Whatever its flaws, in short, multiculturalism raised issues that had been considered "closed and settled," pointing toward new definitions of what it might entail to be British, French, German, or Dutch.[19] As critics across the political spectrum have argued, multiculturalism has been a hugely imperfect instrument for such purposes, often failing adequately to represent a broader range of minority voices or acknowledge the complexity of immigrant politics. But the very fact that it generated such critiques suggests its significance as a discursive space. Indeed, it was only in the criticism of policies defined as multicultural that the ground for something more inclusive started to become visible or even thinkable. This was the crucial insight of British sociologist Stuart Hall, who was all too aware of the various deficiencies of the earliest efforts at state-sponsored multiculturalism at the level of local government. What Hall recognized was that the "multicultural question" was ultimately essential to European democracy because it opened up a terrain of debate that otherwise would likely have remained closed.

A second condition for more effective engagement involves an insistently historical perspective. There is no doubt that the values of liberty and equality must be the starting point for any effort to foster democratic debate in relation to social diversity. These values were hard-won. And of course, they have done enormous work in guaranteeing a broader equity of rights and treatment since they were first developed in the context of the Enlightenment. But we cannot simply return to some originalist conception of Enlightenment individualism, as Ayaan Hirsi Ali and Kenan Malik have suggested.[20] As a half century of critical historical scholarship has demonstrated, the Enlightenment valorization of liberal man and his ability to reason also justified self-interested and hugely destructive European colonial and imperial projects. Indeed, in many instances, it authorized a belief in the fundamental inequality of humanity advanced through scientific racism and ideologies of conquest.

But just as we cannot unself-consciously reaffirm liberty and equality in a vacuum, neither can we cling to a blind, unreconstructed celebration of pluralism and cultural relativism. Cultural pluralist arguments played a crucial role in legitimizing the idea that different groups of people should have the right to express their identities, explore their own histories, and pursue their own lifestyles free of social exclusion or cultural prejudice. They recognized the "complexities of attachment, belongingness and identity" that inhere in community cultures.[21] This pluralistic vision, moreover, went a long way to exposing the unspoken ethnocentrism of a putatively neutral (and universalistic), European liberalism. Yet the initial efforts to implement state policies of multiculturalism in the 1980s and 1990s produced their own dangers. The celebration of ethnicity in its absolutist forms tended to reify cultures as monolithic and unchanging, often relied on conservative representatives of diverse communities to speak for the whole, and at times led to the policing of disagreement.[22] As Hall noted in the midst of these fights, "we cannot enfranchise the claims of community cultures and norms over individuals without at the same time expanding—not ideally but in practice—the right of individuals as bearers of rights to dissent from, exit from and oppose if necessary their communities of origin."[23] What a historical perspective makes clear, in short, is that we need to uphold both liberal conceptions of individual freedom *and* pluralistic communitarianism. Each acts as a check on the excesses of the other.

A final condition for more effective social and political engagement with European diversity is democracy itself. The half-century-long history of the rise and fall of multiculturalism suggests, above all, that it is well past time for European states to get serious about their democratic principles. Meaningful democracy is (of course) an ongoing and often maddeningly difficult project, not something that can be achieved once and for all. But for European nations as they currently exist to live up to these principles, they must first embrace a radical reorientation in their patterns of collective understanding and self-representation. Across the continent, country by country, Europe's population is undeniably multiethnic—and is becoming more so by the day. This is true of not only those nations that relied upon former colonials and guest workers to fuel the postwar economic boom (Great Britain, France, Germany, the Benelux states, the Scandinavian countries), but also nations that traditionally sent workers abroad (Italy, Spain, Greece, the Balkan states). Such on-the-ground diversity can no longer be dismissed as an anomaly, a temporary phenomenon, or the unintended consequence of national resiliency and economic miracles. One might argue, in fact, that it is simply irresponsible for European states to continue to allow significant segments of their populations to be driven by nostalgia for homogeneity. There is no longer room to pretend that European countries will return to some imagined, idealized state of ethnic and cultural sameness. To continue to do so is to condone and ultimately perpetuate the perception of immigrants as aliens, interlopers, and enemies.

At the same time, it is important to recognize that simply acknowledging multicultural diversity does not ensure any particular political outcome. The United States is the most obvious example here. Americans have described their country as a "nation of immigrants" since at least the late nineteenth century. National self-conceptions of the United States as multiethnic have long been invoked by political leaders, public figures, and ordinary folk. Still, in the process of writing this epilogue, the newly elected president—now standard-bearer of the mainstream Republican Party—orchestrated a successful campaign that included a promise to build a wall along the US border with Mexico. Most recently, he issued an executive order to suspend the Syrian refugee program and ban the entry of people from seven Muslim-majority countries. The bedrock notion that most Americans were immigrants at some point provides an important basis on which to challenge policies of border restrictions and contest this president's vision of national belonging. But it is hardly a guarantee of progressive results.

Even this basic recognition of shared histories and lived diversity, however, is still missing in a majority of European countries. The British, as we have seen, have been the most willing to acknowledge the postwar complexities of their demographics. Roy Jenkins alluded to this view in his 1966 efforts to advocate integration; Michael Swann stated it explicitly in his 1985 promotion of multicultural education; and Bhikhu Parekh made it a defining characteristic of the nation in his 2000 assessment of the future of multiethnic Britain. Yet since 2001, even the British have become more suspicious of any politics linked to multiculturalism. Meanwhile, most French leaders have remained steadfastly insistent on a cultural homogeneity based on republican universalism; and

German authorities, although admitting that immigration was the unwanted result of their own guest worker program, have yet to embrace or make a forceful, positive argument (beyond their naked demographic needs) for multiethnic co-existence as a defining feature of their society.[24]

The real danger here, it seems to me, is that these silences and disavowals have created a democratic deficit, a situation in which immigrants are effectively written out of the social body. In light of the recent terrorist tragedies in Paris, Brussels, Nice, Ansbach, and Berlin, Europeans can no longer afford to continue to ostracize their ethnic minorities and signal that they do not belong. Such a stance only fuels disaffection, giving those most embittered greater incentive to join the growing numbers of extremist groups eager to expand their international ranks.

But acknowledging the multicultural contours of twenty-first-century Europe can be only the first step in a larger project of making its democracies more robust. For democracy to be truly meaningful, all members of society must be counted as contributors to its culture, have the ability to make their voices heard, and participate in the broader defining of its social blueprints. Whether or not we choose to call those blueprints multiculturalism is ultimately far less important than that we engage in the democratic struggle to produce new ways of thinking about European diversity, instead of settling for denial, demonization, or disavowal.

NOTES

Introduction:
The Multicultural and Multiculturalism

1. Tony Judt, *Postwar: A History of Europe since 1945* (London: Penguin, 2005).

2. Virtually every scholar or critic who has examined multiculturalism begins with the admission of its multiple meanings and uses. For some of the most cogent statements on this point, see Stuart Hall, "When Was the 'Post-colonial'? Thinking at the Limit," in Iain Chambers and Lidia Curti, eds., *The Post-colonial Question: Common Skies, Divided Horizons* (London: Routledge, 1996), 242–59; Homi K. Bhabha, "Culture's in Between," in David Bennett, ed., *Multicultural States: Rethinking Difference and Identity* (London: Routledge, 1998), 29–36; Barnor Hesse, ed., *Un/settled Multiculturalisms: Diasporas, Entanglements, Transruptions* (London: Zed Books, 2000), 1–3; Stuart Hall, "Conclusion: The Multicultural Question," in Hesse, *Un/settled Multiculturalisms*, 209–11; Steven Vertovec and Susanne Wessendorf, eds., *The Multiculturalism Backlash: European Discourses, Policies and Practices* (London: Routledge, 2010), 2–3; Kenan Malik, *Multiculturalism and Its Discontents: Rethinking Diversity after 9/11* (London: Seagull Books, 2013), 7–9.

3. Bhabha, "Culture's in Between," 31.

4. "Turns with a Bookworm," *New York Herald Tribune*, 13 July 1941, H10.

5. Iris Barry, "Melodrama, Tract, Good Story," *New York Herald Tribune*, 27 July 1941, H3. Another review characterized the protagonist as fighting "not for any particular country, but for a more universal outlook of all people against the greatest obstacle on the road of progress: the segregation of races and the violent forms of nationalism." See Klaus Lambrecht, "Lance," *Saturday Review of Literature*, 2 August 1941, 7.

6. Drake DeKay, "Days of Wrath," *New York Times*, 27 July 1941, BR7.

7. "The MLA Foreign Language Program," *Hispania* 40.3 (1957): 344–52, here 349.

8. David A. Hollinger, *Postethnic America: Beyond Multiculturalism* (New York: Basic Books, 1995), 11–12, 93–94.

9. "Primer Is Recast for City Children," *New York Times*, 9 September 1962, 77.

10. "Primer Is Recast for City Children," 77.

11. "Primer Is Recast for City Children," 77.

12. Trude Weiss-Rosmarin, "Melting Pot Theory Is Discounted," *American Israelite*, 13 February 1964, 4.

13. Hollinger, *Postethnic America*, 11–12. See also Daniel Greene, *The Jewish Origins of Cultural Pluralism: The Menorah Association and American Diversity* (Bloomington: Indiana University Press, 2011). Kallen famously likened American culture to a symphony orchestra in which every instrument played together and produced something new and greater than the sum of its parts, but this creative process did not obviate the individual identities of each instrument.

14. The term "melting pot," according to Hollinger, was coined by Israel Zangwill in the title of his 1908 play of the same name. This ideology imagined that the peculiarities of immigrants would be "melt[ed] down . . . in order to pour the resulting liquid into preexisting molds created in the self-image of the Anglo-Protestants who claimed prior possession of America." See Hollinger, *Postethnic America*, 91–92.

15. "NEA's New Checklist for History Textbooks," *Baltimore Afro-American*, 2 March 1974, B12.

16. "NEA's New Checklist for History Textbooks," B12.

17. Jack Thomas, "Textbook Backlash Spreading across US," *Boston Globe*, 7 April 1975, 2.

18. Richard Bourne, "Forked Tongues," *Guardian*, 13 August 1974, 19.

19. Bourne, "Forked Tongues," 19.

20. Max Farrar, "Multiculturalism in the UK: A Contested Discourse," in Max Farrar, Simon Robinson, Yasmin Valli, and Paul Wetherley, eds., *Islam in the West: Key Issues in Multiculturalism* (Basingstoke: Palgrave Macmillan, 2012), 9–10.

21. E.J.B. Rose, *Colour and Citizenship—A Report on British Race Relations* (London: Oxford University Press, 1969), 25.

22. The Third World Liberation Front at SFSU included the Latin American Students Organization, Asian American Political Alliance, Filipino-American Students Organization, Pilipino American Collegiate Endeavor, and El Renacimiento (a Mexican American student organization).

23. Hall, "Conclusion," 209.

24. Hall, "Conclusion," 209.

25. Hall explicates the multiplicity of multiculturalisms along these lines. See Hall, "Conclusion," 210.

26. Ralph Grillo, "Transmigration and Cultural Diversity in the Construction of Europe" (paper, Cultural Diversity and the Construction of Europe, Barcelona, 2000), cited in Steven Vertovec, "Transnational Challenges to the 'New' Multiculturalism" (paper, ASA Conference, University of Sussex, April 2001), 3.

27. In addition to these examples drawn from Hall's enumeration, Steven Vertovec has compiled a list of eight different kinds of multiculturalism and Gerard Delanty has offered a list of nine varieties. See Steven Vertovec, "Multimulticulturalisms," in Marco Martiniello, ed., *Multicultural Policies and the State* (Utrecht: ERCOMER, 1998), 25–38; and Gerard Delanty, *Community* (London: Routledge, 2003).

28. Hall, "Conclusion," 211.

Chapter One:
The Birth of Multicultural Europe

1. This position has been advanced most recently by Matthijs Lok, "Inventing European Pluralism in History Writing" (paper, Navigating Diversity: Narratives, Politics, and Practices in German-Speaking Europe from 1500 to the Present, Montreal, April 2016), 1–3. Lok specifically singles out Tony Judt for making the claim, "Europe is the smallest continent. . . . But in the intensity of its internal differences and contrasts, Europe is unique." See Tony Judt, *Postwar: A History of Europe since 1945* (London: Penguin, 2005), vii.

2. See John Kulczycki, *The Foreign Worker and the German Labor Movement: Xenophobia and Solidarity in the Coal Fields of the Ruhr, 1871–1914* (Oxford: Berg, 1994); and Ulrich Herbert, *A History of Foreign Labor in Germany, 1880–1980: Seasonal Workers/Forced Laborers/Guest Workers*, trans. William Templer (Ann Arbor: University of Michigan Press, 1990).

3. Eugen Weber, *Peasants into Frenchmen: The Modernization of Rural France, 1870–1914* (Stanford, CA: Stanford University Press, 1976).

4. Maxim Silverman, *Deconstructing the Nation: Immigration, Racism and Citizenship in Modern France* (London: Routledge, 1992), 10. See also Alec G. Hargreaves, *Immigration, "Race" and Ethnicity in Contemporary France* (London: Routledge, 1995), 8–12. For more on the interwar wave of immigration, see Mary D. Lewis, *The Boundaries of the Republic: Migrant Rights and the Limits of Universalism in France, 1918–1940* (Stanford, CA: Stanford University Press, 2007).

5. Gérard Noiriel, *The French Melting Pot: Immigration, Citizenship, and National Identity*, trans. Geoffroy de Laforcade (Minneapolis: University of Minnesota Press, 1996), 5.

6. For more on the racialization of the Irish, see Catherine Hall, "The Nation Within and Without," in Catherine Hall, Keith McClelland, and Jane Rendall, *Defining the Victorian Nation: Class, Race, Gender and the Reform Act of 1867* (Cambridge: Cambridge University Press, 2000), 209–11.

7. E.J.B. Rose, *Colour and Citizenship—A Report on British Race Relations* (London: Oxford University Press, 1969), 17–19. See also David Feldman, *Englishmen and Jews: Social Relations and Political Culture, 1840–1914* (New Haven, CT: Yale University Press, 1994).

8. Kenan Malik, *Multiculturalism and Its Discontents: Rethinking Diversity after 9/11* (London: Seagull Books, 2013), 85.

9. Jan Lucassen and Rinus Penninx, *Newcomers: Immigrants and Their Descendants in the Netherlands, 1550–1995* (Amsterdam: Het Spinhuis, 1998). For the French comparison, see Ralph Schor, *Histoire de l'immigration en France de la fin du XIXe siècle à nos jours* (Paris: Armand Colin, 1996), 14.

10. "I Don't Know Who Sent Them," *Daily Express*, 8 June 1948, quoted in Mike Phillips and Trevor Phillips, *Windrush: The Irresistible Rise of Multiracial Britain* (London: HarperCollins, 1998), 59.

11. "Empire Men Flee No Jobs Land: 500 Hope to Start New Life Today," *Daily Express*, 21 June 1948, quoted in Phillips and Phillips, *Windrush*, 53.

12. British Pathé News, "Empire Windrush" (n.d.), YouTube, https://www.you tube.com/watch?v=QDH4IBeZF-M (accessed 12 November 2014).

13. Phillips and Phillips, *Windrush*, 67–68.

14. Internal memorandum, W. H. Hardman, Ministry of Labour, 19 June 1948, Public Records Office (PRO) Ministry of Labour (LAB) 8/1816, quoted in Phillips and Phillips, *Windrush*, 69.

15. Letter from Clement Attlee, Prime Minister, 5 July 1948, PRO Colonial Office (CO) 876/88, quoted in Phillips and Phillips, *Windrush*, 70.

16. "Empire Men Flee No Jobs Land," quoted in Phillips and Phillips, *Windrush*, 53.

17. For more on the perceptions of black Britons in the immediate postwar period, see Kathleen Paul, "From Subjects to Immigrants: Black Britons and National Identity, 1948–1962," in Richard Weight and Abigail Beach, eds., *The Right to Belong: Citizenship and National Identity in Britain, 1930–1960* (London: I.B. Taurus, 1998), 223–48.

18. Wendy Webster, "The Empire Comes Home: Commonwealth Migration to Britain," in Andrew Thompson, ed., *Britain's Experience of Empire in the Twentieth Century* (Oxford: Oxford University Press, 2012), 126. Webster notes that there was a lot of ignorance in Britain about imperial histories and geographies. She cites a survey in 1948 that found that only 49 percent of those questioned could name one colony. See also Phillips and Phillips, *Windrush*, 99.

19. "Jamaicans Arrive to Seek Work," *Times* (London), 23 June 1948, 2.

20. Kathleen Paul claims that the scholarly verdict is still out on whether the Attlee government recognized the significance of the *Windrush* upon its arrival, or whether its role as harbinger of postwar immigration was understood only after the influx of colonial migrants was complete. See Kathleen Paul, *Whitewashing Britain: Race and Citizenship in the Postwar Era* (Ithaca, NY: Cornell University Press, 1997), 111.

21. "I Don't Know Who Sent Them," quoted in Phillips and Phillips, *Windrush*, 59.

22. Internal memorandum, Privy Council Office to Colonial Office, 15 June 1948, PRO CO 876/88, quoted in Phillips and Phillips, *Windrush*, 68–69.

23. Paul, *Whitewashing Britain*, 114.

24. Letter from Clement Attlee, Prime Minister, 5 July 1948, PRO CO 876/88, quoted in Phillips and Phillips, *Windrush*, 70, emphasis added.

25. Paul, *Whitewashing Britain*, 4.

26. Paul, *Whitewashing Britain*, 4–5.

27. Paul, *Whitewashing Britain*, 6–7.

28. Paul, *Whitewashing Britain*, chap. 3, 64–89.

29. Paul, *Whitewashing Britain*, 119.

30. Paul, *Whitewashing Britain*, 119.

31. See Robert Bickers, ed., *Settlers and Expatriates: Britons over the Seas* (Oxford: Oxford University Press, 2010); and Marjory Harper and Stephen Constantine, eds., *Migration and Empire* (Oxford: Oxford University Press, 2010).

32. Webster, "Empire Comes Home," 123.

33. Webster, "Empire Comes Home," 144. See also Paul, *Whitewashing Britain*, 13–14, 128–30.

34. Paul, *Whitewashing Britain*, 129–30.

35. Paul, *Whitewashing Britain*, 131.

36. Schor, *Histoire de l'immigration*, esp. chaps. 3 and 7.

37. Silverman, *Deconstructing the Nation*, 38. For more on the long-term French demographic crisis, see Joshua Cole, *The Power of Large Numbers: Population, Politics and Gender in Nineteenth-Century France* (Ithaca, NY: Cornell University Press, 2000).

38. Hargreaves, *Immigration, "Race" and Ethnicity*, 10–11; and Patrick Weil, *La France et ses étrangers: L'aventure d'une politique de l'immigration, 1938–1991* (Paris: Calmann-Lévy, 1991), chap. 1.

39. Silverman, *Deconstructing the Nation*, 39.

40. Silverman, *Deconstructing the Nation*, 40.

41. Silverman, *Deconstructing the Nation*, 41.

42. Todd Shepard, *The Invention of Decolonization: The Algerian War and the Remaking of France* (Ithaca, NY: Cornell University Press, 2006), 20.

43. Alice Conklin, Sarah Fishman, and Robert Zaretsky, *France and Its Empire since 1870* (Oxford: Oxford University Press, 2011), 24.

44. Conklin, Fishman, and Zaretsky, *France and Its Empire*, 67.

45. For more on the changing notions of France's civilizing mission, see Alice Conklin, *A Mission to Civilize: The Republican Idea of Empire in France and West Africa, 1895–1930* (Stanford, CA: Stanford University Press, 1997), 1–6, 14–22.

46. Michael Brett, "Legislating for Inequality in Algeria: The Senatus-Consulte of 14 July 1865," *Bulletin of the School of Oriental and African Studies* 51.3 (1988): 440–61.

47. Shepard, *Invention of Decolonization*, 26.

48. Shepard, *Invention of Decolonization*, 22.

49. The one exception to this granting of French citizenship to Jews was the Jews of the M'zab, who lived in the southernmost reaches of the Sahara desert. For more on this group, see Rebecca Wall, "The Jews of the Desert: Colonialism, Zionism, and the Jews of the Algerian M'zab, 1882–1962" (PhD diss., University of Michigan, Ann Arbor, 2014).

50. Conklin, Fishman, and Zaretsky, *France and Its Empire*, 51. For more on the status of Jews in Algeria, see Joshua Schreier, *Arabs of the Jewish Faith: The Civilizing Mission in Colonial Algeria* (New Brunswick, NJ: Rutgers University Press, 2010); and Sarah Abrevaya Stein, *Saharan Jews and the Fate of French Algeria* (Chicago: University of Chicago Press, 2014).

51. Joan W. Scott, *The Politics of the Veil* (Princeton, NJ: Princeton University Press, 2007), 48.

52. Quoted in Scott, *Politics of the Veil*, 46.

53. Scott, *Politics of the Veil*, 46.

54. John Ruedy, *Modern Algeria: The Origins and Development of a Nation* (Bloomington: Indiana University Press, 1992), 111.

55. Hargreaves, *Immigration, "Race" and Ethnicity*, 15; Schor, *Histoire de l'immigration*, 41–44.

56. Lewis, *Boundaries of the Republic*, 190.

57. Hargreaves, *Immigration, "Race" and Ethnicity*, 15. See also Alain Gillette

and Abdelmalek Sayad, *L'immigration algérienne en France*, 2nd ed. (Paris: Entente, 1984).

58. Conklin, Fishman, and Zaretsky, *France and Its Empire*, 244.

59. Lewis, *Boundaries of the Republic*, 189–92.

60. Lewis, *Boundaries of the Republic*, 191.

61. Lewis, *Boundaries of the Republic*, 194–211.

62. Conklin, Fishman, and Zaretsky, *France and Its Empire*, 250–51.

63. Shepard, *Invention of Decolonization*, 39. The granting of political and civic equality was a major breakthrough. But it proved to be too little, too late, especially since this reform created a subcategory of citizen based on ethnic difference that Algerians resented.

64. Patrick Weil and John Crowley argue that the granting of Algerian Muslims French citizenship came on the heels of the establishment of a "coherent, formally egalitarian and liberal, legal framework" for immigration through the ordonnance of 18 October 1945, which, in actual practice, granted "liberal access to French nationality" for the very first time. See "Integration in Theory and Practice: A Comparison of France and Britain," in Martin Baldwin-Edwards and Martin A. Schain, eds., *The Politics of Immigration in Western Europe* (London: Routledge, 1994), 110–39, here, 114.

65. For more on the Japanese occupation of the Dutch East Indies and the process of decolonization in Indonesia, see Elizabeth Buettner, *Europe after Empire: Decolonization, Society, and Culture* (Cambridge: Cambridge University Press, 2016), 84–96.

66. Pamela Pattynama, "Cultural Memory and Indo-Dutch Identity Formations," in Ulbe Bosma, ed., *Post-colonial Immigrants and Identity Formations in the Netherlands* (Amsterdam: Amsterdam University Press, 2013), 182.

67. Pattynama, "Cultural Memory," 182.

68. Buettner, *Europe after Empire*, 217–18.

69. Buettner, *Europe after Empire*, 219.

70. Buettner, *Europe after Empire*, 220–21.

71. Buettner, *Europe after Empire*, 222. As Buettner notes, by the mid-1970s, prominent scholar Hans van Amersfoort declared that the Indisch Dutch were "so completely incorporated into society that a representative study of these people was made virtually impossible." See van Amersfoort, *Immigration and the Formation of Minority Groups: The Dutch Experience, 1945–1975*, trans. Robert Lyng (Cambridge: Cambridge University Press, 1982), 81.

72. Buettner, *Europe after Empire*, 271.

73. Buettner, *Europe after Empire*, 272.

74. Henk Smeets and Justus Veenman, "More and More at Home: Three Generations of Moluccans in the Netherlands," in Hans Vermeulen and Rinus Penninx, eds., *Immigrant Integration: The Dutch Case* (Amsterdam: Het Spinhuis, 2000), 36–39.

75. Jan C. van Ours and Justus Vennman, "The Netherlands: Old Emigrants—Young Immigrant Country" (paper, European Migration: What Do We Know? Conference, Munich, 14 November 1997).

76. Judith Roosblad, "Dutch Trade Unions, Immigrants and Immigration: Myopic Politics of Equality," in Rinus Pennix and Judith Roosblad, eds., *Trade*

Unions, Immigration, and Immigrants in Europe, 1960–1993: A Comparative Study of the Actions of Trade Unions in Seven West European Countries (New York: Berghahn Books, 2000), 92.

77. Marcel Maussen, "Constructing Mosques: The Governance of Islam in France and the Netherlands" (PhD diss., Amsterdam Institute for Social Science Research, 2009), 122.

78. Maussen, "Constructing Mosques," 122.

79. Smeets and Veenman, "More and More at Home," 38.

80. Sita Radhakrishnan, *Welfare Services in the Netherlands and the United Kingdom* (New Delhi: Northern Book Centre, 1992), 108.

81. Maussen, "Constructing Mosques," 123.

82. Paul, *Whitewashing Britain*, chap. 3.

83. Antje Ellermann, "When Can Liberal States Avoid Unwanted Immigration? Self-Limited Sovereignty and Guest Worker Recruitment in Switzerland and Germany," *World Politics* 65.3 (2013): 491–538, here 509–11.

84. Ellermann, "When Can Liberal States Avoid Unwanted Immigration?," 508–9.

85. Ellermann, "When Can Liberal States Avoid Unwanted Immigration?," 511; Rita Chin, *The Guest Worker Question in Postwar Germany* (Cambridge: Cambridge University Press, 2007), 24.

86. Ellermann, "When Can Liberal States Avoid Unwanted Immigration?," 508.

87. Ellermann, "When Can Liberal States Avoid Unwanted Immigration?," 509.

88. Ellermann, "When Can Liberal States Avoid Unwanted Immigration?," 511.

89. Ellermann, "When Can Liberal States Avoid Unwanted Immigration?," 512.

90. Stephen Castles and Godula Kosack, *Immigrant Workers and Class Structure in Europe* (Oxford: Oxford University Press, 1985), 377.

91. Ellermann, "When Can Liberal States Avoid Unwanted Immigration?," 521–22.

92. Herbert, *History of Foreign Labor in Germany*, 209.

93. Neil MacMaster, *Colonial Migrants and Racism: Algerians in France, 1900–62* (New York: St. Martin's, 1997), 189.

94. MacMaster, *Colonial Migrants and Racism*, 189.

95. Many of these shantytowns had actually been established during the interwar period, but grew exponentially in the 1950s. For more on the early history of *bidonvilles*, see MacMaster, *Colonial Migrants and Racism*, 90–91.

96. MacMaster, *Colonial Migrants and Racism*, 193.

97. Hargreaves, *Immigration, "Race" and Ethnicity*, 69.

98. MacMaster, *Colonial Migrants and Racism*, 196.

99. MacMaster, *Colonial Migrants and Racism*, 194.

100. Silverman, *Deconstructing the Nation*, 46.

101. Jim House and Neil MacMaster, *Paris 1961: Algerians, State Terror, and Memory* (Oxford: Oxford University Press, 2006), 67–70.

102. MacMaster, *Colonial Migrants and Racism*, 196–97.

103. C. R. Ageron, "L'Opinion française à travers les sondages," in J.-P. Rioux, ed., *La Guerre d'Algérie et les Français* (Paris: Fayard, 1990), 25–44.

104. MacMaster, *Colonial Migrants and Racism*, 198.

105. MacMaster, *Colonial Migrants and Racism*, 198.

106. For more on the 17 October massacre, see Joshua Cole, "Remembering the Battle of Paris: 17 October 1961 in French and Algerian Memory," *French Politics, Culture, and Society* 21.3 (2003): 21–50.

107. MacMaster, *Colonial Migrants and Racism*, 199–200. See also House and MacMaster, *Paris 1961*, 88–136.

108. "London Racial Outburst Due to Many Factors," *Times* (London), 3 September 1958, 7.

109. For Nottingham numbers, see "Why Racial Clash Occurred," *Times* (London), 27 August 1958, 4; for Notting Hill numbers, see "London Racial Outburst Due to Many Factors," 7.

110. "Why Racial Clash Occurred," 4.

111. "London Racial Outburst Due to Many Factors," 7.

112. Paul, *Whitewashing Britain*, 166–68.

113. "Commonwealth Migrants," memorandum by the Secretary of State for the Home Department, 6 October 1961, CAB 129/107 C (61)153, cited in Paul, *Whitewashing Britain*, 166.

114. Malik, *Multiculturalism and Its Discontents*, 23–24.

115. Ellermann, "When Can Liberal States Avoid Unwanted Immigration?," 512.

116. Ellermann, "When Can Liberal States Avoid Unwanted Immigration?," 513.

117. Ellermann, "When Can Liberal States Avoid Unwanted Immigration?," 513–14.

118. Chin, *Guest Worker Question*, 37.

119. Duncan Miller and Ihsan Çetin, *Migrant Workers, Wages, and Labor Markets: Emigrant Turkish Workers in the Federal Republic of Germany* (Istanbul: Istanbul University Press, 1974).

120. Chin, *Guest Worker Question*, 48–49; Karen Schönwälder, *Einwanderung und ethnische Pluralität: Politische Entscheidungen und öffentliche Debatten in Großbritannien und der Bundesrepublik von den 1950er bis zu den 1970er Jahren* (Essen: Klartext, 2001), 253.

121. Ellermann, "When Can Liberal States Avoid Unwanted Immigration?," 522.

122. Ellermann, "When Can Liberal States Avoid Unwanted Immigration?," 522. During this period, too, West Germany began to import female guest workers in fairly large numbers. See Esra Erdem and Monika Mattes, "Gendered Policies/Gendered Patterns: Female Labour Migration from Turkey to Germany from the 1960s to the 1990s," in Rainer Ohliger, Karen Schönwälder, and Triadafilos Triadafilopoulos, eds., *European Encounters: Migrants, Migrations and European Societies since 1945* (Aldershot: Ashgate, 2003), 167–85; and Monika Mattes, *"Gastarbeiterinnen" in der Bundesrepublik. Anwerbepolitik, Migration und Geschlecht in den 50er bis 70er Jahren* (Frankfurt/Main: Campus Verlag, 2005).

123. Amparo González-Ferrer, "The Process of Family Reunification among Original Guest-Workers in Germany," *Zeitschrift für Familienforschung* 19.1 (2007): 10–33, here 13.

124. Ellermann, "When Can Liberal States Avoid Unwanted Immigration?," 522–23.

125. Ellermann, "When Can Liberal States Avoid Unwanted Immigration?," 522.

126. Rita Chin and Heide Fehrenbach, "German Democracy and the Question of Difference, 1945–1995," in Rita Chin, Heide Fehrenbach, Geoff Eley, and Atina Grossmann, *After the Nazi Racial State: Difference and Democracy in Germany and Europe* (Ann Arbor: University of Michigan Press, 2009), 105–6.

127. Chin, *Guest Worker Question*, 48–49; González-Ferrer, "Process of Family Reunification," 13.

128. Ellermann, "When Can Liberal States Avoid Unwanted Immigration?," 524.

129. Han Entzinger, "Shifting Paradigms: An Appraisal of Immigration in the Netherlands," in Heinz Fassmann and Rainer Münz, eds., *European Migration in the Late Twentieth Century: Patterns, Actual Trends, and Social Implications* (Brookfield, VT: Edward Elgar, 1994), 94.

130. Maussen, "Constructing Mosques," 122.

131. Eytan Meyers, *International Immigration Policy: A Theoretical and Comparative Analysis* (New York: Palgrave Macmillan, 2004), 89–90.

132. Meyers, *International Immigration Policy*, 89.

133. CBS Statistics Netherlands, "Den Haag/Heerlen, Population, Households and Population Dynamics; from 1899," http://statline.cbs.nl/Statweb/publication/?VW=T&DM=SLEN&PA=37556eng&D1=0-44&D2=1,11,21,31,41,51,61,71,81,91,101,l&HD=150108-0152&LA=EN&HDR=G1&STB=T (accessed 7 January 2015).

134. Alexis Spire, *Étrangers à la carte: L'administration de l'immigration en France 1945–1975* (Paris: Grasset, 2005), 212–22.

135. MacMaster, *Colonial Migrants and Racism*, 202.

136. MacMaster, *Colonial Migrants and Racism*, 202–3.

137. James F. Hollifield, "Immigration and Modernization," in James F. Hollifield and George Ross, eds., *Searching for the New France* (New York: Routledge, 1991), 113–50, here 123.

138. Silverman, *Deconstructing the Nation*, 45.

139. Silverman, *Deconstructing the Nation*, 43.

140. Hargreaves, *Immigration, "Race" and Ethnicity*, 135. See also Naomi Davidson, *Only Muslim: Embodying Islam in Twentieth-Century France* (Ithaca, NY: Cornell University Press, 2012), 171.

141. Silverman, *Deconstructing the Nation*, 45.

142. Silverman, *Deconstructing the Nation*, 43.

143. Silverman, *Deconstructing the Nation*, 43.

144. MacMaster, *Colonial Migrants and Racism*, 204.

145. Randall Hansen, *Citizenship and Immigration in Post-war Britain: The Institutional Origins of a Multicultural Nation* (Oxford: Oxford University Press, 2000), 157–59.

146. Hansen, *Citizenship and Immigration*, 159.

147. Hansen, *Citizenship and Immigration*, 169–71.

148. Hansen, *Citizenship and Immigration*, 160.

149. Hansen, *Citizenship and Immigration*, 161.

150. Paul, *Whitewashing Britain*, 179.

151. Hansen, *Citizenship and Immigration*, 163–64.

152. Hansen, *Citizenship and Immigration*, 200–201.

153. Buettner, *Europe after Empire*, 290.

154. Ellermann, "When Can Liberal States Avoid Unwanted Immigration?," 513–18.

155. Ellermann, "When Can Liberal States Avoid Unwanted Immigration?," 519.

156. Silverman, *Deconstructing the Nation*, 45. See also Albano Cordeiro, *L'immigration* (Paris: La Découverte, 1984).

157. Silverman, *Deconstructing the Nation*, 47.

158. Silverman, *Deconstructing the Nation*, 73–77.

159. Hollifield, "Immigration and Modernization," 124.

160. Silverman, *Deconstructing the Nation*, 49–50.

161. Silverman, *Deconstructing the Nation*, 52–53.

162. Silverman, *Deconstructing the Nation*, 48, 77. See also Catherine Wihtol de Wenden, *Les immigrés et la politique* (Paris: Presses de la Fondation nationale des sciences politiques, 1988).

163. Meyers, *International Immigration Policy*, 90.

164. Rob Witte, *Racist Violence and the State: A Comparative Analysis of Britain, France and the Netherlands* (London: Routledge, 2014), 121–23.

165. Witte, *Racist Violence and the State*, 122.

166. Meyers, *International Immigration Policy*, 90.

167. Meyers, *International Immigration Policy*, 91.

168. Ellermann, "When Can Liberal States Avoid Unwanted Immigration?," 527.

169. Ellermann, "When Can Liberal States Avoid Unwanted Immigration?," 526.

170. Jennifer Miller, "Postwar Negotiations: The First Generation of Turkish 'Guest Workers' in West Germany, 1961–1973" (PhD diss., Rutgers University, 2008), see esp. chap. 4.

171. Ellermann, "When Can Liberal States Avoid Unwanted Immigration?," 529.

Chapter Two:
Managing Multicultural Societies

1. Dominic Sandbrook, "Miliband's Marxist Father and the Real Reason He Wants to Drag Us Back to the Nightmare 70s," *Daily Mail*, 25 September 2013, www.dailymail.co.uk/debate/article-2432626/Ed-Milibands-Marxist-father -real-reason-wants-drag-1970s-DOMINIC-SANDBROOK.html (accessed 25 July 2016).

2. Interview with Cecil Holness, quoted in Mike Phillips and Trevor Phillips, *Windrush: The Irresistible Rise of Multi-Racial Britain* (London: Harper-

Collins, 1998), 89. Wendy Webster also makes this point. See Wendy Webster, *Englishness and Empire 1939–1965* (Oxford: Oxford University Press, 2005), 155.

3. Phillips and Phillips, *Windrush*, 96.

4. Phillips and Phillips, *Windrush*, 120.

5. Zig Layton-Henry, *The Politics of Immigration: Immigration, "Race," and "Race" Relations in Postwar Britain* (Oxford: Blackwell, 1992), 13.

6. Webster contrasts the government's efforts to project the public image of an open-door policy with its behind-the-scenes discussions about restricting black and Asian immigration. See Webster, *Englishness and Empire*, 172.

7. CO 1028/22, CWP (53), 6 August 1953, cited in Randall Hansen, *Citizenship and Immigration in Post-war Britain: The Institutional Origins of a Multicultural Nation* (Oxford: Oxford University Press, 2000), 67, notes 11 and 15.

8. Kenan Malik, *The Meaning of Race: Race, History and Culture in Western Society* (New York: New York University Press, 1996), 21.

9. Phillips and Phillips, *Windrush*, 161–80, esp. 165–66.

10. Phillips and Phillips, *Windrush*, 165.

11. "Why Racial Clash Occurred," *Times* (London), 27 August 1958, 4.

12. *Daily Sketch*, 2 September 1958, cited in Malik, *Meaning of Race*, 22.

13. Hansen, *Citizenship and Immigration*, 84.

14. Hansen, *Citizenship and Immigration*, 130.

15. As Hansen has explained, the 1962 Commonwealth Immigrants Act addressed only primary immigration—that is, those who applied to enter Britain to work—but continued to guarantee the entry of spouses, children under eighteen, and grandparents over sixty-five. See Hansen, *Citizenship and Immigration*, 136.

16. Quoted in Robert Miles and Annie Phizacklea, *White Man's Country: Racism in British Politics* (London: Pluto Press, 1984), 55.

17. Cited in Hansen, *Citizenship and Immigration*, 132.

18. Hansen, *Citizenship and Immigration*, 132.

19. Hansen, *Citizenship and Immigration*, 138.

20. Quoted in Miles and Phizacklea, *White Man's Country*, 54.

21. Quoted in Adrian Favell, *Philosophies of Integration: Immigration and the Idea of Citizenship in France and Britain* (Basingstoke: Palgrave, 2001), 104.

22. Hansen, *Citizenship and Immigration*, 139–40. Critics of the first Race Relations Act believed that it did not go far enough: it did not apply to large areas of economic and social life (such as employment); and its enforcement procedures were weak, adjudicated through a Race Relations Board that emphasized conciliation, and not legally binding. See Miles and Phizacklea, *White Man's Country*, 57–58.

23. Further legislation followed in 1968, as an answer to complaints about the limited scope of the initial law. The second Race Relations Act empowered a Race Relations Board to adjudicate complaints and extended the prohibition of discrimination to employment, housing, financial services, education, and all places of public resort. A subsequent bill in 1976 expanded the definition of discrimination to include indirect discrimination and replaced the Race Relations

Board with the Commission for Racial Equality. See Hansen, *Citizenship and Immigration*, 225–27.

24. Erik Bleich, *Race Politics in Britain and France: Ideas and Policymaking since the 1960s* (Cambridge: Cambridge University Press, 2003), 170.

25. Kathleen Paul, *Whitewashing Britain: Race and Citizenship in the Postwar Era* (Ithaca, NY: Cornell University Press, 1997), 140, esp. note 31.

26. Favell, *Philosophies of Integration*, 3–4.

27. Hansen, *Citizenship and Immigration*, 127–29. See also Paul Foot, *Immigration and Race in British Politics* (Harmondsworth: Penguin, 1965); Ira Katznelson, *Black Men, White Cities: Race, Politics, and Migration in the United States, 1900–30 and Britain, 1948–68* (London: Oxford University Press, 1975); and Anthony Messina, *Race and Party Competition in Britain* (Oxford: Clarendon, 1989).

28. Michael Banton, *Promoting Racial Harmony* (Cambridge: Cambridge University Press, 1985), 126.

29. *Parliamentary Debates* (Hansard), vol. 709, cols. 443–44, 23 March 1965, quoted in Hansen, *Citizenship and Immigration*, 141.

30. Local Government Act 1966 (London: HMSO, 1966), 12, www.legislation.gov.uk/ukpga/1966/42/pdfs/ukpga_19660042_en.pdf (accessed 14 January 2017).

31. Enoch Powell, "Speech to the Annual General Meeting of the West Midlands Area Conservative Political Centre, Birmingham, 20 April 1968," in Enoch Powell, *Reflections of a Statesman: The Writings and Speeches of Enoch Powell* (London: Bellew, 1991), 373–79.

32. Quoted in Hansen, *Citizenship and Immigration*, 186.

33. Layton-Henry, *Politics of Immigration*, 81.

34. Favell, *Philosophies of Integration*, 105–6.

35. Favell, *Philosophies of Integration*, 105. Indeed, the decade of the 1970s became a moment when actions by the Irish Republican Army intensified and resulted in significant violence on English soil.

36. Miles and Phizacklea, *White Man's Country*, 67–68.

37. Miles and Phizacklea, *White Man's Country*, 70.

38. Sasha Josephides, "Towards a History of the Indian Workers' Association" (Research Paper in Ethnic Relations no. 18, University of Warwick, December 1991).

39. Danièle Joly, "Race, Ethnicity and Religion: Emerging Policies in Britain," *Patterns of Prejudice* 46.5 (2012): 467–85, here 470.

40. Kenan Malik, *From Fatwa to Jihad: The Rushdie Affair and Its Aftermath* (Brooklyn: Melville House, 2010), 49.

41. Avtar Brah, *Cartographies of Diaspora: Contesting Identities* (London: Routledge, 1996), 229. The protest was prompted by a leaked confidential report, which stated, "On a rough calculation about half the immigrants will be West Indians at 7 of the 11 schools, the significance of this being the general recognition that their I.Q.s work out below their English contemporaries. Thus academic standards will be lower in schools where they form a large group." See Alfred Doulton, "Haringey Comprehensive Schools" (13 January 1969), 5c, George Padmore Institute Archive, BEM/1/2/5.

42. Joly, "Race, Ethnicity and Religion," 471.

43. Anandi Ramamurthy, "The Politics of Britain's Asian Youth Movements," *Race and Class* 48.2 (2006): 38–60, here 40.

44. Phillips and Phillips, *Windrush*, 266.

45. Hansen, *Citizenship and Immigration*, 212–14.

46. Stuart Hall, Chas Critcher, Tony Jefferson, John Clarke, and Brian Roberts, *Policing the Crisis: Mugging, the State, and Law and Order* (London: Macmillan, 1978), 6–9.

47. John Solomos, *Black Youth, Racism and the State: The Politics of Ideology and Policy* (Cambridge: Cambridge University Press, 1992), 117–18.

48. Solomos, *Black Youth, Racism and the State*, 109.

49. Phillips and Phillips, *Windrush*, 303.

50. Layton-Henry, *Politics of Immigration*, 129.

51. Bethnal Green and Stepney Trades Council, "Blood on the Streets: A Report by the Bethnal Green and Stepney Trades Council on Racial Attacks in East London" (London: Bethnal Green and Stepney Trades Council, September 1978).

52. Bethnal Green and Stepney Trades Council, "Blood on the Streets," 8.

53. Layton-Henry, *Politics of Immigration*, 139.

54. Mike Brake and Chris Hale, *Public Order and Private Lives: The Politics of Law and Order* (London: Routledge, 1992), 49. See also Malik, *From Fatwa to Jihad*, 54–55.

55. Quoted in Sarah Neal, "The Scarman Report, the Macpherson Report and the Media: How Newspapers Respond to Race-Centered Social Policy Interventions," *Journal of Social Policy* 32.1 (2003): 55–74, here 63.

56. Malik, *From Fatwa to Jihad*, 57.

57. Layton-Henry, *Politics of Immigration*, 134.

58. David Walker, "Defusing the Time-Bombs in Britain's Inner Cities," *Times* (London), 14 May 1985, 12.

59. "A Good Knight's Solution," *Sunday Times*, 10 October 1982, quoted in Keith Thompson, *Under Siege: Racism and Violence in Britain Today* (London: Penguin, 1988), 91.

60. These funds were provided under section 11 of the Local Government Act 1966. Section 11 was initiated to provide additional funding for local authorities to address the specific needs of "Commonwealth immigrants whose language or culture differed from the rest of the community." These funds were initially used to pay for English-language teaching and cultural projects. See Kathryn Ray, "Constituting 'Asian Women': Political Representation, Identity Politics and Local Discourses of Participation," *Ethnic and Racial Studies* 26.5 (2003): 854–78, here 862; Joly, "Race, Ethnicity and Religion," 474; and Thompson, *Under Siege*, 94–97.

61. This arrangement was partly expedient, as most immigrants—community leaders and ordinary folks alike—saw the Conservative Party as the "party of racism" and therefore did not trust the central government. See Malik, *From Fatwa to Jihad*, 57–58.

62. Ali Rattansi, *Multiculturalism: A Very Short Introduction* (Oxford: Oxford University Press, 2011), 26.

63. Other initiatives included adopting an equal opportunity policy statement, establishing a race relations committee, appointing special race/ethnic advisers, providing antiracist training for staff, creating consultation programs with ethnic minority groups, supporting minority self-help. See Thompson, *Under Siege*, 99; and Joly, "Race, Ethnicity and Religion," 473.

64. Phillips and Phillips, *Windrush*, 372.

65. James Curran, Ivor Gaber, and Julian Petley, *Culture Wars: The Media and the British Left* (Edinburgh: Edinburgh University Press, 2005), 85.

66. Eytan Meyers, *International Immigration Policy: A Theoretical and Comparative Analysis* (New York: Palgrave Macmillan, 2004), 91.

67. Meyers, *International Immigration Policy*, 92.

68. Hans van Amersfoort, *Immigration and the Formation of Minority Groups: The Dutch Experience, 1945–1975*, trans. Robert Lyng (Cambridge: Cambridge University Press, 1982), 5.

69. Hans van Amersfoort and Rinus Penninx, "Regulating Migration in Europe: The Dutch Experience, 1960–92," *Annals of the American Academy of Political and Social Science* 534 (1994): 133–46, here 137. See also Elizabeth Buettner, *Europe after Empire: Decolonization, Society, and Culture* (Cambridge: Cambridge University Press, 2016), 102.

70. Buettner, *Europe after Empire*, 102–3.

71. Meyers, *International Immigration Policy*, 92; Buettner, *Europe after Empire*, 276.

72. Hans van Amersfoort, "How the Dutch Government Stimulated the Unwanted Migration from Suriname" (Working Paper 47, International Migration Institute, Oxford, 2011), 8.

73. Martijn Rasser, "The Dutch Response to Moluccan Terrorism, 1970–1978," *Studies in Conflict and Terrorism* 28.6 (2005): 481–92, here 483.

74. Rasser, "Dutch Response," 484–87.

75. Meyers, *International Immigration Policy*, 93.

76. Peter Scholten, *Framing Immigrant Integration: Dutch Research-Policy Dialogues in Comparative Perspective* (Amsterdam: University of Amsterdam Press, 2011), 89–90.

77. Sita Radhakrishnan, *Welfare Services in the Netherlands and the United Kingdom* (New Delhi: Northern Book Centre, 1992), 108.

78. Marcel Maussen, "Constructing Mosques: The Governance of Islam in France and the Netherlands" (PhD diss., Amsterdam Institute for Social Science Research, 2009), 122.

79. Radhakrishnan, *Welfare Services*, 109.

80. Scholten, *Framing Immigrant Integration*, 97.

81. Scholten, *Framing Immigrant Integration*, 91.

82. Scholten, *Framing Immigrant Integration*, 99.

83. Radhakrishnan, *Welfare Services*, 115–16.

84. Scholten, *Framing Immigrant Integration*, 100.

85. Rob Witte, *Racist Violence and the State: A Comparative Analysis of Britain, France and the Netherlands* (London: Routledge, 2014), 126–27.

86. Han Entzinger, "Changing the Rules while the Game Is On: From Multiculturalism to Assimilation in the Netherlands," in Y. Michal Bodemann and

Gökçe Yurdakul, eds., *Migration, Citizenship, Ethnos: Incorporation Regimes in Germany, Western Europe and North America* (New York: Palgrave Macmillan, 2006), 121–46, here 124.

87. Jan Rath, "Research on Immigrant Ethnic Minorities in the Netherlands," in Peter Ratcliffe, ed., *The Politics of Social Science Research: Race, Ethnicity and Social Change* (London: Palgrave Macmillan, 2001), 137–59, here 150–51.

88. Scholten, *Framing Immigrant Integration*, 114.

89. Jaap van Donselaar and Peter R. Rodrigues, eds., *Racism and Extremism Monitor Eighth Report*, trans. Nancy Forest-Flier (Leiden: Anne Frank Stichting, Leiden University, 2008), 4.

90. Meyers, *International Immigration Policy*, 94.

91. Scholten, *Framing Immigrant Integration*, 115–16. See also Rath, "Research on Immigrant Ethnic Minorities," 150–51.

92. Meyers, *International Immigration Policy*, 93–94.

93. Kees Groenendijk and Eric Heijs, "Immigration, Immigrants and Nationality Law in the Netherlands," in Randall Hansen and Patrick Weil, eds., *Towards a European Nationality: Citizenship, Immigration, and Nationality Law in the EU* (London: Palgrave Macmillan, 2001), 143–72, here 147.

94. Marc Morjé Howard, *The Politics of Citizenship in Europe* (Cambridge: Cambridge University Press, 2009), 84.

95. Patrick Simon and Valérie Sala Pala, "'We're Not All Multiculturalists Yet': France Swings between Hard Integration and Soft Anti-discrimination," in Steven Vertovec and Susanne Wessendorf, eds., *The Multiculturalism Backlash: European Discourses, Policies and Practices* (London: Routledge, 2010), 92. See also Maxim Silverman, *Deconstructing the Nation: Immigration, Racism and Citizenship in Modern France* (London: Routledge, 1992), 98–99; Jeremy Jennings, "Citizenship, Republicanism, and Multiculturalism in Contemporary France," *British Journal of Political Science* 30.4 (2000): 575–98; and Cécile Laborde, "The Culture(s) of the Republic: Nationalism and Multiculturalism in French Republican Thought," *Political Theory* 29.5 (2001): 716–35.

96. Frederick Cooper, *Citizenship between Empire and Nation: Remaking France and French Africa, 1945–1960* (Princeton, NJ: Princeton University Press, 2014), 442–45. As Cooper emphasizes, ex-colonial peoples had once been citizens and "had become immigrants."

97. Silverman, *Deconstructing the Nation*, 53. See also Alec G. Hargreaves, *Immigration, "Race" and Ethnicity in Contemporary France* (London: Routledge, 1995), 179–80.

98. Favell, *Philosophies of Integration*, 48. See also Yvan Gastaut, *L'immigration et l'opinion en France sous la Vᵉ République* (Paris: Seuil, 2000), 466–71.

99. Patrick Weil and John Crowley, "Integration in Theory and Practice: A Comparison of France and Britain," in Martin Baldwin-Edwards and Martin A. Schain, eds., *The Politics of Immigration in Western Europe* (London: Routledge, 1994), 110–39, here 113–15.

100. Silverman, *Deconstructing the Nation*, 54.

101. Weil and Crowley, "Integration in Theory and Practice," 114–15.

102. Favell, *Philosophies of Integration*, 47.

103. Favell, *Philosophies of Integration*, 47–48.

104. Todd Shepard, *The Invention of Decolonization: The Algerian War and the Remaking of France* (Ithaca, NY: Cornell University Press, 2006), 22. See also Tyler Stovall, *Transnational France: The Modern History of a Universal Nation* (Boulder, CO: Westview, 2015), 342.

105. Silverman, *Deconstructing the Nation*, 46.

106. Buettner, *Europe after Empire*, 290.

107. Neil MacMaster, *Colonial Migrants and Racism: Algerians in France, 1900–62* (New York: St. Martin's, 1997), 106.

108. Patrick Ireland, *The Policy Challenge of Ethnic Diversity: Immigrant Politics in France and Switzerland* (Cambridge, MA: Harvard University Press, 1994), 38, quoted in Maussen, "Constructing Mosques," 113.

109. Naomi Davidson, *Only Muslim: Embodying Islam in Twentieth-Century France* (Ithaca, NY: Cornell University Press, 2012), 172.

110. Davidson, *Only Muslim*, 174.

111. Martin Schain, "Policy and Policy-Making in France and the United States: Models of Incorporation and the Dynamics of Change," *Modern and Contemporary France* 3.4 (1995): 401–13, here 409–10. By 1990, FAS had a budget of nearly 1.4 billion francs, had 400 administrators around the country, and offered financial support to 3,000 associations.

112. Maussen, "Constructing Mosques," 112–13.

113. Maussen, "Constructing Mosques," 113.

114. Davidson, *Only Muslim*, 178–79. Davidson states that the Portuguese made up 27.6 percent of all foreigners in SONACOTRA hostels in the Paris region, as compared to 21 percent for Algerians, 11 percent for Spaniards, 7.1 percent for Moroccans, 4.9 percent for Tunisians, and 3.4 percent for Africans.

115. Favell, *Philosophies of Integration*, 47.

116. Favell, *Philosophies of Integration*, 47.

117. Silverman, *Deconstructing the Nation*, 53.

118. Maussen, "Constructing Mosques," 115.

119. Ralph D. Grillo, *Ideologies and Institutions in Urban France: The Representation of Immigrants* (Cambridge: Cambridge University Press, 2006), 110.

120. Favell, *Philosophies of Integration*, 57.

121. Patrick Weil, "Racisme et discrimination dans la politique française de l'immigration 1938–1945, 1974–1995," *Vingtième Siècle* 47 (1995): 77–102.

122. Thomas R. Christofferson, *The French Socialists in Power, 1981–1986: From Autogestation to Cohabitation* (Newark: University of Delaware Press, 1991), 116.

123. Christofferson, *French Socialists*, 117.

124. Christofferson, *French Socialists*, 116.

125. Weil and Crowley, "Integration in Theory and Practice," 114.

126. Robert C. Lieberman, *Shaping Race Policy: The United States in Comparative Perspective* (Princeton, NJ: Princeton University Press, 2011), 112; and Christine Garin, "ZEP: La grande désillusion," *Autrement* 136 (March 1993): 95–101, here 97.

127. James Shields, *The Extreme Right in France: From Pétain to Le Pen* (London: Routledge, 2007), 202.

128. Miriam Feldblum, *Reconstructing Citizenship: The Politics of Nationality Reform and Immigration in Contemporary France* (Albany: State University of New York Press, 1999), 33–34.

129. For more on the peasants of Larzac, see Herman Lebovics, *Bringing the Empire Back Home: France in the Global Age* (Durham, NC: Duke University Press, 2004), esp. chap. 1.

130. Quoted in Feldblum, *Reconstructing Citizenship*, 33.

131. Favell, *Philosophies of Integration*, 51. See also Henri Giordan, *Démocratie culturelle et droit à la différence: rapport présenté à Jack Lang, ministre de la Culture* (Paris: La Documentation française, 1982).

132. See Buettner, *Europe after Empire*, 339; and Stovall, *Transnational France*, 449.

133. Feldblum, *Reconstructing Citizenship*, 35.

134. Feldblum, *Reconstructing Citizenship*, 36.

135. *Le Monde*, 21 September 1982, quoted in Feldblum, *Reconstructing Citizenship*, 36.

136. Favell, *Philosophies of Integration*, 53–54.

137. Favell, *Philosophies of Integration*, 54.

138. Favell, *Philosophies of Integration*, 54.

139. Feldblum, *Reconstructing Citizenship*, 39.

140. Favell, *Philosophies of Integration*, 55.

141. Laura Coello, *Significant Difference? A Comparative Analysis of Multicultural Policies in the United Kingdom and the Netherlands* (Amsterdam: Amsterdam University Press, 2010), 15.

142. Rita Chin, *The Guest Worker Question in Postwar Germany* (Cambridge: Cambridge University Press, 2007), 62.

143. Triadafilos Triadafilopoulos, *Becoming Multicultural: Immigration and the Politics of Membership in Canada and Germany* (Vancouver: University of British Columbia Press, 2012), 79. This number was for 1967.

144. Triadafilopoulos, *Becoming Multicultural*, 80.

145. Triadafilopoulos, *Becoming Multicultural*, 80.

146. Hans Dietrich Genscher, interview in the *Westdeutsche Allgemeine Zeitung*, 5 October 1972, cited in Triadafilopoulos, *Becoming Multicultural*, 82.

147. Triadafilopoulos, *Becoming Multicultural*, 81.

148. Triadafilopoulos, *Becoming Multicultural*, 82–83.

149. Jennifer Miller, "Postwar Negotiations: The First Generation of Turkish 'Guest Workers' in West Germany, 1961–1973" (PhD diss., Rutgers University, 2008), 33–34.

150. Chin, *Guest Worker Question*, 100–102. For more on the activities of the Wohlfartsverbände, see Dietrich Thränhardt, "Patterns of Organization among Different Ethnic Minorities," *New German Critique* 46 (1989): 15–16. For more on the DGB, see Cynthia W. Rolling, "But People Came: Responses to the Guestworkers in the Federal Republic of Germany, 1961–1976" (PhD diss., University of Wisconsin–Madison, 1982), 145–57; and Brett Klopp, *German Multiculturalism: Immigrant Integration and the Transformation of Citizenship* (Westport, CT: Praeger, 2002), 60–69.

151. Klopp, *German Multiculturalism*, 63.

152. Chin, *Guest Worker Question*, 91.

153. Cited in Karen Schönwälder, "Zukunftsblindheit oder Steuerungsversagen? Zur Ausländerpolitik der Bundesregierung der 1960er und frühen 1970er Jahre," in Jochen Oltmer, ed., *Migration steuern und verwalten* (Göttingen: V and R Unipress, 2003), 140.

154. Chin, *Guest Worker Question*, 92–93.

155. CDU, *Konzept der CDU Ausländerpolitik* (Bonn, 1977), 3, quoted in Klaus Unger, *Ausländerpolitik in der Bundesrepublik Deutschland* (Saarbrücken: Verlag Breitenbach, 1980), 21.

156. Chin, *Guest Worker Question*, 98.

157. Chin, *Guest Worker Question*, 99.

158. Sarah T. Vierra, "At Home in Almanya? Turkish-German Spaces of Belonging in the Federal Republic of Germany" (PhD diss., University of North Carolina, Chapel Hill, 2011), chap. 3.

159. Vierra, "At Home in Almanya?," chap. 4.

160. Triadafilopoulos, *Becoming Multicultural*, 120.

161. Vierra, "At Home in Almanya?," 42–44.

162. Vierra, "At Home in Almanya?," 129.

163. Vierra, "At Home in Almanya?," 132–33.

164. Vierra, "At Home in Almanya?," 177–78.

165. Rauf Ceylan, *Ethnische Kolonien: Entstehung, Funktion und Wandel am Beispiel türkischer Moscheen und Cafés* (Wiesbaden: VS Verlag für Sozialwissenschaften, 2006), 133–38.

166. Ceylan, *Ethnische Kolonien*, 185–93.

167. Triadafilopoulos, *Becoming Multicultural*, 122.

168. Triadafilopoulos, *Becoming Multicultural*, 123.

169. Chin, *Guest Worker Question*, 99.

170. Heinz Kühn, *Stand und Weiterentwicklung der Integration der ausländischen Arbeitnehmer und ihrer Familien in der Bundesrepublik Deutschland. Memorandum des Beauftragten der Bundesregierung* (Bonn, 1979), 2, 11, cited in Chin, *Guest Worker Question*, 104.

171. Chin, *Guest Worker Question*, 104–5.

172. Chin, *Guest Worker Question*, 144, 150–51.

173. Bundestag, *Verhandlungen des Deutschen Bundestages: Stenographische Berichte*, 9. Wahlperiode, vol. 120 (Bonn: Deutscher Bundestag und Bundesrat, 1982), 4892.

174. Triadafilopoulos, *Becoming Multicultural*, 125.

Chapter Three:
Race, Nation, and Multicultural Society

1. Adrian Favell, *Philosophies of Integration: Immigration and the Idea of Citizenship in France and Britain* (Basingstoke: Palgrave, 2001), 42.

2. Margaret Thatcher, TV interview with Gordon Burns, Granada *World in Action*, 27 January 1978, www.margaretthatcher.org/document/103485 (accessed 17 March 2015).

3. Martin Barker, *New Racism: Conservatives and the Ideology of the Tribe* (London: Junction Books, 1981), 1; Zig Layton-Henry, *The Politics of Immigration: Immigration, "Race" and "Race" Relations in Post-war Britain* (Oxford: Blackwell, 1992), 187.

4. Thatcher, TV interview with Gordon Burns.

5. Thatcher, TV interview with Gordon Burns.

6. Barker, *New Racism*, 1.

7. Barker, *New Racism*, chaps. 2 and 3; Paul Gilroy, *There Ain't No Black in the Union Jack: The Cultural Politics of Race and Nation* (Chicago: University of Chicago Press, 1991), chap. 2; Yasmin Alibhai-Brown, *Imagining the New Britain* (New York: Routledge, 2001), chap. 3; Layton-Henry, *Politics of Immigration*, chap. 8.

8. Enoch Powell, *Reflections of a Statesman: The Writings and Speeches of Enoch Powell* (London: Bellew, 1991), 373–79.

9. Enoch Powell, speech delivered to the annual conference of the Rotary Club of London, Eastbourne, 16 November 1968, quoted in Layton-Henry, *Politics of Immigration*, 82.

10. Layton-Henry, *Politics of Immigration*, 82.

11. Layton-Henry, *Politics of Immigration*, 82.

12. Elazar Barkan, *The Retreat of Scientific Racism: Changing Concepts of Race in Britain and the United States between the World Wars* (Cambridge: Cambridge University Press, 1993).

13. UNESCO, Conference for the Establishment of the United Nations Educational, Scientific and Cultural Organization, 16 November 1945, 93, quoted in Kenan Malik, *The Meaning of Race: Race, History and Culture in Western Society* (New York: New York University Press, 1996), 15.

14. George Frederickson, *Racism: A Short History* (Princeton, NJ: Princeton University Press, 2002), 2; Rita Chin and Heide Fehrenbach, "Introduction: What's Race Got to Do With It? Postwar German History in Context," in Rita Chin, Heide Fehrenbach, Geoff Eley, and Atina Grossmann, *After the Nazi Racial State: Difference and Democracy in Germany and Europe* (Ann Arbor: University of Michigan Press, 2009), 1–29.

15. Universal Declaration of Human Rights, www.un.org/en/universal-declaration-human-rights (accessed 28 January 2017).

16. UNESCO, *UNESCO and Its Programme* (Paris: UNESCO, 1950), quoted in Michael Banton, *The International Politics of Race* (Cambridge: Polity Press, 2002), 28.

17. UNESCO, "The Race Question," in *UNESCO and Its Programme*, 2.

18. UNESCO, "Race Question," 3.

19. Triadafilos Triadafilopoulos, *Becoming Multicultural: Immigration and the Politics of Membership in Canada and Germany* (Vancouver: University of British Columbia Press, 2012), 53.

20. UNESCO, "Race Question," 8.

21. Barkan, *Retreat of Scientific Racism*, 1.

22. Race was also employed as a Cold War weapon. Soviet censure of American racism, especially in the US South, stung—and ultimately motivated both the Americans and their Western European allies to renounce racism. In this sense, European countries such as Britain and France paid a steep price for their efforts to combat communism; it meant relinquishing the vestiges of colonialism and empire.

23. Chin and Fehrenbach, "Introduction," 20.

24. Dienke Hondius, "Race and the Dutch: On the Uneasiness Surrounding Racial Issues in the Netherlands," in Sharam Alghasi, Thomas Hylland Eriksen, and Halleh Ghorashi, eds., *Paradoxes of Cultural Recognition: Perspectives from Northern Europe* (London: Ashgate, 2009), 41.

25. Éric Fassin, "(Sexual) Whiteness and National Identity: Race, Class and Sexuality in Colour-Blind France," in Karim Murji and John Solomos, eds., *Theories of Race and Ethnicity: Contemporary Debates and Perspectives* (Cambridge: Cambridge University Press, 2014), 233–50. See also Alana Lentin, "Europe and the Silence about Race," *European Journal of Social Theory* 11.4 (2008): 487–503, here 496.

26. Shirley Joshi and Bob Carter, "The Role of Labour in the Creation of a Racist Britain," *Race and Class* 25.3 (1984): 53–70.

27. Layton-Henry, *Politics of Immigration*, 71.

28. Geoff Eley, "The Trouble with 'Race': Migrancy, Cultural Difference, and the Remaking of Europe," in Chin et al., *After the Nazi Racial State*, 161.

29. Banton, *International Politics of Race*, 127.

30. Robert Miles and Annie Phizacklea, *White Man's Country: Racism in British Politics* (London: Pluto Press, 1984), 58, quoted in Malik, *Meaning of Race*, 25. See also Colin Brown, "Ethnic Pluralism in Britain: The Demographic and Legal Background," in Nathan Glazer and Ken Young, eds., *Ethnic Pluralism and Public Policy: Achieving Equality in the United States and Britain* (Portsmouth, NH: Heinemann, 1983), 48–49.

31. Randall Hansen, *Citizenship and Immigration in Post-war Britain: The Institutional Origins of a Multicultural Nation* (Oxford: Oxford University Press, 2000), 132.

32. Parliamentary Debates, Commons (Hansard), vol. 701, col. 71, 3 November 1964, quoted in Layton-Henry, *Politics of Immigration*, 78.

33. Gilroy, *There Ain't No Black in the Union Jack*, 46.

34. Enoch Powell, "Speech to the Annual General Meeting of the West Midlands Area Conservative Political Centre, Birmingham, 20 April 1968," in Powell, *Reflections of a Statesman*, 373–79.

35. Malik, *Meaning of Race*, 186–87; Paul Gilroy, "The End of Antiracism," in James Donald and Ali Rattansi, eds., *"Race," Culture and Difference* (London: Sage, 1992), 49–61, here 53.

36. Margaret Thatcher, Speech to Conservative Rally at Cheltenham, 3 July 1983, www.margaretthatcher.org/document/104989 (accessed 25 March 2015).

37. Peregrine Worsthorne, *Sunday Telegraph*, 23 May 1982, quoted in Gilroy, *There Ain't No Black in the Union Jack*, 51.

38. Gilroy, *There Ain't No Black in the Union Jack*, 74.

39. Select Committee on Race Relations and Immigration, *Police/Immigrant Relations* (1972), 71, quoted in John Solomos, *Black Youth, Racism and the State: The Politics of Ideology and Policy* (Cambridge: Cambridge University Press, 1988), 96.

40. Solomos, *Black Youth, Racism and the State*, 97.

41. Stuart Hall, Chas Critcher, Tony Jefferson, John Clarke, and Brian Roberts, *Policing the Crisis: Mugging, the State, and Law and Order* (London: Macmillan, 1978), 321–22.

42. Gilroy, *There Ain't No Black in the Union Jack*, 98.

43. *South London Press*, 5 August 1977. See also Ben Carrington, "Living the Crisis through Ten Moments," *Soundings: A Journal of Politics and Culture* 64 (2016–17): 148–59, here 150.

44. Solomos, *Black Youth, Racism and the State*, 110–11; Gilroy, *There Ain't No Black in the Union Jack*, 98.

45. Gilroy, *There Ain't No Black in the Union Jack*, 99.

46. "Outbreak of an Alien Disease," *Financial Times*, 11 July 1981, 12.

47. Siobhan Kattago, *Ambiguous Memory: The Nazi Past and German National Identity* (New York: Greenwood, 2001), 52.

48. Quoted in Charles S. Maier, *The Unmasterable Past: History, Holocaust, and German National Identity* (Cambridge, MA: Harvard University Press, 1988), 121. See also Christian Wicke, *Helmut Kohl's Quest for Normalty: His Representation of the German Nation* (New York: Berghahn Books, 2015), 159.

49. Geoff Eley, "Nazism, Politics and the Image of the Past: Thoughts on the West German Historikerstreit, 1986–1987," *Past and Present* 121 (1988): 171–208, here 176.

50. Rita Chin, *The Guest Worker Question in Postwar Germany* (Cambridge: Cambridge University Press, 2007), 156–57.

51. Jan-Werner Müller, *Another Country: German Intellectuals, Unification and National Identity* (New Haven, CT: Yale University Press, 2000), 59. See also Wulf Kansteiner, *In Pursuit of German Memory: History, Television, and Politics after Auschwitz* (Athens: Ohio University Press, 2006), 54–64.

52. Jürgen Habermas, "Apologectic Tendencies," in Jürgen Habermas, *The New Conservatism: Cultural Criticism and the Historians' Debate*, ed. and trans. Shierry Weber Nicholsen (Cambridge, MA: MIT Press, 1989), 212–28.

53. Müller, *Another Country*, 61. See also Maier, *Unmasterable Past*, 2.

54. Franz Josef Strauß, "Mehr aufrechten Gang," *Frankfurter Rundschau*, 14 January 1987, quoted in Eley, "Nazism, Politics and the Image of the Past," 182.

55. James M. Markham, "An Unabashedly Patriotic Strauss Goes Stumping," *New York Times*, 13 January 1987, A4.

56. Bundestag, *Verhandlungen des Deutschen Bundestages: Stenographische Berichte*, 9. Wahlperiod, vol. 120 (Bonn: Deutscher Bundestag und Bundesrat, 1982), 4892.

57. Bundestag, *Verhandlungen des Deutschen Bundestages*, 4893.

58. Heide Fehrenbach, "Black Occupation Children and the Devolution of the Nazi Racial State," in Chin et al., *After the Nazi Racial State*, 34.

59. Heide Fehrenbach, *Race after Hitler: Black Occupation Children in Postwar Germany and America* (Princeton, NJ: Princeton University Press, 2005).

60. Jeremy Varon, *Bringing the War Home: The Weather Underground, the Red Army Faction, and Revolutionary Violence in the Sixties and Seventies* (Berkeley: University of California Press, 2004), 31.

61. Rita Chin, "Democratization, Turks, and the Burden of German History," in Warren Breckman, Peter E. Gordon, A. Dirk Moses, Samuel Moyn, and Elliot Neaman, eds., *The Modernist Imagination: Intellectual History and Critical Theory* (New York: Berghahn Books, 2009), 242–67, here 248.

62. Hanno Kühnert, "Rassistische Klänge," *Die Zeit*, 5 February 1982, 61.

63. Nina Grunenberg, "Die Politiker müssen Farbe bekennen," *Die Zeit*, 5 February 1982, 5–6; Kühnert, "Rassistische Klänge," 61; Hanno Kühnert, "Von Flöhen und vielen unklugen Menschen," *Frankfurter Rundschau*, 25 February 1982; "Unser Land hat keinen Nachholbedarf für Nationalismus und Rassismus," *Frankfurter Rundschau*, 4 March 1982.

64. Hans Schueler, "Die Angst vor den Fremden," *Die Zeit*, 1 January 1982, 3.

65. Chin, *Guest Worker Question*, 144–47.

66. Scheuler, "Die Angst," 3.

67. Hans Schueler, "Last des Vorurteils," *Die Zeit*, 23 April 1982, 5.

68. Theodor Blank, "Ein Schritt zur Völkerverständigung," *Der Arbeitgeber* 17 (1965): 280.

69. Miriam Feldblum, *Reconstructing Citizenship: The Politics of Nationality Reform and Immigration in Contemporary France* (Albany: State University of New York Press, 1999), chap. 3.

70. Jonathan Marcus, *The National Front and French Politics: The Resistible Rise of Jean-Marie Le Pen* (Basingstoke: MacMillan, 1995), 53.

71. Feldblum, *Reconstructing Citizenship*, 37.

72. *Le Monde*, 2 November 1982, cited in Feldblum, *Reconstructing Citizenship*, 37.

73. Feldblum, *Reconstructing Citizenship*, 37–38. See also Pierre-André Taguieff, "The Doctrine of the National Front in France (1972–1989): A 'Revolutionary Programme'? Ideological Aspects of a National-Populist Mobilization," *New Political Science* 8.1–2 (1989): 29–70.

74. James G. Shields, "Politics and Populism: The French Far Right in the Ascendant," *Contemporary French Civilization* 11.1 (1987): 39–52, here 40. For more on the FN's electoral success in Dreux, see Françoise Gaspard, *A Small City in France: A Socialist Mayor Confronts Neofascism*, trans. Arthur Goldhammer (Cambridge, MA: Harvard University Press, 1995).

75. Shields, "Politics and Populism," 45; Feldblum, *Reconstructing Citizenship*, 52.

76. Shields, "Politics and Populism," 39–41. It's worth noting that the FN's 10 percent of the national vote, in both the European (1984) and legislative elections (1986), placed the party on par with the performance of the French Communist Party. It's also important to acknowledge that part of the FN's success had to do with Mitterrand's decision to determine the elections according to proportional vote.

77. *Le Quotidien de Paris*, 22–23 June 1985, quoted in Feldblum, *Reconstructing Citizenship*, 41.

78. *Le Figaro*, 26 October 1985, quoted in Feldblum, *Reconstructing Citizenship*, 41–42.

79. Feldblum, *Reconstructing Citizenship*, 44–45.

80. Feldblum, *Reconstructing Citizenship*, 42.

81. Feldblum, *Reconstructing Citizenship*, 44.

82. Tyler Stovall, "From Red Belt to Black Belt: Race, Class, and Urban Marginality in Twentieth Century Paris," in Sue Peabody and Tyler Stovall, eds., *The Color of Liberty: Histories of Race in France* (Durham, NC: Duke University Press, 2003), 355.

83. Feldblum, *Reconstructing Citizenship*, 60.

84. Feldblum, *Reconstructing Citizenship*, 59, 64.

85. RPR and UDF, 1986, quoted in Feldblum, *Reconstructing Citizenship*, 62.

86. Feldblum, *Reconstructing Citizenship*, 66.

87. RPR and UDF, 1986, quoted in Feldblum, *Reconstructing Citizenship*, 63.

88. *Le Monde*, 8 June 1985, quoted in Feldblum, *Reconstructing Citizenship*, 66. See also Bernard Stasi, *L'immigration: Une chance pour la France* (Paris: Laffont, 1984).

89. Favell, *Philosophies of Integration*, 54.

90. Although not against reform in principle, French bureaucrats resisted eliminating the territorial basis of citizenship because it clashed with administrative practices—that is, jus soli served as a primary way of attributing French nationality and was the preferred method of proving French citizenship (over the tedious process of demonstrating filial ties). For more on the French state's objections, see Feldblum, *Reconstructing Citizenship*, 78–88. The Conseil d'État declared that the government's effort was inopportune and contradicted republican tradition. It specifically rejected the nativist motivations of the right's proposals: the "measures of exclusion of populations already in France" (Feldblum, *Reconstructing Citizenship*, 89). This ruling, moreover, offered a kind of legitimation for activist groups that opposed the reform, enabling them to claim for themselves the role of "defenders of the republican tradition." In effect, the Conseil's decision sharpened the contrast between the right as champions of an exclusionary national identity and the left as guardians of French humanist, republican values.

91. David Assouline and Sylvia Zappi, *Notre printemps en hiver: Le mouvement étudiant de décembre 1986* (Paris: Éditions La Découverte, 1987), 263.

92. *Le Quotidien de Paris*, 16 January 1987, quoted in Feldblum, *Reconstructing Citizenship*, 96–97.

93. Favell, *Philosophies of Integration*, 55.

94. The Commission was chaired by Marceau Long, vice president of the Conseil d'État. Its other members included two other state bureaucrats (P. P. Kaltenback and J. J. de Bresson), four law professors and one lawyer (B. Goldman, P. Catala, Y. Loussouarn, J. Rivero, and J. M. Varaut), three historians (P. Chaunu, H. Carrère d'Encausee, and E. Le Roy Ladurie), two sociologists (A. Touraine and D. Schnapper), two doctors (S. Kacet and L. Boutbien),

and one filmmaker (H. Verneuil). See Feldblum, *Reconstructing Citizenship* 103–4.

95. Favell, *Philosophies of Integration*, 42.

96. Pierre Catala, "Notes Sur le Droit de la Nationalité" (2 November 1987, 6 pages), Nationality Commission Archives, 6, quoted in Feldblum, *Reconstructing Citizenship*, 107.

97. The classic discussion of such a national integration process is Eugen Weber, *Peasants into Frenchmen: The Modernization of Rural France, 1870–1914* (Stanford, CA: Stanford University Press, 1976).

98. Marceau Long, "Présentation du Rapport de la Commission de la Nationalité par Marceau Long" (11 April 1988, 14 pages), Nationality Commission Archives, 4, quoted in Feldblum, *Reconstructing Citizenship*, 109, emphasis original.

99. Long, "Présentation du Rapport," 8, quoted in Feldblum, *Reconstructing Citizenship*, 110.

100. Marceau Long, *Etre français aujourd'hui et demain: Rapport de la Commission de la Nationalité presenté par M. Marceau Long au Premier Ministre*, 2 vols. (Paris: La Documentation Française, 1988), 1:28, quoted in Feldblum, *Reconstructing Citizenship*, 111.

101. Long, *Etre Français ajourd'hui et demain*, 2:87, quoted in Jeremy Jennings, "Citizenship, Republicanism, and Multiculturalism in Contemporary France," *British Journal of Political Science* 30.4 (2000): 575–98, here 582.

102. Dominique Schnapper, *La Communauté des citoyens: sur l'idée moderne de nation* (Paris: Gallimard, 1994), 48.

103. Ernest Renan, "Qu'est-ce qu'une nation?," in *Oeuvres complètes* (Paris: Calmann-Lévy, 1947), 887–906, here 904.

104. Dominique Schnapper, *La France de l'integration* (Paris: Gallimard, 1991), 63, quoted in Jennings, "Citizenship, Republicanism, and Multiculturalism," 577.

105. Long, *Etre Français aujourd'hui et demain*, 1:595–96, quoted in Feldblum, *Reconstructing Citizenship*, 118.

106. Long, *Etre Français aujourd'hui et demain*, 1:418–19, quoted in Feldblum, *Reconstructing Citizenship*, 119.

107. Feldblum, *Reconstructing Citizenship*, 103.

108. Peter Nyers and Kim Rygiel, *Citizenship, Migrant Activism and the Politics of Movement* (London: Routledge, 2012), 27.

109. Long, *Etre Français aujourd'hui et demain*, 1:558–59, quoted in Feldblum, *Reconstructing Citizenship*, 113.

110. Long, *Etre Français aujourd'hui et demain*, 1:473–74, quoted in Feldblum, *Reconstructing Citizenship*, 113.

111. Favell, *Philosophies of Integration*, 56–57.

112. Atam Vetta, "A Contract with the Devil," *Impact International*, 23 February–8 March 1990, 5–8, here 5.

113. M. H. Faruqi, "The Satanic Verses: Dear Mr. Baker, Please Do Not Rush to Judgment," *Impact International*, 10–23 February 1989, 7–8, here 8. See also Kenan Malik, *From Fatwa to Jihad: The Rushdie Affair and Its Aftermath* (New York: Melville House, 2009), 1.

114. Daniel Pipes, *The Rushdie Affair: The Novel, the Ayatollah, and the West* (New Brunswick, NJ: Transaction, 2003), 19–20.

115. Elaine R. Thomas, *Immigration, Islam, and the Politics of Belonging in France: A Comparative Framework* (Philadelphia: University of Pennsylvania Press, 2012), 212.

116. Malik, *From Fatwa to Jihad*, 14–16.

117. Thomas, *Immigration, Islam*, 240.

118. Malik, *From Fatwa to Jihad*, 18–19.

119. Thomas, *Immigration, Islam*, 215.

120. "Hurd Preaches Non-violence to Muslims," *Guardian*, 25 February 1989, 2.

121. John Patten, "The Muslim Community in Britain," *Times* (London), 5 July 1989, 13.

122. Patten, "Muslim Community in Britain," 13.

123. Talal Asad, *Genealogies of Religion: Discipline and Reasons of Power in Christianity and Islam* (Baltimore: Johns Hopkins University Press, 1993), 240.

124. Max Farrar, "Multiculturalism in the UK: A Contested Discourse," in Max Farrar, Simon Robinson, Yasmin Valli, and Paul Wetherley, eds., *Islam in the West: Key Issues in Multiculturalism* (Basingstoke: Palgrave Macmillan, 2012), 13.

125. Patten, "Muslim Community in Britain," 13.

126. Patten, "Muslim Community in Britain," 13.

127. John Patten, "On Being British" (London: Home Office), 18 July 1989, quoted in Asad, *Genealogies of Religion*, 244.

128. Martin Jones, "Ground Rules for the British Way of Life," *Sunday Times*, 23 July 1989, quoted in Thomas, *Immigration, Islam*, 220.

129. James Lynch, "Cultural Pluralism, Structural Pluralism and the United Kingdom," in Commission for Racial Equality and Runnymede Trust, *Britain, a Plural Society: Report of a Seminar* (London: Commission for Racial Equality, 1990), 34, quoted in Thomas, *Immigration, Islam*, 224.

130. Patten, "Muslim Community in Britain," 13.

131. *Economist*, 5 January 1991, quoted in Thomas, *Immigration, Islam*, 225.

132. *New Statesman & Society*, 15 February 1991, quoted in Thomas, *Immigration, Islam*, 225.

133. *Economist*, 5 January 1991, quoted in Thomas, *Immigration, Islam*, 225–26.

134. Fay Weldon, *Sacred Cows: A Portrait of Britain, Post-Rushdie, Pre-Utopia* (London: Chatto & Windus, 1989), 31.

135. Weldon, *Sacred Cows*, 32.

136. Thomas, *Immigration, Islam*, 222.

137. Weldon, *Sacred Cows*, 16.

138. Roy Hattersley, "The Racism of Asserting That 'They' Must Behave Like 'Us,'" *Independent*, 21 July 1989.

139. Asad, *Genealogies of Religion*, 266.

140. Edward Pearce, "Wielding a Racist Stick in God-Fearing Politics," *Sunday Times*, 23 July 1989, quoted in Asad, *Genealogies of Religion*, 266 note 25.

141. "One Thousand Muslim Fundamentalists Demonstrate in Paris," *Le Monde*, 27 February 1989, quoted in Lisa Appignanesi and Sara Maitland, eds., *The Rushdie File* (London: Fourth Estate, 1989), 132.

142. *Le Monde*, 28 February 1989, quoted in Appignanesi and Maitland, *Rushdie File*, 132.

143. James M. Markham, "Fallout over Rushdie; The Muslim Presence in Western Europe Is Suddenly Starker," *New York Times*, 5 March 1989, E2.

144. Claus Leggewie, "Multikulturelle Gesellschaft oder: die Naivität der Ausländerfreunde," *Deutsche Volkszeitung/Die Tat*, 10 March 1989, 3.

145. Dankwart Guratzsch, "Rushdie und die Multikultur," *Die Welt*, 20 March 1989.

Chapter Four:
Muslim Women, Sexual Democracy, and the Defense of Freedom

1. John R. Bowen, *Why the French Don't Like Headscarves: Islam, the State, and Public Space* (Princeton, NJ: Princeton University Press, 2006), 83.

2. Paul A. Silverstein, "Sporting Faith: Islam, Soccer, and the French Nation-State," *Social Text* 18.4 (2000): 25–53, here 25.

3. Elaine R. Thomas, *Immigration, Islam, and the Politics of Belonging in France: A Comparative Framework* (Philadelphia: University of Pennsylvania Press, 2012), 163–64.

4. Thomas, *Immigration, Islam*, 164–65.

5. Thomas, *Immigration, Islam*, 165.

6. Joan W. Scott, *The Politics of the Veil* (Princeton, NJ: Princeton University Press, 2007), 91–92.

7. Jeremy Jennings, "Citizenship, Republicanism, and Multiculturalism in Contemporary France," *British Journal of Political Science* 30.4 (2000): 575–98, here 578.

8. Jennings, "Citizenship, Republicanism, and Multiculturalism," 579.

9. Scott, *Politics of the Veil*, 99; Thomas, *Immigration, Islam*, 165.

10. Thomas, *Immigration, Islam*, 166.

11. Thomas, *Immigration, Islam*, 167.

12. Bowen, *Why the French Don't Like Headscarves*, 84.

13. Miriam Feldblum, *Reconstructing Citizenship: The Politics of Nationality Reform and Immigration in Contemporary France* (Albany: State University of New York Press, 1999), 138–39.

14. Scott, *Politics of the Veil*, 90.

15. *Le Nouvel Observateur*, 2 November 1989, quoted in Scott, *Politics of the Veil*, 24.

16. *Le Quotidien de Paris*, 18 October 1989, quoted in Thomas, *Immigration, Islam*, 173.

17. Saïd Bouamama, "Au-delà du foulard . . . la laïcité," *Revue Mémoire Fertile* 1 (1989): 4–12, here 7.

18. *Journal Officiel*, 25 October 1989, 4114, quoted in Maxim Silverman, *Deconstructing the Nation: Immigration, Racism and Citizenship in Modern France* (London: Routledge, 1992), 25.

19. *Journal Officiel*, 8 November 1989, 4752, quoted in Thomas, *Immigration, Islam*, 178.

20. Quoted in Silverman, *Deconstructing the Nation*, 25–26.

21. Feldblum, *Reconstructing Citizenship*, 142.

22. Scott, *Politics of the Veil*, 27.

23. "Wearing of Ostentatious Signs in Schools," *Bulletin officiel de l'éducation nationale* 35 (29 September 1994): 2528–29, quoted in Nicky Jones, "Beneath the Veil: Muslim Girls and Islamic Headscarves in Secular France, *Macquarie Law Journal* 9 (2009): 47–69, here 55–56, emphasis added.

24. Scott, *Politics of the Veil*, 27.

25. Scott, *Politics of the Veil*, 28.

26. Scott, *Politics of the Veil*, 28–29.

27. Scott, *Politics of the Veil*, 34.

28. Christine Delphy, *Separate and Dominate: Feminism and Racism after the War on Terror*, trans. David Broder (London: Verso, 2015), 101.

29. Scott, *Politics of the Veil*, 35.

30. Scott, *Politics of the Veil*, 124.

31. Alma Lévy and Lila Lévy, *Des filles comme les autres: au-delà du foulard* (Paris: La Découverte, 2004), 63, quoted in Scott, *Politics of the Veil*, 125.

32. Scott, *Politics of the Veil*, 125.

33. Cited in Emmanuel Terray, "L'hystérie politique," in Charlotte Nordmann, ed., *Le foulard islamique en questions* (Paris: Editions Amsterdam, 2004), 113.

34. "Et vous, qu'en pensez-vous?," *France-Soir*, 21 October 1989, quoted in Jones, "Beneath the Veil," 64.

35. Bowen, *Why the French Don't Like Headscarves*, 112.

36. Alex Duval Smith, "France Divided as Headscarf Ban Is Set to Become Law," *Observer*, 1 February 2004; and Claire Murphy, "Headscarves: Contentious Cloths," *BBC News Online*, 11 December 2003.

37. Scott, *Politics of the Veil*, 27.

38. Françoise Gaspard and Farhad Khosrokhavar, *Le foulard et la République* (Paris: La Découverte, 1995), 210, quoted in Scott, *Politics of the Veil*, 28.

39. *Libération*, 13 May 2003, quoted in Bowen, *Why the French Don't Like Headscarves*, 107.

40. Vron Ware, "Moments of Danger: Race, Gender, and Memories of Empire," *History and Theory* 31.4 (1992): 116–37, here 133.

41. Leti Volpp, "Feminism versus Multiculturalism," *Columbia Law Review* 101.5 (2001): 1181–1218, here 1195.

42. Uma Chakravarti, "Whatever Happened to the Vedi Dasi? Orientalism, Nationalism and a Script for the Past," in Kumkum Sangari and Sudesh Vaid, eds., *Recasting Women: Essays in Indian Colonial History* (New Brunswick, NJ: Rutgers University Press, 1990), 27–87, here 35.

43. James Mill, *The History of British India* (London: Baldwin, Cradock and Joy, 1817), vol. 1, bk. 2, 295–96.

44. Mill, *History of British India*, vol. 1, bk. 2, 274–75. Many other British scholars of and commentators on India focused on *sati*. For an early Orientalist treatment of the women's question in India, see H. T. Colebrooke, "On the Duties of the Faithful Hindu Widow," *Asiatic Researches* 4 (1795): 202–19.

45. Lata Mani, *Contentious Traditions: The Debate on Sati in Colonial India* (Berkeley: University of California Press, 1998), 3.

46. Antoinette M. Burton, *Burdens of History: British Feminists, Indian Women, and Imperial Culture* (Chapel Hill: University of North Carolina Press, 1994), 8.

47. Burton, *Burdens of History*, 7.

48. Leila Ahmed, *Women and Gender in Islam: Historical Roots of a Modern Debate* (New Haven, CT: Yale University Press, 1992), 152.

49. Ahmed, *Women and Gender in Islam*, 152.

50. Ahmed, *Women and Gender in Islam*, 152–53.

51. Julia Clancy-Smith, "Islam, Gender, and Identities in the Making of French Algeria, 1830–1962," in Julia Clancy-Smith and Frances Gouda, eds., *Domesticating Empire: Race, Gender, and Family Life in French and Dutch Colonialism* (Charlottesville: University of Virginia Press, 1998), 154–74, here 154–55.

52. Eugène Daumas, "La femme arabe," *Revue Africaine* 56.284 (1912): 1, quoted in Clancy-Smith, "Islam, Gender, and Identities," 163. As Clancy-Smith notes, Daumas actually wrote this piece near the end of his life (1871), but it was not published until 1912.

53. Neil MacMaster, *Burning the Veil: The Algerian War and the "Emancipation" of Muslim Women, 1954–62* (Manchester: Manchester University Press, 2009), 30.

54. Jeanne Bowlan, "Civilizing Gender Relations in Algeria: The Paradoxical Case of Marie Bugéja, 1919–39," in Clancy-Smith and Gouda, eds., *Domesticating Empire*, 175–92, here 175.

55. Frantz Fanon, *A Dying Colonialism*, trans. Haakon Chevalier (New York: Grove Press, 1994), 38.

56. MacMaster, *Burning the Veil*, 5.

57. *L'Écho d'Alger*, 19 May 1958, quoted in MacMaster, *Burning the Veil*, 131–32.

58. MacMaster, *Burning the Veil*, 132.

59. James F. Hollifield, "Immigration and Modernization," in James F. Hollifield and George Ross, eds., *Searching for the New France* (New York: Routledge, 1991), 113–50, see esp. Tables 5.3 and 5.4.

60. Amelia H. Lyons, *The Civilizing Mission in the Metropole: Algerian Families and the French Welfare State during Decolonization* (Stanford, CA: Stanford University Press, 2013), 70–74.

61. Lyons, *Civilizing Mission in the Metropole*, 78.

62. Amelia H. Lyons, "The Civilizing Mission in the Metropole: Algerian Immigrants in France and the Politics of Adaptation during Decolonization," *Geschichte und Gesellschaft* 32.4 (2006): 489–516, here 507.

63. Lyons, *Civilizing Mission in the Metropole*, 75, 79.

64. Lyons, *Civilizing Mission in the Metropole*, 77, 75.

65. Franz Brandt, *Situationsanalyse nichterwerbstätiger Ehefrauen auslän-discher Arbeitnehmer in der Bundesrepublik Deutschland* (Bonn: Bundesminis-terium für Jugend, Familie und Gesundheit, 1977), 180.

66. Susanne von Paczensky, "Frauen aus Anatolien: Vorwort," in Andrea Baumgartner-Karabak and Gisela Landesberger, eds., *Die verkauften Bräute: Türkische Frauen zwischen Kreuzberg und Anatolien* (Hamburg: Rowohlt, 1978), 7. For more on the nuanced German efforts at cultural understanding of Turkish women, see Rita Chin, "Turkish Women, West German Feminists, and the Gen-dered Discourse on Muslim Cultural Difference," *Public Culture* 22.3 (2010): 557–81, here 563–64.

67. Von Paczensky, "Frauen aus Anatolien," 7.

68. Baumgartner-Karabak and Landesberger, *Die verkauften Bräute*, 67–68.

69. Avtar Brah, "Reframing Europe: Engendered Racisms, Ethnicities and Nationalisms in Contemporary Western Europe," *Feminist Review* 45 (1993): 9–28, here 19–20.

70. Kathryn Ray, "Constituting 'Asian Women': Political Representation, Iden-tity Politics and Local Discourses of Participation," *Ethnic and Racial Studies* 26.5 (2003): 854–78, here 861.

71. Pratibha Parmar, "Gender, Race, and Class: Asian Women in Resistance," in Centre for Contemporary Cultural Studies, *The Empire Strikes Back: Race and Racism in 70s Britain* (London: Hutchinson, 1982), 236–75, here 259.

72. Ali Rattansi, "Changing the Subject? Racism, Culture and Education," in James Donald and Ali Rattansi, eds., *"Race," Culture and Difference* (London: Sage, 1992), 11–48, here 19. Rattansi notes that British discourse also figured the Asian woman as "full of sexual charm and allure produced by a demure seductiveness replete with the promise of a mysterious Oriental eroticism."

73. Rattansi, "Changing the Subject?," 19.

74. For more on French feminist movements, see Claire Duchen, *Feminism in France: From May '68 to Mitterrand* (London: Routledge, 1986). For a good summary, see Claire Goldberg Moses, "French Feminism's Fortunes," *Women's Review of Books* 5.1 (1987): 16–17.

75. Alice Schwarzer, "Die Betrogenen," *EMMA*, May 1979, 12–19, here 19. This early essay was recently reprinted in Alice Schwarzer, ed., *Die große Ver-schleierung: Für Integration, gegen Islamismus* (Cologne: Kiepenheuer & Witsch, 2010).

76. Hazel V. Carby, "White Women Listen! Black Feminism and the Bound-aries of Sisterhood," in Centre for Contemporary Cultural Studies, *Empire Strikes Back*, 212–35, here 216.

77. Fatemeh Serdani, "Erste Kongreß der ausländischen und deutschen Frauen vom 24. Bis 26. März 1984 in Frankfurt am Main," *Feministische Studien* 3.2 (1984): 170–71, here 170.

78. Wendy Pojmann, *Immigrant Women and Feminism in Italy* (Aldershot: Ashgate, 2006), 146.

79. Carby, "White Women Listen!," 232.

80. Yasemin Yıldız, "Governing European Subjects: Tolerance and Guilt in the Discourse of 'Muslim Women,'" *Cultural Critique* 77 (2011): 70–101, here 75.

81. Beverly Weber, "Hijab Martyrdom, Headscarf Debates: Rethinking Violence, Secularism, and Islam in Germany," *Comparative Studies of South Asia, Africa and the Middle East* 32.1 (2012): 102–15, here 108.

82. Beverly Weber, "Cloth on Her Head, Constitution in Hand: Germany's Headscarf Debates and the Cultural Politics of Difference," *German Politics and Society* 22.3 (2004): 33–64, here 47.

83. Weber, "Cloth on Her Head," 44.

84. Susan B. Rottmann and Myra Marx Ferree, "Citizenship and Intersectionality: German Feminist Debates about Headscarf and Antidiscrimination Laws," *Social Politics* 15.4 (2008): 481–513, here 491.

85. Wulf Reimer, "Kopftuchstreit in Pluederhausen. Eine muslimische Pädagogin verwirrt Baden-Württemberg," *Süddeutsche Zeitung*, 8 July 1998, cited in Weber, "Cloth on Her Head," 48.

86. Anita Heilinger, "Kopftuch-Debatte und Feminismus," *Kofra* 108/04, www.kofra.de/htm/Zeitung/Zeitung108.pdf, quoted in Rottmann and Marx Ferree, "Citizenship and Intersectionality," 495.

87. Myra Marx Ferree, *Varieties of Feminism: German Gender Politics in Global Perspective* (Stanford, CA: Stanford University Press, 2012), 216.

88. Rottmann and Marx Ferree, "Citizenship and Intersectionality," 499–500.

89. Gaby Strassburger, "Nicht westlich und doch modern: Partnerwahlmodi türkischer Migrant(inn)en in Diskurs und Praxis," *Beiträge zur feministischen Theorie und Praxis: Wenn Heimat global wird* . . . 63/64 (2003): 15–28, cited in Rottmann and Marx Ferree, "Citizenship and Intersectionality," 495.

90. Rottmann and Marx Ferree, "Citizenship and Intersectionality," 498.

91. Jack Straw, "I Felt Uneasy Talking to Someone I Couldn't See," *Guardian*, 5 October 2006, www.guardian.co.uk/commentisfree/2006/oct/06/politics.uk (accessed 20 March 2012).

92. Straw, "I Felt Uneasy."

93. Sevgı Kılıç, "The British Veil Wars," *Social Politics* 15.4 (2008): 433–54, here 450.

94. Kılıç, "British Veil Wars," 450.

95. Brittany Murray and Diane Perpich, eds., *Taking French Feminism to the Streets: Fadela Amara and the Rise of Ni Putes Ni Soumises* (Urbana: University of Illinois Press, 2011), 1.

96. Mayanthi Fernando, "Exceptional Citizens: Secular Muslim Women and the Politics of Difference in France," *Social Anthropology/Anthropologie Sociale* 17.4 (2009): 379–92.

97. Murray and Perpich, *Taking French Feminism to the Streets*, 88.

98. Murray and Perpich, *Taking French Feminism to the Streets*, 88.

99. Fadela Amara, *Ni Putes Ni Soumises* (Paris: La Découverte, 2003). See also Fadela Amara with Sylvia Zappi, *Breaking the Silence: French Women's Voices from the Ghetto* (Berkeley: University of California Press, 2006).

100. Fernando, "Exceptional Citizens," 382.

101. Amara with Zappi, *Breaking the Silence*, 48–49, quoted in Fernando, "Exceptional Citizens," 382.

102. Murray and Perpich, *Taking French Feminism to the Streets*, 72.

103. Murray and Perpich, *Taking French Feminism to the Streets*, 14.

104. Murray and Perpich, *Taking French Feminism to the Streets*, 49.

105. Fernando, "Exceptional Citizens," 382.

106. Murray and Perpich, *Taking French Feminism to the Streets*, 16–17.

107. Murray and Perpich, *Taking French Feminism to the Streets*, 18–19.

108. See Sheila Pullham, "Inflammatory Language," *Guardian*, 8 November 2005, www.guardian.co.uk/news/blog/2005/nov/08/inflammatoryla (accessed 19 August 2016). She cites Doug Ireland's opinion: " 'Racaille' is infinitely more pejorative than 'scum' to French-speakers—it has the flavor of characterizing an entire group of people as subhuman, inherently evil and criminal, worthless, and is, in other words, one of the most serious insults one could launch at the rebellious ghetto youth."

109. Fernando, "Exceptional Citizens," 379.

110. Quoted in Scott, *Politics of the Veil*, 158.

111. Alice Schwarzer, "Offene Antwort an '60 Deutsche Migrantionsforscher,' " in Schwarzer, *Die große Verschleierung*, 156.

112. Fernando, "Exceptional Citizens," 380.

113. Amara, *Ni Putes Ni Soumises*, 48–49, quoted in Fernando, "Exceptional Citizens," 382.

114. Ayaan Hirsi Ali, *The Caged Virgin: An Emancipation Proclamation for Women and Islam* (New York: Free Press, 2006), 62.

115. Fernando, "Exceptional Citizens," 384.

116. Yıldız, "Governing European Subjects," 82.

117. Human Rights Watch declared the Dutch test discriminatory because very specific groups of foreign nationals were exempted from the test. These include people from the European Union, Norway, Iceland, Switzerland, Australia, Japan, Canada, New Zealand, South Korea, and the United States. Surinamese citizens who could demonstrate that they had had basic schooling in Dutch were also excused from this requirement.

118. See the description of the film *Coming to the Netherlands* at Naar Nederland, www.naarnederland.nl/en/the-examination-package/filmen (accessed 21 March 2012).

119. Naar Nederland, www.naarnederland.nl/en/the-examination-package/filmen (accessed 21 March 2012).

120. Éric Fassin, "National Identities and Transnational Intimacies: Sexual Democracy and the Politics of Immigration in Europe," *Public Culture* 22.3 (2010): 507–29, here 517.

121. Nicholas Sarkozy's presidential campaign video, www.dailymotion.com/video/x1qz2d_1-identite-national, quoted in Fassin, "National Identities and Transnational Intimacies," 513, emphasis added.

122. Anne Norton, *On the Muslim Question* (Princeton, NJ: Princeton University Press, 2013), 54.

123. Norton, *On the Muslim Question*, 54.

124. Ian Buruma, *Murder in Amsterdam: Liberal Europe, Islam, and the Limits of Tolerance* (New York: Penguin, 2006), 46–47.

125. Norton, *On the Muslim Question*, 56.

126. Scott, *Politics of the Veil*, 102.

127. Scott, *Politics of the Veil*, 102.

128. Schwarzer, *Die große Verschleierung*, 1.

129. Fassin, "National Identities and Transnational Intimacies," 513.

130. Halina Bendkowski et al., "Offener Brief an die Integrationsbeauftragte Frau Marieluise Beck, die Frauenministerin Frau Renate Schmidt und die Justizministerin Frau Brigitte Zypries," www.isioma.net/sds06203.html (accessed 31 March 2012).

131. Hirsi Ali, *Caged Virgin*, 7.

132. Necla Kelek, *Himmelreise: Mein Streit mit den Wächtern des Islam* (Munich: Goldmann, 2011), 12.

133. Kelek, *Himmelreise*, 270, quoted in Yildiz, "Governing European Subjects," 89.

134. Carl Degler, *In Search of Human Nature: The Decline and Revival of Darwinism in American Social Thought* (Oxford: Oxford University Press, 1991), 61.

Chapter Five:
The "Failure" of Multiculturalism

1. "Integration: Merkel erklärt Multikulti für gescheitert," *Spiegel Online*, 16 October 2010, www.spiegel.de/politik/deutschland/integration-merkel-erklaert-multikulti-fuer-gescheitert-a-723532.html (accessed 17 July 2013).

2. On the web, for instance, Merkel's pronouncement produced immediate headlines: "Merkel Says German Multicultural Society Has Failed," *BBC News*, 17 October 2010, www.bbc.co.uk/news/world-europe-11559451 (accessed 16 September 2013); "Chancellor Merkel Says German Multiculturalism Has 'Utterly Failed,'" *Deutsche Welle*, 17 October 2010, www.dw.de/chancellor-merkel-says-german-multiculturalism-has-utterly-failed/a-6118859 (accessed 16 September 2013); "Merkel Says German Multiculturalism Has Failed," *Reuters*, 16 October 2010, www.reuters.com/article/2010/10/16/us-germany-merkel-immigration-idUSTRE69F1K320101016 (accessed 16 September 2013).

3. Tom Heneghan, "Sarkozy Joins Allies Burying Multiculturalism," *Reuters*, 11 February 2011, www.reuters.com/article/us-france-sarkozy-multiculturalism-idUSTRE71A4UP20110211 (accessed 11 November 2016).

4. Alana Lentin and Gavan Titley, *The Crises of Multiculturalism: Racism in a Neoliberal Age* (London: Zed Books, 2011), 18–29.

5. Quoted in E.J.B. Rose, *Colour and Citizenship—A Report on British Race Relations* (London: Oxford University Press, 1969), 25.

6. Andrew Adonis and Keith Thomas, *Roy Jenkins: A Retrospective* (Oxford: Oxford University Press, 2004), 142.

7. Swann Committee, "Education for All" (London: HMSO, 1985), 199.

8. Swann Committee, "Education for All," 200.

9. Swann Committee, "Education for All," 198.

10. Swann Committee, "Education for All," 199–200.

11. Swann Committee, "Education for All," 222.

12. Swann Committee, "Education for All," 221–22.

13. Swann Committee, "Education for All," 225.

14. Swann Committee, "Education for All," 5, 228.

15. Swann Committee, "Education for All," 225–26.

16. Swann Committee, "Education for All," 227.

17. Alfred Sherman, "Schooling by Race," *Daily Telegraph*, 19 January 1985, quoted in Nancy Murray, "Anti-Racists and Other Demons: The Press and Ideology in Thatcher's Britain," *Race & Class* 27.3 (1986): 1–19, here 12.

18. Simon Pearce, "Swann and the Spirit of the Age," in Frank Palmer, ed., *Anti-racism: An Assault on Education and Value* (London: Sherwood Press, 1986), 136–48, here 136.

19. Ray Honeyford, "Education and Race—An Alternative View," *Salisbury Review*, Winter 1984, 30–32, here 30.

20. Honeyford, "Education and Race," 30.

21. Honeyford, "Education and Race," 30.

22. Honeyford, "Education and Race," 32.

23. Ray Honeyford, "Multi-ethnic Intolerance," *Salisbury Review*, Summer 1983, 12–13, here 13.

24. Honeyford, "Education and Race," 31.

25. Honeyford, "Education and Race," 31.

26. "Education and Race—An Alternative View," *Telegraph*, 27 August 2006, www.telegraph.co.uk/culture/3654888/Education-and-Race-an-Alternative-View.html (accessed 24 July 2015).

27. Roger Scruton, "Bigots in a Class of Their Own," *Times* (London), 24 April 1984, 12.

28. "The Judge and the Head and the Children," *Guardian*, 7 September 1985, 10.

29. James Curran, "A New Political Generation," in James Curran, Ivor Gaber, and Julian Petley, *Culture Wars: The Media and the British Left* (Edinburgh: Edinburgh University Press, 2005), 3–38, here 16.

30. Curran, "New Political Generation," 11.

31. Curran, "New Political Generation," 11–12.

32. Curran, "New Political Generation," 16.

33. John Nagle, *Multiculturalism's Double-Bind: Creating Inclusivity, Cosmopolitanism and Difference* (London: Routledge, 2016), 15–16.

34. James Curran, "Goodbye to the Clowns," in Curran, Gaber, and Petley, *Culture Wars*, 39–55, here 41.

35. *Daily Mail*, 30 March 1984, quoted in Curran, "Goodbye to the Clowns," 42.

36. Julian Petley, "Hit and Myth," in Curran, Gaber, and Petley, *Culture Wars*, 85–107, here 87.

37. Yasmin Alibhai-Brown, *Imagining the New Britain* (New York: Routledge, 2001), 82.

38. Petley, "Hit and Myth," 86.

39. "Labour Councils Accused of Being Big Spenders of Other People's Money," *Times* (London), 8 April 1981, 9.

40. Conor O'Clery, "GLC Dead, But Won't Lie Down," *Irish Times*, 9 July 1985, 5.

41. Paul Gilroy, "Melancholia and Multiculture," *Open Democracy*, 3 August 2004, https://www.opendemocracy.net/arts-multiculturalism/article_2035 .jsp (accessed 18 September 2016).

42. Ali Rattansi, *Multiculturalism: A Very Short Introduction* (Oxford: Oxford University Press, 2011), 28.

43. Bhikhu Parekh, *The Future of Multi-ethnic Britain* (London: Profile Books, 2000), viii.

44. Parekh, *Future of Multi-ethnic Britain*, xi.

45. Parekh, *Future of Multi-ethnic Britain*, 48.

46. Parekh, *Future of Multi-ethnic Britain*, 56.

47. Rita Chin, *The Guest Worker Question in Postwar Germany* (Cambridge: Cambridge University Press, 2007), 202–4.

48. Konrad Adam, "Der Preis der Multikultur. Ausländer und Detusche—eine kritische Masse?," *Frankfurter Allgemeine Zeitung*, 23 November 1982, quoted in Chin, *Guest Worker Question*, 204.

49. In certain pockets of the CDU/CSU, skepticism toward multiculturalism ran deep. In 1988, Interior Minister Friedrich Zimmerman attempted to revise the 1965 Foreigner Law and justified his proposed restrictions by warning "the self-understanding of the Federal Republic of Germany as a German state is at stake." Allowing the migration of foreigners to continue, he argued, "would mean abandoning the homogeneity of society, which is defined by membership in the nation. . . . The Federal Republic of Germany would develop into a multinational and multicultural society, which would be permanently plagued by minority problems." Christian Schneider, "Aus Fremden warden Mitbürger und Landsleute," *Süddeutsche Zeitung*, 10–11 September 1988, quoted in Christian Joppke, "Multiculturalism and Immigration: A Comparison of the United States, Germany, and Great Britain," *Theory and Society* 25 (1996): 471.

50. It replicated the federal post that had been inaugurated in 1979 by the SPD but was rendered largely inactive after the CDU came to power in 1982.

51. Gökçe Yurdakul, "Mobilizing Kreuzberg: Political Representation, Immigrant Incorporation, and Turkish Associations in Berlin" (PhD diss., University of Toronto, 2006), 157.

52. Elisa Klapheck, "Multikulturell—was ist das?," *Die Tageszeitung*, 22 February 1989, quoted in Chin, *Guest Worker Question*, 191.

53. Dankwart Guratzsch, "Rushdie und die Multikultur," *Die Welt*, 20 March 1989.

54. Claus Leggewie, "Multikulturelle Gesellschaft oder: die Naivität der Ausländerfreunde," *Deutsche Volkszeitung/Die Tat*, 10 March 1989, 3.

55. Brett Klopp, *German Multiculturalism: Immigrant Integration and the Transformation of Citizenship* (Westport, CT: Praeger, 2002), 165.

56. Klopp, *German Multiculturalism*, 167.

57. Klopp, *German Multiculturalism*, 168.

58. Chin, *Guest Worker Question*, 250–54.

59. Triadafilos Triadafilopoulos, *Becoming Multicultural: Immigration and the Politics of Membership in Canada and Germany* (Vancouver: University of British Columbia Press, 2012), 140.

60. Quoted in Triadafilopoulos, *Becoming Multicultural*, 149.

61. Triadafilopoulos, *Becoming Multicultural*, 151.

62. Paul A. Silverstein, *Algeria in France: Transpolitics, Race, and Nation* (Bloomington: Indiana University Press, 2004), 92–95.

63. Riva Kastoryano, *Negotiating Identities: States and Immigrants in France and Germany*, trans. Barbara Harshav (Princeton, NJ: Princeton University Press, 2002), 69–70.

64. For more on the emergence of a spatial approach to the urban crisis in France, see Sylvie Tissot, *L'État et les quartiers: Genèse d'une catégorie d'action publique* (Paris: Le Seuil, 2007).

65. Marie-Thérèse Espinasse, "A Brief Look at the Development of Urban Policy in France, 1977 to 1996," in Organisation for Economic Co-operation and Development, *Immigrants, Integration and Cities: Exploring the Links* (Paris: OECD, 1998), 92.

66. Fabien Jobard, "An Overview of French Riots: 1981–2004," in David Waddington, Fabien Jobard, and Mike King, eds., *Rioting in the UK and France: A Comparative Analysis* (Milton: Willan, 2009), 27–38, here 32.

67. Sylvie Tissot, "'French Suburbs': A New Problem or a New Approach to Social Exclusion?" (Center for European Studies Working Paper 160, 2008), 6.

68. Tissot, "French Suburbs," 7.

69. Tissot, "French Suburbs," 8.

70. Espinasse, "Brief Look," 96.

71. Espinasse, "Brief Look," 94.

72. Jobard, "Overview of French Riots," 33.

73. Jobard, "Overview of French Riots," 30. He notes that in the first half of the 1990s, there were ten to fifteen conflicts between *banlieue* youth and the police each year.

74. George W. Pugh and Jean H. Pugh, "Measures for Malaise: Recent French 'Law and Order' Legislation," *Louisiana Law Review* 42.4 (1982): 1301–21, here 1302. The new law changed many French criminal justice codes, including giving greater power to the prosecution, increasing sentences for violent crimes, decreasing judicial discretion, and adopting measures to speed up the entire process.

75. Yvan Gastaut, *L'immigration et l'opinion en France sous la Ve République* (Paris: Seuil, 2000), 482–91.

76. Tissot, "French Suburbs," 6.

77. Cathy Lisa Schneider has argued that French scholars and most of the French political establishment "fail to acknowledge racial inequality or racial discrimination on the part of the state or any part of its security apparatus." See *Police Power and Race Riots: Urban Unrest in Paris and New York* (Philadelphia: University of Pennsylvania Press, 2014), 88.

78. Graham Murray, "France: The Riots and the Republic," *Race & Class* 47.4 (2006): 26–45, here 28.

79. "French Muslims Face Job Discrimination," *BBC News*, 2 November 2005, http://news.bbc.co.uk/2/hi/europe/4399748.stm (accessed 10 November 2016).

80. Ambalavaner Sivanandan, "Attacks on Multicultural Britain Pave the Way for Enforced Assimilation," *Guardian*, 13 September 2006, www.pressmon.com/cgi-bin/press_view.cgi?id=902179 (accessed 30 October 2014).

81. Ambalavaner Sivanandan, *Communities of Resistance: Writings on Black Struggles for Socialism* (London: Verso, 1990), 80.

82. Rattansi, *Multiculturalism*, 27.

83. Sivanandan, "Attacks on Multicultural Britain."

84. Gita Sahgal, "Fundamentalism and the Multi-cultural Fallacy," in Southall Black Sisters, *Against the Grain: A Celebration of Survival and Struggle* (Middlesex: Southall Black Sisters, 1990), 16.

85. Sahgal, "Fundamentalism and the Multi-cultural Fallacy," 16.

86. Sahgal, "Fundamentalism and the Multi-cultural Fallacy," 17.

87. Sahgal, "Fundamentalism and the Multi-cultural Fallacy," 18.

88. Southall Black Sisters, "Multiculturalism in Secondary Schools: Managing Conflicting Demands" (unpublished report, December 2006), 11.

89. Kenan Malik, *From Fatwa to Jihad: The Rushdie Affair and Its Aftermath* (Brooklyn, NY: Melville House, 2010), 65–66.

90. Malik, *From Fatwa to Jihad*, 66.

91. Malik, *From Fatwa to Jihad*, 67.

92. Malik, *From Fatwa to Jihad*, 67.

93. Kenan Malik, *Multiculturalism and Its Discontents: Rethinking Diversity after 9/11* (London: Seagull Books, 2013), 57.

94. Malik, *Multiculturalism and Its Discontents*, 24.

95. Malik, *Multiculturalism and Its Discontents*, 28–29.

96. Kenan Malik, *The Meaning of Race: Race, History and Culture in Western Society* (New York: New York University Press, 1996), 150–60.

97. "Limits to Mutual Tolerance," *Independent*, 18 February 1989, cited in Paul Weller, *A Mirror for Our Times: "The Rushdie Affair" and the Future of Multiculturalism* (London: Continuum, 2009), 80.

98. Political theorist Susan Moller Okin raised this very question in *Is Multiculturalism Bad for Women?* (Princeton, NJ: Princeton University Press, 1999).

99. Frits Bolkestein, "On the Collapse of the Soviet Union" (speech, Liberal International Conference, Lucerne, Switzerland, 6 September 1991), www.liberal-international.org/contentFiles/files/Bolkestein%201991.pdf (accessed 20 October 2014).

100. Baukje Prins, "The Nerve to Break Taboos: New Realism in the Dutch Discourse on Multiculturalism," *Journal of International Migration and Integration* 3.3–4 (2002): 363–79, here 367.

101. Bolkestein, "On the Collapse of the Soviet Union."

102. Bernard Lewis, "The Roots of Muslim Rage," *Atlantic Monthly*, 1 September 1990, www.theatlantic.com/magazine/archive/1990/09/the-roots-of-muslim-rage/304643/ (accessed 16 October 2014). An earlier version of this essay was delivered by Lewis as the Jefferson Lecture, the highest honor for achievement in the humanities selected by the National Endowment for the Humanities. Three years later, the American political scientist Samuel Hunting-

ton popularized the concept. In a 1993 essay for *Foreign Affairs*, Huntington argued that cultural divisions would provide the primary source of antagonism in the post–Cold War world. "The battle lines of the future," he predicted, "will occur between nations and groups of different civilizations. The clash of civilizations will dominate global politics." Samuel P. Huntington, "The Clash of Civilizations?," *Foreign Affairs*, Summer 1993, 22–49, here 22.

103. Bolkestein, "On the Collapse of the Soviet Union."

104. Prins, "Nerve to Break Taboos"; and Baukje Prins and Sawitri Saharso, "From Toleration to Repression: The Dutch Backlash against Multiculturalism," in Steven Vertovec and Susanne Wessendorf, eds., *The Multiculturalism Backlash: European Discourses, Policies and Practices* (London: Routledge, 2010), 72–91.

105. Prins and Saharso, "From Toleration to Repression," 74–75.

106. Prins and Saharso, "From Toleration to Repression," 74–75.

107. Paul Scheffer, "Het multiculturele drama," *NRC Handelsblad*, 29 January 2000.

108. Prins, "Nerve to Break Taboos," 370.

109. Han Entzinger, "Changing the Rules while the Game Is On: From Multiculturalism to Assimilation in the Netherlands," in Y. Michal Bodemann and Gökçe Yurdakul, eds., *Migration, Citizenship, Ethnos: Incorporation Regimes in Germany, Western Europe and North America* (New York: Palgrave Macmillan, 2006), 121–44, here 128.

110. Christian Joppke, "The Retreat of Multiculturalism in the Liberal State: Theory and Policy," *British Journal of Sociology* 55.2 (2004): 237–57, here 248.

111. Quoted in Entzinger, "Changing the Rules," 128.

112. Prins, "Nerve to Break Taboos," 371.

113. Ayaan Hirsi Ali, *The Caged Virgin: An Emancipation Proclamation for Women and Islam* (New York: Free Press, 2006), 35–36. The Dutch original appeared as *De Maagdenkooi* in 2004.

114. Hirsi Ali, *Caged Virgin*, 48.

115. David Goodhart, "Too Diverse?," *Prospect*, February 2004, www .prospectmagazine.co.uk/features/too-diverse-david-goodhart-multiculturalism -britain-immigration-globalisation (accessed 28 October 2014).

116. Goodhart, "Too Diverse?" This is a position that the British American academic and public intellectual Tony Judt also championed in his final lecture, "What Is Living and What Is Dead in Social Democracy?" (New York University, 19 October 2009).

117. Goodhart, "Too Diverse?"

118. Trevor Phillips, "Genteel Xenophobia Is as Bad as Any Other," *Guardian*, 15 February 2004, www.theguardian.com/world/2004/feb/16/race.equality (accessed 28 October 2014).

119. Phillips, "Genteel Xenophobia."

120. Goodhart, "Too Diverse?"

121. Trevor Phillips, "Multiculturalism's Legacy Is 'Have a Nice Day' Racism," *Guardian*, 28 May 2004, www.theguardian.com/society/2004/may/28 /equality.raceintheuk (accessed 28 October 2014).

122. Phillips, "Multiculturalism's Legacy."

123. Trevor Phillips, "After 7/7: Sleepwalking to Segregation" (speech, Manchester Council for Community Relations, Manchester, 22 September 2005).

124. Arun Kundnani, "Multiculturalism and Its Discontents: Left, Right and Liberal," *European Journal of Cultural Studies* 15.2 (2012): 155–66, here 157.

125. Phillips, "After 7/7."

126. Tony Blair, "The Duty to Integrate: Shared British Values" (speech, 10 Downing Street, London, 8 December 2006), www.vigile.net/The-Duty-to-Integrate-Shared (accessed 29 October 2014).

127. All quotes from Merkel's speech are from a transcript I made from the YouTube video of Merkel's entire speech at the Deutschlandstag der Junge Union, 16 October 2010, www.youtube.com/watch?v=WaEg8aM4fcc (accessed 19 July 2013).

128. David Cameron, speech at Munich Security Conference, Munich, 5 February 2011, https://www.gov.uk/government/speeches/pms-speech-at-munich-security-conference (accessed 31 January 2014).

129. Oliver Wright and Jerome Taylor, "Cameron: My War on Multiculturalism," *Independent*, 5 February 2011, www.independent.co.uk/news/uk/politics/cameron-my-war-on-multiculturalism-2205074.html (accessed 6 October 2014).

130. Cameron speech.

131. Cameron speech.

132. TF1 News, 10 February 2011, www.youtube.com/watch?v=N-woTrjH-Do (accessed 8 October 2014).

133. "Sarkozy: le multiculturalisme, 'un échec,' " *Le Figaro*, 10 February 2011, www.lefigaro.fr/flash-actu/2011/02/10/97001-20110210FILWWW00731-sarkozy-le-multiculturalisme-un-echec.php (accessed 8 October 2014).

134. Peggy Hollinger, "Sarkozy Joins Multiculturalism Attack," *Financial Times*, 10 February 2011, www.ft.com/intl/cms/s/0/05baf22e-356c-11e0-aa6c-00144feabdc0.html#axzz3FZWycbAR (accessed 7 October 2014).

135. "Sarkozy: le multiculturalisme."

Epilogue:
The Future of Multicultural Europe?

1. See, for example, Kenan Malik, *The Meaning of Race: Race, History and Culture in Western Society* (New York: New York University Press, 1996); Kenan Malik, *Multiculturalism and Its Discontents: Rethinking Diversity after 9/11* (London: Seagull Books, 2013); Paul Gilroy, *After Empire: Melancholia or Convivial Culture?* (London: Routledge, 2004); and Paul Gilroy, *Postcolonial Melancholia* (New York: Columbia University Press, 2005).

2. David A. Hollinger, *Postethnic America: Beyond Multiculturalism* (New York: Basic Books, 1995), 68.

3. Hollinger, *Postethnic America*, 68, emphasis original.

4. For a detailed discussion of liberalism as it relates to multiculturalism, see George Crowder, *Theories of Multiculturalism: An Introduction* (Cambridge: Polity Press, 2013), 38–80.

5. Malik, *Meaning of Race*, 129.

6. Malik, *Meaning of Race*, 150.

7. Ambalavaner Sivanandan, *Communities of Resistance: Writings on Black Struggles for Socialism* (London: Verso, 1990), 63.

8. Malik, *Multiculturalism and Its Discontents*, 62.

9. Ambalavaner Sivanandan, "Attacks on Multicultural Britain Pave the Way for Enforced Assimilation," *Guardian*, 13 September 2006, https://www.almendron.com/tribuna/attacks-on-multicultural-britain-pave-the-way-for-enforced-assimilation/ (accessed 29 January 2017); Malik *Multiculturalism and Its Discontents*, 61.

10. Malik, *Multiculturalism and Its Discontents*, 60.

11. Birmingham City Council, "Joint Report of Head of Equalities and Director of Birmingham Race Action Partnership: Development of Issue-Based Community Action Forums" (Birmingham: Birmingham City Council, 1999), 4, quoted in Malik, *Multiculturalism and Its Discontents*, 61.

12. See Malik, *Multiculturalism and Its Discontents*, 91–94.

13. Ian Buruma, *Murder in Amsterdam: Liberal Europe, Islam, and the Limits of Tolerance* (New York: Penguin, 2006), 30–31.

14. Karl Polanyi, *The Great Transformation: The Political and Economic Origins of Our Time* (Boston: Beacon, 1957), 254.

15. Polanyi, *Great Transformation*, 256.

16. One could easily replace these examples with many others from countless Western European cities. Indeed, one of my larger hopes is that the present study, which focuses on state policy and national public debate, will help to spark new waves of social and cultural histories documenting more of the lived experience of postwar multiculturalism on the ground.

17. On the afterlives of race thinking in postwar German society, see Rita Chin, Heide Fehrenbach, Geoff Eley, and Atina Grossmann, *After the Nazi Racial State: Difference and Democracy in Germany and Europe* (Ann Arbor: University of Michigan Press, 2009); and Rita Chin, "Thinking Difference in Postwar Germany: Some Epistemological Obstacles around 'Race,'" in Cornelia Wilhelm, ed., *Migration, Memory and Diversity in Germany* (New York: Berghahn Books, 2016). On the problem of race in France, see Herrick Chapman and Laura L. Frader, eds., *Race in France: Interdisciplinary Perspectives on the Politics of Difference* (New York: Berghahn Books, 2004); and Didier Fassin and Éric Fassin, eds., *De la question sociale à la question raciale? Représenter la société française* (Paris: La Découverte, 2006).

18. Michele Wallace, "The Search for the Good-Enough Mammy," in David Theo Goldberg, ed., *Multiculturalism: A Critical Reader* (London: Blackwell, 1994), quoted in Stuart Hall, "Conclusion: The Multicultural Question," in Barnor Hesse, ed., *Un/settled Multiculturalisms: Diasporas, Entanglements, Transruptions* (London: Zed Books, 2000), 211.

19. Hall, "Conclusion," 237.

20. Ayaan Hirsi Ali, *The Caged Virgin: An Emancipation Proclamation for Women and Islam* (New York: Free Press, 2006); see also Buruma, *Murder in Amsterdam*, 167–71. In the wake of the *Charlie Hebdo* massacre, Kenan Malik has begun to describe himself as a "free speech fundamentalist," a statement he made during a discussion with the students in my course "Muslims in Contemporary Europe" (University of Michigan, Ann Arbor, 4 October 2015).

21. Hall, "Conclusion," 236.

22. Paul Gilroy, *Small Acts: Thoughts on the Politics of Black Cultures* (London: Serpent's Tail, 1994), 65.

23. Hall, "Conclusion," 236.

24. At best, the Germans put themselves in the posture of "we welcome you" vis-à-vis guest workers and asylum seekers. What's missing in the German discourse is any embrace or appreciation of the positive effects that accrue from a diverse population.

SUGGESTIONS FOR
FURTHER READING

The question of multiculturalism has been treated at length by scholars in various fields. Among the most influential efforts to theorize multiculturalism are Iris Marion Young, *Justice and the Politics of Difference* (Princeton, NJ: Princeton University Press, 1990); Charles Taylor, *Multiculturalism and the Politics of Recognition* (Princeton, NJ: Princeton University Press, 1992); Will Kymlicka, *Multicultural Citizenship: A Liberal Theory of Minority Rights* (Oxford: Oxford University Press, 1996); Bhikhu Parekh, *Rethinking Multiculturalism: Cultural Diversity and Political Theory* (Cambridge, MA: Harvard University Press, 2002); and Anne Phillips, *Multiculturalism without Culture* (Princeton, NJ: Princeton University Press, 2007). A helpful primer on these theories is George Crowder, *Theories of Multiculturalism: An Introduction* (Cambridge: Polity Press, 2013). Two especially trenchant critiques of multiculturalism include Brian Barry, *Culture and Equality: An Egalitarian Critique of Multiculturalism* (Cambridge: Polity Press, 2000), who tackles the question from the perspective of redistribution and equal treatment; and Kenan Malik, *The Meaning of Race: Race, History and Culture in Western Society* (New York: New York University Press, 1996), who criticizes multiculturalism for treating culture as a predetermined, natural, and unchanging phenomenon. For a useful overview of the most recent European backlash against multiculturalism, see Steven Vertovec and Susanne Wessendorf, eds., *The Multiculturalism Backlash: European Discourses, Policies and Practices* (London: Routledge, 2010). Paul Gilroy, *Postcolonial Melancholia* (New York: Columbia University Press, 2005), provides an important defense of the vibrant, ordinary culture of "conviviality" that is produced in multicultural societies in Britain and across Europe; while Alana Lentin and Gavan Titley, *The Crises of Multiculturalism: Racism in a Neoliberal Age* (London: Zed Books, 2011), offer a thought-provoking critique of the backlash against multiculturalism.

This book has focused on social policies and national public debates about multiculturalism, but a number of recent studies examine the lived experiences of postwar multiculturalism on the ground. These include Ruth Mandel, *Cosmopolitan Anxieties: Turkish Challenges to Citizenship and Belonging in Germany* (Durham, NC: Duke University Press, 2008); Nina Glick Schiller and Ayşe Çağlar, eds., *Locating Migration: Rescaling Cities and Migrants* (Ithaca, NY: Cornell University Press, 2011); Naomi Davidson, *Only Muslim: Embodying Islam in Twentieth-Century France* (Ithaca, NY: Cornell University Press, 2012); Maria Stehle, *Ghetto Voices in Contemporary Germany: Textscapes, Filmscapes, and Soundscapes* (Rochester, NY: Camden House, 2012); Amelia Lyons, *The Civilizing Mission in the Metropole: Algerian Families and the French Welfare State during Decolonization* (Stanford, CA: Stanford University Press, 2013); Marc Matera, *Black London: The Imperial Metropolis and Decolonization in the Twentieth Century* (Berkeley: University of California Press, 2015); Kennetta Hammond Perry, *London Is the Place for Me: Black Britons, Citizenship, and the Politics of Race* (Oxford: Oxford University Press, 2015); and Minayo Nasiali, *Native to the Republic:*

Empire, Social Citizenship, and Everyday Life in Marseille since 1945 (Ithaca, NY: Cornell University Press, 2016).

There is currently no broad history of immigration to postwar (Western) Europe. Tony Judt, *Postwar: A History of Europe since 1945* (London: Penguin, 2005), is a masterful account of the continent and its decades-long rebuilding process in the wake of the Second World War, but this narrative registers only the presence of labor migrants and the broader phenomenon of immigration. Other broad syntheses such as William I. Hitchcock, *The Struggle for Europe: The Turbulent History of a Divided Continent, 1945 to the Present* (New York: Anchor Books, 2003), deal with immigrants as a coda to this history. Most treatments of immigration, race, and ethnicity in postwar Europe, then, have been handled country by country. For Britain, Zig Layton-Henry, *The Politics of Immigration: Immigration, "Race," and "Race" Relations in Postwar Britain* (Oxford: Blackwell, 1992), continues to provide an important foundation in early policy and politics for understanding this set of questions, while Kathleen Paul, *Whitewashing Britain: Race and Citizenship in the Postwar Era* (Ithaca, NY: Cornell University Press, 1997), remains a crucial introduction from a historical perspective. Paul Gilroy, *There Ain't No Black in the Union Jack: The Cultural Politics of Race and Nation* (Chicago: University of Chicago Press, 1991), offers a dense critique of the interdependent relationship of nationalism and racism in Thatcher-era Britain that is still relevant for understanding European responses to postwar immigration more generally. In *Afterlife of Empire* (Berkeley: University of California Press, 2012), Jordanna Bailkin provides a window onto the processes of decolonization—including multiple waves of migration—that shaped postwar British society.

For Germany, there remain relatively few studies in English on the topic of guest workers and postwar diversity.

Among the earliest studies in this area, Ray C. Rist, *Guest-workers in Germany: The Prospects for Pluralism* (Westport, CT: Praeger, 1978), still stands as an important starting point for understanding how guest worker recruitment presented the possibility for a more plural conception of German society. The longer history of immigrant labor in Germany is the subject of Ulrich Herbert's field-defining investigation, *A History of Foreign Labor in Germany, 1880–1980: Seasonal Workers/Forced Laborers/Guest Workers*, trans. William Templer (Ann Arbor: University of Michigan Press, 1990). Brett Klopp, *German Multiculturalism: Immigrant Integration and the Transformation of Citizenship* (Westport, CT: Praeger, 2002), provides an institutional and political account of guest worker integration. Rita Chin, *The Guest Worker Question in Postwar Germany* (Cambridge: Cambridge University Press, 2007), traces the history of public debate and political discourse about guest workers from the beginning of foreign labor recruitment to German reunification.

For France, too, the English-language treatments of immigration and diversity are relatively few and far between. *The French Melting Pot: Immigration, Citizenship, and National Identity*, trans. Geoffroy de Laforcade (Minneapolis: University of Minnesota Press, 1996), by leading French social scientist Gérard Noiriel, is still the work with which to begin for anyone interested in immigration in France. Two early studies, Maxim Silverman, *Deconstructing the Nation: Immigration, Racism and Citizenship in Modern France* (London: Routledge, 1992), and Alec G. Hargreaves, *Immigration, "Race" and Ethnicity in Contemporary France* (London: Routledge, 1995), remain crucial starting points for understanding the postwar situation. More recently, anthropologist Paul A. Silverstein, *Algeria in France: Transpolitics, Race, and Nation* (Bloomington: Indiana University Press, 2004), has sought to understand the experience of Algerians in France through immigration policy, the legacy of colonial governance, urban planning, and corporate advertising.

By contrast, there is a voluminous literature on the headscarf controversies. John R. Bowen, *Why the French Don't Like Headscarves: Islam, the State, and Public Space* (Princeton, NJ: Princeton University Press, 2006), approaches the topic from an anthropological perspective, focusing on the question of *laïcité* and especially French sensitivity to religion in the schools. In *The Politics of the Veil* (Princeton, NJ: Princeton University Press, 2007), Joan W. Scott offers a penetrating historical analysis of the headscarf affairs that probes the racist and gendered aspects of political discourse. Cécile Laborde, *Critical Republicanism: The Hijab Controversy and Political Philosophy* (Oxford: Oxford University Press, 2008), situates the headscarf debates within the broader tradition of republican citizenship.

Similarly, the scholarly work on the place of Muslims and Islam in Europe is extensive. Among the most readable treatments of these questions is Ian Buruma's *Murder in Amsterdam: Liberal Europe, Islam, and the Limits of Tolerance* (New York: Penguin, 2006), which uses the murder of cultural critic Theo van Gogh as the focal point for a fine-grained portrait of Muslim immigrants in the Netherlands. Olivier Roy, *Secularism Confronts Islam*, trans. George Holoch (New York: Columbia University Press, 2007), uses France as the context for recasting debates about Islam and democracy through a detailed analysis of immigrant Muslim life. The flashpoint controversies of the Danish cartoons of Muhammad and the murder of Theo van Gogh serve as the entry point for Anne Norton's insightful interrogation of the clash of civilizations argument, *On the Muslim Question* (Princeton, NJ: Princeton University Press, 2013). In *The Muslim Question:*

Political Controversies and Public Philosophies (Philadelphia: Temple University Press, 2016), Peter O'Brien analyzes familiar issues of citizenship, veiling, secularism, and terrorism through the political theory lenses of liberalism, nationalism, and postmodernism.

INDEX

France, immigrants/minorities
in (*continued*)
   188–89; second-generation immigrants, 122–23, 167, 169–71; shift
   in demographics of immigrants,
   210–11; tensions over citizenship
   and religion of Algerians, 39–40; and
   terrorism, 53–54, 57; and "threshold
   of tolerance," 114, 135. *See also* Algerians; France, policies and legislation;
   West Africans
France, policies and legislation in:
   amnesty program, 120; citizenship
   issues, 43–44, 67, 116–17, 169–72,
   175, 194, 199, 329n90; conservative
   backlash against immigrants, 139,
   166–78; criminal justice codes, 263,
   341n74; Evian Accords (1962), 65,
   116–17; immigration curtailed in
   the 1970s, 74–75, 78, 81, 113–14;
   insertion policies, 112–24, 136, 260;
   Marcellin-Fontanet circulars, 74–75;
   National Immigration Office (ONI),
   36–37; Nationality Commission
   and debate over nationality code,
   172–78, 193; nationality policy
   allowing free colonial migration,
   40–41, 43, 65; and politics of national belonging, 6, 166–78; preservation of immigrant culture and
   promotion of ties to Islam, 117, 136;
   recruitment of European laborers,
   35, 36, 41, 43, 49, 67; rejection of
   multiculturalism as strategy, 112–13;
   repatriation efforts, 41–42, 119–20,
   122; and "right to difference," 122–
   23, 167, 169, 176–77, 292; Secretary
   of State for Foreign Workers, 114,
   117–20; and secularism (*laïcité*), 175,
   194, 197–203, 232, 272; Security and
   Liberty Law (1981), 263; Stasi Commission report on secularism as fundamental to French identity, 202–3,
   232; urban renewal projects, 260–63;
   welfare aid to immigrants, 115–19,
   211–12. See also *France, immigrants/
   minorities in*

Free Democratic Party (FDP; West
   Germany), 130, 259
freedom, 184, 246, 288–90, 295–97,
   346n20
Front National (FN; France), 123–24,
   166–69, 260, 328n76

Gaspard, Françoise, 204–5
Germany/West Germany: contrast
   to Switzerland, 52, 61; economic
   downturn following oil embargo,
   76–79, 125; foreign policy imperatives, 63; and free speech, 189; Germany viewed as a "non-immigration
   country," 164, 166, 255; pre-WWII
   ethnic and religious diversity in, 25;
   public consideration of National
   Socialist past, 155–62; repudiation
   of Nazi racial project, 146, 160,
   163; reunification, 259; and sexual
   democracy, 228–30; and status of
   women, 282. See also *specific leaders,
   political parties, and the following
   headings*
Germany/West Germany, immigrants/
   minorities in: and assimilation/
   integration, 6, 127–35, 154, 158–60,
   165, 189–90, 219–20, 254–59, 282–
   83; demographics/statistics, 125, 132,
   211; and education, 132, 134; and
   "failure" of multiculturalism, 237,
   254–60; and family reunification,
   62, 76, 125, 130–32, 211; guest workers viewed as immigrants, 154–55;
   guest workers viewed as temporary
   residents, 62–63, 129–30, 136, 163–
   66, 281; headscarf controversy, 217–
   20; and housing, 131–32; immigrant
   activism, 77, 131; immigrant women,
   212–13; and Islam, 132–33, 160,
   164–65, 219–20, 233–34; post-WWII
   refugees, 51, 61; public perception
   of immigrants, 162–63, 257–58; religious welfare organizations, 128;
   and Rushdie affair, 189; second-
   generation immigrants, 134; and
   "threshold of tolerance," 136. *See also*